Online Incivility and Public Debate

Gina Masullo Chen

Online Incivility and Public Debate

Nasty Talk

Gina Masullo Chen
School of Journalism
The University of Texas at Austin
Austin, TX
USA

ISBN 978-3-319-85872-2   ISBN 978-3-319-56273-5 (eBook)
DOI 10.1007/978-3-319-56273-5

© The Editor(s) (if applicable) and The Author(s) 2017
Softcover reprint of the hardcover 1st edition 2017
This work is subject to copyright. All rights are solely and exclusively licensed by the Publisher, whether the whole or part of the material is concerned, specifically the rights of translation, reprinting, reuse of illustrations, recitation, broadcasting, reproduction on microfilms or in any other physical way, and transmission or information storage and retrieval, electronic adaptation, computer software, or by similar or dissimilar methodology now known or hereafter developed.
The use of general descriptive names, registered names, trademarks, service marks, etc. in this publication does not imply, even in the absence of a specific statement, that such names are exempt from the relevant protective laws and regulations and therefore free for general use.
The publisher, the authors and the editors are safe to assume that the advice and information in this book are believed to be true and accurate at the date of publication. Neither the publisher nor the authors or the editors give a warranty, express or implied, with respect to the material contained herein or for any errors or omissions that may have been made. The publisher remains neutral with regard to jurisdictional claims in published maps and institutional affiliations.

Cover design by Sam Johnson

Printed on acid-free paper

This Palgrave Macmillan imprint is published by Springer Nature
The registered company is Springer International Publishing AG
The registered company address is: Gewerbestrasse 11, 6330 Cham, Switzerland

For Mom and Dad, my first teachers.

Acknowledgements

The idea for this book came to me 20 years ago, although I did not know it at the time. I was on a weekend getaway in Manhattan with my then-boyfriend. We had just watched *Dead Man Walking*, an acclaimed film about the death penalty. Afterward, we talked about the movie, and I realized that this man I was dating disagreed with me about whether the U.S. government should have the right to put a criminal to death. He supported it. I opposed it. We debated for a while. He offered rational arguments and evidence to support his point of view. He asked pointed questions about why I believed as I did. I did the same. It was tense but not acrimonious. Neither of us persuaded the other to change views. But I gained a deeper understanding of why someone might support this penalty I abhor. At the end, I knew this guy was a keeper. Anyone who could express a point of view so passionately and offer well-thought-out reasons for his opinions was someone I wanted in my life—even if he was to disagree with me much of the time. Less than two years later, I married this man, and we have raised two children together. I thank my husband, Peter, for having the strength to disagree with me on so many things. I thank him, along with our children, Ian and Chloe, for giving me the time and mental space to complete this book. I also thank my dogs, Phoebe and Finn, who slept at my feet as I wrote many of these pages.

I believed then, and still do now, that vigorous debate, especially with those you disagree with, is vital to our society. We all gain when differences get aired in a rational way. These types of discussions are even more important today in the aftermath a particularly uncivil and divisive presidential campaign that has turned friends into foes and generated angry and sometimes abusive discourse across the nation. In this climate, we cannot shut off debate, even if it is tremendously uncomfortable or hurtful at times.

Many others supported my efforts to write this book. I am sure I have missed some, and I apologize in advance for that. First, I must thank my editor, Shaun Vigil, for believing in my idea and helping it come to fruition. I feel lucky to have an editor who so readily understands my vision. I also thank Hinda Mandell, co-editor of my first book, *Scandal in a Digital Age*, for encouraging me to venture forth on this solo project even though I was terrified of doing a book on my own. To Pam Shoemaker, I extend my deepest gratitude for sparking my interest in research that changed the trajectory of my life. As I wrote this book, I heard your words in my head often: "Write clearly; say what you think; don't just quote other people." You will never know what a tremendous influence you have had on me.

I thank Jay Bernhardt, R.B. Brenner, and Steve Reese at The University of Texas at Austin (UT Austin) for supporting my request for a dean's fellowship to provide the time to complete this book. I am also indebted to the School of Journalism at UT Austin for providing a grant from the Student Enrichment Fund that allowed me to hire students to collect the comments that became the experimental stimuli in Chap. 7. Paromita Pain, Shannon Price, Paige Turner, and Taylor Weese; I greatly appreciate your efforts. I also thank the Center for Women's and Gender Studies at UT Austin for supporting me with a faculty development award. This award allowed me to hire Jackson Prewitt, who collected most of the comments that form the data for Chap. 5 and helped me code them. This award also allowed me to pay research subjects for the experiment in Chap. 7. Jinglun Zheng, who gathered some of the comments for Chap. 5, also has my thanks. Additionally, I thank the doctoral students who were part of my research group over the past 2.5 years for your insights and help with related projects about incivility and commenting that shaped my thinking on this book: Jordon Brown, Vickie Chen, Shuning Lu, Yee Man Margaret Ng, Mustafa Oz, Deepa Fadnis, Pain, Martin J. Riedl, Jeremy L. Shermak, Ori Tenenboim, Kelsey Whipple, and Pei Zheng. In particular, the earlier studies Lu and Zheng helped me with regarding emotional responses to incivility paved the way for the experiment in Chap. 7. I am likewise grateful to Natalie Jomini Stroud, who directs UT Austin's Engaging News Project (ENP), where I am a faculty research associate. I also thank all my colleagues at ENP: Alexis Alizor, Alishan Alibhai, Melody E. Avant, Alex Curry, Jay Jennings, Cameron Lang, Shannon McGregor, Ashley

Muddiman, Joshua Scacco, Cynthia Peacock, Katie Steiner, Tenenboim, and Emily Van Duyn. Your enthusiasm, suggestions, and kind words kept me going when this project seemed daunting. It was so good to find fellow scholars who share my interest (obsession) with online commenting.

Contents

Part I Incivility and Why It Matters

1 Introduction: Incivility in Today's World   3

2 Online Incivility and Public Discourse   29

3 Nasty Talk Online   57

Part II Online Incivility: Three Examples in the News

4 Can Incivility and Deliberation Co-exist?   81

5 Analyzing Comments in the News   105

Part III Incivility and Political Participation

6 Incivility and Speaking Out   133

7 Testing the "Defensive Effect"   149

Part IV What This Means for Public Debate

8 Conclusion: Where Do We Go from Here? 175

Bibliography 195

Index 215

List of Figures

Fig. 4.1	Conceptual model of how incivility and deliberation may overlap	85
Fig. 5.1	Comment length by topic and news organization	112
Fig. 5.2	Percentages of attributes of incivility and deliberation in 3508 comments	113
Fig. 5.3	Incivility by topic and news organization	114
Fig. 5.4	Deliberation by topic and news organization	115
Fig. 6.1	Proposed direct effects of "defensive effect" model	138
Fig. 6.2	Proposed indirect effect of "defensive effect" model	139
Fig. 7.1	Direct effects of "defensive effect" model	159
Fig. 7.2	Indirect effect of "defensive effect" model	159

LIST OF TABLES

Table 5.1	Breakdown of comments that were analyzed by topic and news organization	106
Table 5.2	Gender of commenters by news organization and topic	110
Table 5.3	Anonymous comments by news organization and topic	111
Table 5.4	Frequency of incivility and deliberation attributes	117
Table 7.1	Demographic descriptions of the 953 experiment participants compared to the U.S. population	151
Table 7.2	Demographic descriptions of the 205 pre-test experiment participants	152
Table 7.3	Comments used in the experiment	154
Table 7.4	Correlations between all variables	156
Table 7.5	Unstandardized OLS path analysis coefficients for direct effects of uncivil and civil disagreement	158

PART I

Incivility and Why It Matters

CHAPTER 1

Introduction: Incivility in Today's World

In late November of 2016, *New York Times* columnist Nicholas Kristof tweeted a fundamental truth: "When people you follow annoy you and cause your temperature to rise—congratulations! You've escaped the echo chamber."[1] The tweet came mere weeks after Republican candidate Donald Trump clinched the presidency of the United States of America, after a contentious campaign that pitted friend against friend and family against family. In the aftermath of the election that shocked many, Kristof was not alone in calling for people to talk and listen to others whose political views differed from their own. The idea was that this type of talk would help people better understand others' views and prevent the tunnel vision that some blamed for the widespread but ultimately false media predictions that Trump would lose to Hillary Clinton, the Democrats' candidate. This tunnel vision is created when people are exposed mainly to opinions that support their own, so they see constant reinforcement—or echoing—of their own worldviews. This echoing entrenches their viewpoints.[2] People believe something and then seek out media and friends who support this view in a process called selective exposure.[3] Then, when they see their beliefs represented, they have that "a-ha moment": See, I was right! This strengthens their beliefs—even if those beliefs are actually incorrect. During the post-election months, exposing oneself to crosscutting viewpoints[4] or media outlets[5] that express opinions that differ from one's own became a rallying cry. But as Kristof's tweet demonstrates, doing this may help democracy, but it challenges people. Basically, even if trying to see the world through others' eyes helps people understand society better, it still may make them angry or even prompt a nasty retort.

This tension—over the need to talk even when we disagree while understanding that this may spark incivility—lies at the heart of this book. The central goal of this book is to answer two main questions: Can online comment streams on news websites ever foster the robust and important public debate that democracy requires? What influence does incivility in these streams have on political participation and the larger public discussion about important issues? This book theorizes online incivility—defined as nasty, attacking remarks[6]—by proposing a conceptual model that explains when incivility may step outside the lines of deliberative speech. It also analyzes news comments across five media sites to examine how uncivil they really are and whether incivility can ever co-exist with deliberation, defined as a form of public talk that aims for rational discussions across disagreement.[7] I also propose and test the "defensive effect," which predicts that incivility may prompt people to get politically involved because it triggers an emotional response that jolts them into action. I argue that incivility is not something to be feared. Rather, it is a natural, yet undesirable, part of the human condition. In some cases, it is a necessary evil that we must tolerate to have the type of engaged electorate that informs a strong democracy, but some forms of incivility are so harsh that they offer no contribution to public discourse. Rather than wring our hands and wish for a mythical "civil society," I suggest that understanding how and when incivility operates helps us arrive at strategies to reclaim the online public debate.

I begin this chapter by defining what I mean by incivility and providing a brief history of why people are uncivil. I then cast a broader net to make the seminal point that lack of civility is not confined to online debate. Rather, it oozes throughout society. It operates in a variety of experiences, from the everyday rudeness of people chatting loudly on a cell phone in public[8] to the more severe forms of aversive communication like workplace bullying,[9] social media attacks on young people,[10] flaming trolls who enjoy sparking discord in comment sections,[11] and anti-feminist assaults on female gamers.[12] I also consider the lack of civility in mediated contexts, such as through political attack ads, presidential debates,[13] and so-called "outrage media,"[14] such as talk radio and cable opinion shows. I note how so-called "fake news" sites—which include parodies, satire, fabricated news intended to provoke, and even outright propaganda[15]—may produce uncivil exchanges. In addition, I explore how people may view incivility as entertaining[16] or fail to see it as distressing because it targets a person who is not a member of their group. Sometimes incivility may be used more for shock value in mediated contexts ranging in variety from reality television shows to tweets on Twitter. Yet, incivility can offer real harm to society by damaging people's self-esteem and increasing their anxiety, destroying social relationships,[17] and reducing the quality of public debate.[18] The goal of this chapter is to make two important points: First, the lack of civility has seeped into almost all aspects of human life and is not exclusive to the online experience. Second, online incivility in comment streams has become a particular problem that challenges the potential for a vigorous public discussion.

After providing this overview, this chapter will transition to the main focus of this book: online incivility's influence on public debate and political participation. I submit that this topic is an essential area to examine because the online space has become where people talk about politics, the news, and even family life. As I explore in greater detail throughout this book, incivility may be intensified in the often-anonymous[19] environment of news site comment streams and social media, and this may influence public debate. As a result, a free-flowing, but mainly civil, online discourse is crucial to the public deliberation necessary in a vigorous democracy.[20] I will conclude, by providing an overview of what the rest of the book will offer.

What Is Incivility?

Incivility can be a slippery notion. What constitutes incivility varies from person to person, so it is difficult to come up with a rule of what incivility means or even describe discourse that is consistently viewed as uncivil. Part of the reason for the confusion is that our own experiences influence what we see as uncivil. For example, I might be offended if you call me uneducated because education is something I value strongly. But you might be proud to be called uneducated because you see yourself as a "regular Joe." So is that name-calling? Is it an insult? Is it uncivil? Similarly, I might be perfectly comfortable expressing a strong opinion on my Facebook wall because I feel it is important to voice my beliefs, but you view my post as impolite or uncivil because you disagree with it or it makes you feel uncomfortable. Think of the old adage that it is impolite to talk about politics or religion. Why? These topics bring up sharp emotions that make people feel ill at ease. Some people, with low tolerance for this tension, see any assertion of opinion as uncivil, particularly if they disagree with the viewpoint. Imagine also a heated back and forth between two people debating whether climate change is caused by humans or is just a natural weather fluctuation. They are intense. They are engaged. They may even raise their voices in the heat of passion. Is that uncivil? It depends on whom you ask.

For this book, I focus on a very narrow definition of incivility. It is not merely the expression of a counter view, regardless of how uncomfortable people may feel hearing that opinion. It is not a two- or three-sided debate that grows strident. That is disagreement,[21] not incivility. It is also not bullying, which requires negative words or actions that escalate over a period of time to socially exclude a specific person or group.[22] Bullying requires an imbalance of power between the bully and victim[23] and a clear intent to harm another. People may be harmed by uncivil speech, but incivility does not require that the perpetrators' intention was to harm.[24] Incivility is also not merely criticism, unless the words used are insulting or demeaning. So-called constructive criticism ("You need to practice your breast stroke more if you want to win") is not uncivil, although a more pointed remark ("You have no idea what you're talking about; you're a complete idiot") would be. My definition of incivility is drawn from ample prior research[25] that categorizes speech based on the characteristics of a message. In this definition, incivility must exhibit at least one of three main attributes: insulting language or name-calling; profanity; and a larger category that encompasses stereotypes, and homophobic, racist, sexist, and xenophobic terms that may at times dip into hate speech. All these types of messages would be considered rude, but I also do not see incivility as synonymous with rudeness. Instead, I suggest that incivility goes beyond rudeness. It might be rude to express a strongly held religious viewpoint among people who disagree with you, but it would not be uncivil. Telling someone her new dress is unbecoming is certainly impolite, but not uncivil. Incivility is part of a larger continuum of aversive speech that both violates[26] what is considered normal in conversation and also has the potential to cause harm. On the mildest side, calling someone "stupid" would fit my definition of incivility. On the more aversive side, President Donald Trump's assertion, in his 2015 campaign announcement speech, that Mexican immigrants were "rapists"[27] would also constitute uncivil discourse because it is a sweeping pejorative statement that defames a group. Incivility moves along the continuum from less to more aversive, depending on the intensity and harshness of the words.

Why Are We Uncivil?

The Internet did not create incivility, even though sometimes it may feel as if it did. In fact, incivility has been with us since humans learned to communicate with each other. But why are people uncivil? What do they gain from it? To understand this, it helps to step back a bit and imagine people as their more primitive ancestors were. For the earliest humans, the main driving force was survival, to live long enough to pass on one's genes to the next generation. That is the basic tenet of evolutionary psychology—everything people do stems in some way from this early drive to survive. However, even if we acknowledge, as I think we must, that people today are more complicated than that, clearly the predilections instilled in humans from these early days still may play a subconscious role in behavior. For example, one of the most powerful early drives was the need to be part of a group. As primitive beings, inclusion in a group was the only way people could survive.[28] Being alone meant certain death from starvation or predators. This background has hardwired humans to subconsciously perceive any type of social exclusion or rejection as a threat to their value as relational partners with others.[29] As a result, this "need to belong"[30] with others has become a powerfully adaptive urge that predisposes people today to seek to affirm again and again that they are worthy to be part of the group.

So why would that make people likely to be uncivil? It doesn't. Incivility is relatively rare. It is a form of deviance[31] that tramples what is normal in polite society,[32] so it does not fit into what is considered acceptable communication. It has shock value. It commands attention. As a result, incivility becomes a way for people to exert control over others, assert their own position, and jockey for power. By being uncivil, people decrease the value of the person whom they attack and, perhaps, increase their own value, by showing dominance much as a wolf baring its teeth or growling. In essence, incivility is a way to hurt others while elevating one's own place in the group, in the competition of human society.[33] But that does not mean incivility predominates. In fact, people's natural need to belong with others keeps incivility in check most of the time. Certain personal attributes, such as self-esteem or poor emotional regulation, may make it easier for people to become uncivil,[34] and people are more likely to become uncivil when their negative emotions are inflamed.[35] People become uncivil when at a subconscious level a need to elevate oneself or a lack of inhibition from stress or emotion overrides people's natural need to remain civil so as not to damage their connection with others.

THE LARGER CONTEXT

This examination of online incivility comes at a particular moment, when our society seems to have lost its sense of civility. While our generation is hardly the first to encounter aversive forms of speech, the growth of online incivility mirrors the spread of other forms of hurtful communication both online and offline. Workplace bullying has long been a problem, whereby aggressive supervisors or nasty co-workers subject their colleagues to harmful words and actions that make the workplace inhospitable and unproductive.[36] The schoolyard bullying of teasing, insults, or kicks, and punches[37] has moved online and become more virulent, spiking depression and suicide among the young.[38] The digital realm has made it easier and faster to bully in more potent ways than in the pre-Internet world. A teen bully, for example, can share an embarrassing image of a classmate with the whole school via text messages, sending shockwaves through the community of youth. Aggressive adults can be just as bad. For example, a wave of racist abuse against actor Leslie Jones, an African-American star of the all-female remake of "Ghostbusters," was so vicious that Twitter banned one of the ringleaders, writer Milo Yiannopoulos, from the platform forever.[39] The speed and ease of online communication makes it particularly easy to single out groups with less societal power, such as women or people of color, for attacks. The publicness of the online space amplifies the effects of harsh words.[40] For example, women have been subjected to online threats of being raped[41] or virulent attacks in the male-dominated culture of online gaming.[42] Hashtags, short keywords with a hash or pound mark, have been used to disseminate some of this rage. #JadaPose, for instance, was used to a mock a 16-year-old African-American rape victim online, although black feminists challenged that attack by developing more positive hashtags.[43] This decay in productive communication provides a backdrop to the focus of this book: online incivility in comment streams. One in five comments has been found to exhibit at least some attribute of uncivil speech,[44] highlighting the importance of this topic.

The political sphere also has been no stranger to uncomfortable and damaging communication. Politicians of days gone by took to duels and fights to make their points.[45] Political battles for civil rights, women's rights, and gay rights all included elements of violence. The belief that things were so much softer and gentler in days gone by is largely a myth.[46] Strife has always been part of the political process since the Sons of Liberty dumped 342 chests of British tea into Boston Harbor in 1773, protesting taxation without representation and sparking the American Revolution from England.[47] However, today's incivility is part of an aggressive cultural shift in politics that makes it easier for the public and politicians to speak directly to the world without the filter of traditional media. Controversial media content in small pockets has been around for decades, but "outrage media"—opinion-based cable news, talk radio, and blogs—really launched this trend toward incivility in political talk.[48] Outrage media aims to provoke an emotional response by using overgeneralizations, sensationalism, and misleading or partially inaccurate information.[49] The goal is to gain an audience and profits[50] but it also politically polarizes people by reinforcing fringe views and making extremists more extreme.[51] Outrage media gives people with viewpoints outside the mainstream a "safe space" to spout their views without being challenged by more moderate statements, and the fear-mongering and vilification that comes with this type of speech undermines a larger public discussion.[52] At the same time, politics has become more "in your face," as political scientist Diana C. Mutz calls it.[53] This describes when politicians wage in-person battles in the television media, dripping with incivility and acrimony. The public may tune in to be informed, but they are riveted by incivility.[54] Incivility becomes a form of entertainment, much like watching people bash each other on reality television shows. The result is people who watch a vitriolic political debate on TV feel almost as angry or aroused as if they were part of the argument.[55] The casualties are political trust and legitimacy.[56]

In the 2016 presidential election, examples of these types of threatening political discourse reached a fever pitch. During the campaign, Trump mocked a disabled reporter; disparaged the courage of Sen. John McCain, a former prisoner of war; insulted the parents of a Muslim U.S. soldier killed in Iraq;[57] and called his opponent a "nasty woman" during the final presidential debate.[58] In addition, a 2005 recording surfaced in which Trump bragged about grabbing women by the genitals without their consent.[59] Clinton remarked that half of Trump's supporters fit in a "basket of deplorables,"[60] but it would be incorrect to suggest the two candidates were equally uncivil. At the same time, fake news sites extolled untrue conspiracy theories but appeared much like real news websites on Facebook,[61] playing a role similar to outrage media in earlier campaigns. Fake news stories that spread about Clinton were blamed in part for her loss to Trump, and after intense pressure after the election, Facebook founder Mark Zuckerberg outlined a plan to curb fake stories on his platform.[62] Like outrage media, many of these sites were created for profit, sometimes by teenagers in the Balkans.[63] Yet, some were created for purely partisan reasons with more nefarious ends.[64] At this writing, this issue has reached epic proportions: The Central Intelligence Agency (CIA), the Federal Bureau of Investigation (FBI), and the National Security Agency (NSA) have concluded that Russian President Vladimir Putin ordered an initiative to influence the 2016 presidential campaign to favor the election of Trump.[65] These efforts include leaking hacked information from Democratic National Committee emails and hiring social media trolls to spread disparaging information about Clinton.[66] Bipartisan lawmakers are investigating.[67]

The main question of this book—can we debate important topics like politics and news online despite the incivility that mars the discourse?—takes on greater meaning against a backdrop where incivility has encroached on nearly every part of our lives. Therefore, it is worth reviewing all these types of aversive speech because they are part of what feels like a sweeping shift toward a less civil and benevolent society. They are all part of what appears as an onslaught of rudeness, a general disregard for norms of society that diminishes and demeans others.[68] However, this background provides only a reference point because it is online interpersonal incivility that is my focus, not bullying, or face-to-face nastiness, or acerbic speech among political actors.

Focus of This Book

This book concerns online debate that may be heated or even nasty, but cannot be definitely identified as intending to harm. Clearly, that does not mean no harm occurs. In contrast, I argue this specific type of aversive speech may cause much of the same damage as more intensive forms of verbal violence, including harming people's relationships, increasing their tension,[69] and reducing the potential for fruitful public discussions.[70] But the intent of the speaker to cause harm is not always clear in incivility, as it might be in a bullying situation. One may argue about the value of the Affordable Care Act, a federal health care program, in a newspaper comment stream, for example, and grow so angry that one peppers her speech with profanity. Yet, that does not mean the commenter intends to hurt other people, just that she is using a mode of speech that uses an aspect of incivility to highlight the intensity of her words.

The focus of this book is also on one narrow aspect of uncivil communication: the digital space of online comments. I limit my focus not because other areas of incivility are unworthy of notice, but because my aim is to drill deeply into this one specific uncivil experience. Comment streams, which started on news sites nearly 20 years ago,[71] have emerged into a virtual space for discussions about politics, news, current events, and life in general. Comment streams are flawed for sure, rife with vitriol[72] so fierce that some news organizations no longer allow them.[73] Yet, they have developed into an important public space[74] with the give and take that offers potential—although often unrealized—for deliberation.[75] Deliberation is a process in which people see themselves as part of a public discussion with a goal of solving society's ills.[76] It aims to be open to all, based in reason, and focused on consensus, although it allows for differences in opinion.[77] The evidence is mixed on whether comments can be places for deliberation because of their incivility.[78] I argue, however, that as a society we need this online space to welcome the type of debate across disagreement that a democratic society requires. My aim is to understand if deliberation—or at least "deliberative moments"—is possible in this online space, amid or despite the incivility.

Plan for This Book

This book is divided into three main parts. The first part, which includes this chapter and the next two chapters, explores incivility and why it matters. In Chap. 2, I lay out my belief more broadly that comment streams have the potential to be the salons and cafés of days gone by, where people gathered together—drawn by the news—to talk about important issues of the day.[79] I explore how the theory of deliberative democracy relates to comment streams and offer a framework to understand how these public, quasi-journalistic spaces may contribute to public debate. Chapter 3 focuses more specifically on online incivility and examines why the digital space is so susceptible to this type of communication. Using theories from interpersonal and computer-mediated communication, I unpack how the immediacy and publicness of online discourse along with the feeling of deindividuation[80]—the sense that nobody knows who you are online—combine to create a perfect storm for incivility to thrive. This chapter also explores more fully the harm caused by uncivil speech to the individuals who consume it and to the larger public discourse.

The second part examines incivility through the lens of a quantitative content analysis of 3508 comments posted on news stories from five different news websites. The comments were posted on stories about three controversial topics in the news during the writing of this book: the 2016 presidential race, the 2015 decision by the U.S. Supreme Court legalizing same-sex marriage, and the battle over removing the Confederate flag from government spaces. These topics were chosen because they offer the type of topics with clear sides that are most likely to elicit public debate[81] as well as foment the heated emotions that may lead to uncivil speech.

These topics provide a lens to examine core questions of this book: Can comment streams foster a robust debate? Can these conversations exhibit attributes of deliberations, such as use of evidence to make a point and asking legitimate questions? Can incivility and deliberation co-exist in comment streams? In Chap. 4, I propose a conceptual model of how uncivil speech and deliberative speech may overlap in the public discourse. Chapter 5 provides a test of this model, by analyzing the 3508 user-generated comments for attributes of incivility and deliberation.

My third part offers the second empirical contribution of this book. This section deals with incivility and its specific impact on political participation. I propose what I call the "defensive effect," which predicts that when people are confronted with uncivil disagreement—marred by name-calling, insults, or profanity—this ignites an emotional response. Then this emotional response triggers a defense mechanism that makes them more likely to speak out or get politically involved in whatever issue they had been discussing. In essence, the emotional response from the incivility diminishes a normative drive to remain silent when confronted with opposing opinions. Chapter 6 proposes a conceptual model of how this effect works, drawing on literature from communication, political science, and psychology, and explains the four core mechanisms of the effect. Chapter 7 tests the effect, using an experiment with 953 participants. My findings demonstrate that the effect works in the same way across three different topics, the 2016 presidential campaign, the same-sex marriage decision, and the battle over the Confederate flag, suggesting a robust theoretical contribution of how incivility influences political participation.

The last part of this book consists of Chap. 8, which synthesizes findings from the content analysis and experiment and answers the main question of this book: What influence does incivility in the digital discourse have on the free exchange of ideas necessary to a deliberative democracy? This chapter also situates my findings in the relevant literature to make a larger statement about incivility more generally, as well as specifically in the computer-mediated realm of user-generated comments. Finally, I look to what these findings mean to future discourse online and how that will shape our world.

Classroom Discussion Prompts

1. How does the author define online incivility?
2. How does incivility differ from related concepts, such as bullying or criticism?
3. Why are people uncivil?
4. Explain some of the history of incivility in politics.

Notes

1. Nicholas Kristof, "When people you follow annoy you and cause your temperature to rise—congratulations! you've escaped the echo chamber," Twitter tweet, November 23, 2016. https://twitter.com/NickKristof/status/801577315276886016.
2. Kathleen Hall Jamieson and Joseph N. Cappella, *Echo Chamber: Rush Limbaugh and the Conservative Media Establishment*, (New York, NY: Oxford University Press, 2008; Matthew Levendusky, *How Partisan Media Polarize America*, (Chicago, IL: The University of Chicago Press, 2013); Michael D. Slater, "Reinforcing Spirals: The Mutual Influence of Media Selectivity and Media Effects and Their Impact on Individual Behavior and Society Identity," *Communication Theory* 17 (2007): 281–303; Natalie J. Stroud, "Media Use and Political Dispositions: Revisiting the Concept of Selective Exposure," *Political Behavior* 30 (2008): 341–366; Natalie J. Stroud, "Polarization and Partisan Selective Exposure," *Journal of Communication* 60 (2010): 556–576 (Jamieson and Cappella 2008; Levendusky 2013; Slater 2007; Stroud 2008, 2010).
3. Levendusky, *How Partisan Media Polarize America*; Slater, "Reinforcing Spirals: The Mutual Influence of Media Selectivity and Media Effects and Their Impact on Individual Behavior and Society Identity"; Stroud, "Media Use and Political Dispositions: Revisiting the Concept of Selective Exposure"; Stroud, "Polarization and Partisan Selective Exposure."
4. Diana C. Mutz, "Cross-Cutting Social Networks: Testing Democratic Theory in Practice," *American Political Science Review* 96, no. 1 (2002): 111–126 (Mutz 2002).
5. Slater, "Reinforcing Spirals: The Mutual Influence of Media Selectivity and Media Effects and Their Impact on Individual Behavior and Society Identity"; Stroud, "Media Use and Political Dispositions: Revisiting the Concept of Selective Exposure"; Stroud, "Polarization and Partisan Selective Exposure."

6. Hyunseo Hwang, Zhondang Pan, and Ye Sun, "Influence of Hostile Media Perceptions on Willingness to Engage in Discursive Activities: An Examination of Mediating Role of Media Indignation," *Media Psychology* 11, no. 1 (2008): 76–97; Zizi Papacharissi, "Democracy Online: Civility, Politeness, and the Democratic Potential of Online Political Discussion Groups," *New Media & Society* 6 (2004): 259–283; Natalie J. Stroud, Joshua M. Scacco, Ashley Muddiman, and Alexander L. Curry, "Changing Deliberative Norms on News Organizations' Facebook Sites," *Journal of Computer-Mediated Communication* 20 (2015): 188–203 (Hwang et al. 2008; Papacharissi 2004; Stroud et al. 2015).
7. James S. Fishkin, *Democracy and Deliberation*, (New Haven, CT: Yale University Press, 1991); John Gastil, *Political Communication and Deliberation*, (Thousand Oaks, CA: Sage, 2008); John Gastil and Laura W. Black, "Public Deliberation as the Organizing Principle of Political Communication Research," *Journal of Public Deliberation* 4, no. 1 (2008): Article 3l; Amy Gutmann and Dennis Thompson, *Democracy and Disagreement*, (Cambridge, MA: Harvard University Press, 1996); Lawrence R. Jacobs, Fay Lomax Cook, and Michael X. Delli Carpini, *Talking Together: Public Deliberation and Political Participation in America*, (Chicago, IL: The University of Chicago Press, 2009); Hélène Landemore, "Democratic Reason: The Mechanism of Collective Intelligence in Politics," in *Collective Wisdom: Principles and Mechanisms*, edited by Hélène Landemore and John Elster, (New York, NY: Cambridge University Press, 2012): 251–289 (Fishkin 1991; Gastil 2008; Gastil and Black 2008; Gutmann and Thompson 1996; Jacobs et al. 2009; Landemore 2012).
8. P.M. Forni, *The Civility Solution: What to Do When People are Rude*, (New York, NY: St. Martin's Press, 2008) (Forni 2008).
9. M. Sandy Herschcovis, "'Incivility, Social Undermining, Bullying ... Oh My!': A Call to Reconcile Constructs Within Workplace Aggression Research," *Journal of Organizational Communication* 32, no. 3 (2011): 499-519; Linda L. Putnam and Dennis K. Mumby, *The Sage Handbook of Organizational Communication*, (Thousand Oaks, CA: Sage, 2014) (Herschcovis 2011; Putnam and Mumby 2014).
10. Francine Dehue, Catherine Bolman, and Trinjntje Völlink, "Cyberbullying: Youngsters' Experiences and Parental Perception," *Cyberpsychology & Behavior* 11, no. 2 (2008): 217–223 (Dehue et al. 2008).
11. Patrick B. O'Sullivan and Andrew J. Flanagin, "Reconceptualizing Flaming and Other Problematic Messages," *New Media & Society* 5, no. 1 (2003): 69–94; Erin E. Buckels, Paul D. Trapnell, and Delroy L. Paulhus, "Trolls Just Want to Have Fun," *Personality and Individual*

Differences 62 (2104): 97–102 (O'Sullivan and Flanagin 2003; Buckels et al. 2014).
12. Andrea Braithwaite, "It's About Ethics in Games Journalism? Gamergaters and Geek Masculinity," *Social Media + Society* October/December, no. 4 (2016): 1–10; Shira Chess and Adrienne Shaw, "A Conspiracy of Fishes, or, How We Learned to Stop Worrying About #GamerGate and Embrace Hegemonic Masculinity," *Journal of Broadcasting & Electronic Media* 59, no. 1 (2015): 208–220 (Braithwaite 2016; Chess and Shaw 2015).
13. John G. Geer, *In Defense of Negativity: Attack Ads in Presidential Campaigns*, (Chicago, IL: The University of Chicago Press, 2006) (Geer 2006).
14. Jeffrey J. Berry and Sarah Sobieraj, *The Outrage Industry: Political Opinion Media and the New Incivility*, (New York, NY: Oxford University Press, 2014) (Berry and Sobieraj 2014).
15. Nsikan Akpan, "The Very Real Consequences of Fake News Stories and Why Our Brain Can't Ignore Them," *PBS News Hour*, December 5, 2016. http://www.pbs.org/newshour/updates/real-consequences-fake-news-stories-brain-cant-ignore/; Irina Khaldarova and Mervi Pantti, "Fake News," *Journalism Practice* 10, no. 7 (2016): 891–901; Regina Marchi, "With Facebook, Blogs, and Fake News, Teens Reject Journalistic 'Objectivity,'" *Journal of Communication Inquiry* 36, no. 3 (2012): 246–262 (Akpan 2016; Khaldarova and Pantti 2016; Marchi 2012).
16. Diana C. Mutz, *In-Your-Face Politics: The Consequences of Uncivil Media*, (Princeton, NJ: Princeton University Press, 2015) (Mutz 2015).
17. Roy F. Baumeister and Mark R. Leary, "The Need to Belong: Desire for Interpersonal Attachments as a Fundamental Human Need," *Psychological Bulletin* 117, no. 3 (1995): 497–529; Mark R. Leary and Roy F. Baumeister, "The Nature and Function of Self-Esteem: Sociometer Theory," *Advances in Experimental Social Psychology* 32 (2000): 1–62 (Baumeister and Leary 1995; Leary and Baumeister 2000).
18. Jack Rosenberry, "Users Support Anonymity Despite Increasing Negativity," *Newspaper Research Journal* 32, no. 1 (2011): 6–19; Nicholas Diakopoulos and Mor Naaman, "Towards Quality Discourse in Online News Comments," *Proceedings of the CSCW, Hangzhou*, China, March 19–23, 2011 (Rosenberry 2011; Diakopoulos and Naaman 2011).
19. Arthur D. Santana, "Virtuous or Vitriolic: The Effects of Anonymity on Civility in Online Newspaper Reader Comment Boards," *Journalism Practice* 8 (2014): 18–33 (Santana 2014).

20. Fishkin, *Democracy and* Deliberation; Gastil, *Political Communication and Deliberation*; Gastil and Black, "Public Deliberation as the Organizing Principle of Political Communication Research"; Landemore, "Democratic Reason: The Mechanism of Collective Intelligence in Politics"; Cliff Zukin, Scott Keeter, Molly Andolina, Krista Jenkins, and Michael X. Delli Carpini, *A New Engagement? Political Participation, Civic Life, and the Changing American Citizen*, (New York, NY: Oxford University Press, 2006); Jacobs, Cook, Delli Carpini, *Talking Together: Public Deliberation and Political Participation in America* (Zukin et al. 2006).
21. Casey A. Klofstad, Anand Edward Sokhey, and Scott D. McClurg, "Disagreeing About Disagreement: How Conflict in Social Networks Affects Political Behavior," *American Journal of Political Science* 57 (2013): 120–134 (Klofstad et al. 2013).
22. Dan Olweus, *Bullying at School: What we Know and What We can Do*, (Oxford, UK: Blackwell 1993) (Olweus 1993).
23. Masaki Matsunaga, "Underlying Circuits of Social Support for Bullied Victims: An Appraisal-Based Perspective on Supportive Communication and Postbullying Adjustment," *Human Communication Research* 37 (2011): 174–206; Olweus, *Bullying at School: What we Know and What We can Do*; Adrzej Podsiadly and Malgorzata Gamain-Wilk, "Personality Traits as Predictors or Outcomes of Being Exposed to Bullying in the Workplace," *Personality and Individual Differences*, Advance Online Publication, 2016. doi:10.1016/2016.08.001 (Matsunaga 2011; Adrzej and Gamain-Wilk 2016).
24. Herschcovis, "'Incivility, Social Undermining, Bullying ... Oh My!': A Call to Reconcile Constructs Within Workplace Aggression Research"; Matsunaga, "Underlying Circuits of Social Support for Bullied Victims: An Appraisal-Based Perspective on Supportive Communication and Postbullying Adjustment"; Lynne M. Andersson and Christine M. Pearson, "Tit for Tat? The Spiraling Effect of Incivility in the Workplace," *Academy of Management Review* 24, no. 3 (1999): 452–471 (Andersson and Pearson 1999).
25. Berry and Sobieraj, *The Outrage Industry: Political Opinion Media and the New Incivility*; Papacharissi, "Democracy Online: Civility, Politeness, and the Democratic Potential of Online Political Discussion Groups"; Stroud et al., "Changing Deliberative Norms on News Organizations' Facebook Sites."
26. Papacharissi, "Democracy Online: Civility, Politeness, and Democratic Potential of Online Political Discussion Groups"; H.P. Grice, "Utterer's Meaning and Intention," *The Philosophical Review*, 78, no. 2 (1969): 147–177 (Grice 1969).

27. Michelle Ye Hee Lee, "Donald Trump's False Comments Connecting Mexican Immigrants and Crime," *The Washington Post*, July 18, 2015. https://www.washingtonpost.com/news/fact-checker/wp/2015/07/08/donald-trumps-false-comments-connecting-mexican-immigrants-and-crime/?utm_term=.ccfc38734c56 (Lee 2015).
28. Baumeister and Leary, "The Need to Belong: Desire for Interpersonal Attachments as a Fundamental Human Need"; Leary and Baumeister, "The Nature and Function of Self-esteem: Sociometer Theory."
29. Baumeister and Leary, "The Need to Belong: Desire for Interpersonal Attachments as a Fundamental Human Need"; Mark R. Leary, "Affiliation, Belonging, and Acceptance: The Pursuit of Interpersonal Connection," in *Handbook of Social Psychology*, eds. Susan T. Fiske, Daniel T. Gilbert, and Gardner Lindzey, (Hoboken, NJ: Wiley, 2010): 864–897; Lisa Zadro, Kipling D. Williams, and Rick Richardson, "Riding the 'O' Train: Comparing the Effects of Ostracism and Verbal Dispute on Targets and Sources," *Group Processes and Intergroup Relations* 8, no. 2 (2005): 125–143 (Leary 2010; Zadro et al. 2005).
30. Baumeister and Leary, "The Need to Belong: Desire for Interpersonal Attachments as a Fundamental Human Need."
31. Pamela J. Shoemaker, "The Perceived Legitimacy of Deviant Political Groups: Two Experiments in Media Effects," *Communication Research* 9, no. 2 (1982): 249–286; Pamela J. Shoemaker, "Media Treatment of Deviant Groups," *Journalism Quarterly* 61, no. 1 (1984): 66–82 (Shoemaker 1982, 1984).
32. Grice, "Utterer's Meaning and Intention"; Papacharissi, "Democracy Online: Civility, Politeness, and the Democratic Potential of Online Political Discussion Groups."
33. Jeanne M. Brett, Mara Olekains, Ray Friedman, Nathan Goates, Cameron Anderson, and Cara Cherry Lisco, "Sticks and Stones: Language, Face, and Online Dispute Resolution," *Academy of Management Journal* 50, no. 1 (2007): 85–99 (Brett et al. 2007).
34. Qiyu Bai, Weipeng Lin, and Lei Wang, "Family Incivility and Counterproductive Work Behavior: A Moderated Mediation Model of Self-esteem and Emotional Regulation," *Journal of Vocational Behavior* 94 (2016): 11–19 (Bai et al. 2016).
35. Gina Masullo Chen and Shuning Lu, "Online Political Discourse: Exploring Differences in Effects of Civil and Uncivil Disagreement in News Website Comments," *Journal of Broadcasting & Electronic Media* 61, no. 1 (2017). doi:10.1080/08838151/2016/1273922; Leonie Rösner, Stephan Winter, and Nicole C. Krämer, "Dangerous Minds? Effects of Online Comments on Aggressive Cognitions, Emotions, and

Behavior," *Computers in Human Behavior* 58 (2016): 461–470 (Chen and Lu 2017; Rösner et al. 2016).
36. Podsiadly and Gamain-Wilk, "Personality Traits as Predictors or Outcomes of Being Exposed to Bullying in the Workplace"; Herschcovis, "'Incivility, Social Undermining, Bullying … Oh My!': A Call to Reconcile Constructs Within Workplace Aggression Research"; Putnam and Mumby, *The Sage Handbook of Organizational Communication*.
37. Olweus, *Bullying at School: What we Know and What We can Do*.
38. Gianluca Gini and Dorothy L. Espelage, "Peer Victimization, Cyberbullying, and Suicide Risk in Children and Adolescents," *Journal of the American Medical Association* 312, no. 5 (2014): 545–546. (Gini and Espelage 2014).
39. Abby Ohlheiser, "Just How Offensive Did Milo Yiannopoulos Have to Be to Get Banned from Twitter?" *The Washington Post*, July 21, 2016. https://www.washingtonpost.com/news/the-intersect/wp/2016/07/21/what-it-takes-to-get-banned-from-twitter/?utm_term=.27ca27d651fa (Ohlheiser 2016).
40. Kristi K. Cole, "'It's Like She's Eager to be Verbally Abused': Twitter, Trolls, and (En)Gendering Disciplinary Rhetoric," *Feminist Media Studies* 15, no. 2 (2015): 356–358 (Cole 2015).
41. Cole, "'It's Like She's Eager to be Verbally Abused': Twitter, Trolls, and (En)Gendering Disciplinary Rhetoric."
42. Chess and Shaw, "A Conspiracy of Fishes, or, How We Learned to Stop Worrying About #GamerGate and Embrace Hegemonic Masculinity."
43. Sherri Williams, "Digital Defense: Black Feminists Resist Violence and Hashtag Activism," *Feminist Media Studies* 15, no. 2 (2015): 341–344 (Williams 2015).
44. Kevin, Coe, Kate Kenski, and Stephen A. Rains, "Online and Uncivil? Patterns and Determinants of Incivility in Newspaper Website Comments," *Journal of Communication* 64 (2014): 658–679 (Coe et al. 2014).
45. Cornell W. Clayton, "Historical Perspectives on the Role of Civility in American Democracy," in *Civility and Democracy in America: A Reasonable Understanding*, eds. Cornell W. Clayton and Richard Elgar, (Pullman, WA: Washington State University Press, 2012); Mutz, *In-Your-Face-Politics: The Consequences of Uncivil Media* (Clayton 2012).
46. Fredrik Logevall, "The Paradox of Civility," in *Civility and Democracy in America: A Reasonable Understanding*, eds. Cornell W. Clayton and Richard Elgar, (Pullman, WA: Washington State University Press, 2012) (Logevall 2012).

47. Encyclopaedia Britannica, "Boston Tea Party: United States History," https://www.britannica.com/event/Boston-Tea-Party.
48. Berry and Sobieraj, *The Outrage Industry: Political Opinion Media and the New Incivility*.
49. Berry and Sobieraj, *The Outrage Industry: Political Opinion Media and the New Incivility*.
50. Berry and Sobieraj, *The Outrage Industry: Political Opinion Media and the New Incivility*.
51. Jamieson and Cappella, *Echo Chamber*; Levendusky, *How Partisan Media Polarize America*.
52. Berry and Sobieraj, *The Outrage Industry: Political Opinion Media and the New Incivility*.
53. Mutz, *In-Your-Face Politics: The Consequences of Uncivil Media*.
54. Mutz, *In-Your-Face Politics: The Consequences of Uncivil Media*.
55. Mutz, *In-Your-Face Politics: The Consequences of Uncivil Media*.
56. Mutz, *In-Your-Face Politics: The Consequences of Uncivil Media*.
57. Karen Yourish, Larry Buchanan, and Alicia Parlapiano, "More Than 160 Republican Leaders Don't Support Donald Trump. Here's When They Reached Their Breaking Point," *The New York Times*, August 28, 2016. http://www.nytimes.com/interactive/2016/08/29/us/politics/at-least-110-republican-leaders-wont-vote-for-donald-trump-heres-when-they-reached-their-breaking-point.html (Yourish et al. 2016).
58. Alan Rappeport, "Who Won the Debate? Hillary Clinton, the 'Nasty Woman,'" *The New York Times*, October 20, 2016. http://www.nytimes.com/2016/10/21/us/politics/who-won-the-third-debate.html (Rappeport 2016).
59. Alexander Burns, Maggie Haberman, and Jonathan Martin, "Donald Trump Apology Caps Day of Outrage Over Lewd Tape," *The New York Times*, October 7, 2016. http://www.nytimes.com/2016/10/08/us/politics/donald-trump-women.html (Burns et al. 2016).
60. Amy Chozik, "Hillary Clinton Calls Many Trump Backers 'Deplorables,' and GOP Pounces," *The New York Times*, September 10, 2016. http://www.nytimes.com/2016/09/11/us/politics/hillary-clinton-basket-of-deplorables.html (Chozik 2016).
61. Akpan, "The Very Real Consequences of Fake News Stories and Why Our Brain Can't Ignore Them."
62. Geoffrey Mohan, "Facebook's Zuckerberg Offers Plan to Counter Fake News Sites," *Los Angeles Times*, November 19, 2016. http://www.latimes.com/business/la-fi-fakenews-facebook-20161119-story.html (Mohan 2016).

63. Sapna Maheshwari, "How Fake News Goes Viral: A Case Study," *The New York Times*, November 201, 2016. http://www.nytimes.com/2016/11/20/business/media/how-fake-news-spreads.html (Maheshwari 2016).
64. Akpan, "The Very Real Consequences of Fake News Stories and Why Our Brain Can't Ignore Them"; Maheshwari, "How Fake News Goes Viral: A Case Study"; Mohan, "Facebook's Zuckerberg Offers Plan to Counter Fake News Sites."
65. An unclassified version of the intelligence report was released to the public through the media on January 6, 2017. http://www.nytimes.com/interactive/2017/01/06/us/politics/document-russia-hacking-report-intelligence-agencies.html?smid=tw-nytimes&smtyp=cur&_r=0.
66. An unclassified version of the intelligence report was released to the public through the media on January 6, 2017. http://www.nytimes.com/interactive/2017/01/06/us/politics/document-russia-hacking-report-intelligence-agencies.html?smid=tw-nytimes&smtyp=cur&_r=0; Adam Entous, Ellen Nakashima, and Greg Miller, "Secret CIA assessment says Russia was Trying to Help Trump Win White House," *The Washington Post*, December 9, 2016. https://www.washingtonpost.com/world/national-security/obama-orders-review-of-russian-hacking-during-presidential-campaign/2016/12/09/31d6b300-be2a-11e6-94ac-3d324840106c_story.html?utm_term=.e589066144fe (Entous et al. 2016).
67. Ed O'Keefe and Paul Kane, "McConnell Announces Senate Probe of Suspected Russian Election Interference: 'The Russians Are Not Our Friends,'" *The Washington Post*, December 12, 2016. https://www.washingtonpost.com/news/powerpost/wp/2016/12/12/schumer-on-congressional-probe-of-russia-i-dont-want-this-to-turn-into-a-benghazi-investigation/?utm_term=.880d5944b09b (O'Keefe and Kane 2016).
68. Forni, *The Civility Solution: What to Do When People are Rude*.
69. Baumeister and Leary, "The Need to Belong: Desire for Interpersonal Attachments as a Fundamental Human Need"; Leary and Baumeister, "The Nature and Function of Self-Esteem: Sociometer Theory."
70. Rosenberry, "Users Support Anonymity Despite Increasing Negativity"; Diakopoulos and Naaman, "Towards Quality Discourse in Online News Comments."
71. Arthur D. Santana, "Online Readers' Comments Represent New Opinion Pipeline," *Newspaper Research Journal* 32, no. 3 (2011): 66–88 (Santana 2011).
72. Coe, Kenski, and Rains, "Online and Uncivil? Patterns and Determinants of Incivility in Newspaper Website Comments."
73. Scott Montgomery, "Beyond Comments: Finding Better Ways to Connect with You," *NPR.org*, August 17, 2016. http://www.npr.

org/sections/thisisnpr/2016/08/17/490208179/beyond-comments-finding-better-ways-to-connect-with-you; Elizabeth Jensen, "NPR Website to Get Rid of Comments," *NPR.org*, August 17, 2016. http://www.npr.org/sections/ombudsman/2016/08/17/489516952/npr-website-to-get-rid-of-comments; Justin Ellis, "What Happened When 7 News Sites Got Rid of Reader Comments," *Nieman Journalism Lab*, September 16, 2015. http://www.niemanlab.org/2015/09/what-happened-after-7-news-sites-got-rid-of-reader-comments/ (Montgomery 2016; Jensen 2016; Ellis 2015).

74. Gina Masullo Chen and Paromita Pain, "Normalizing Online Comments," *Journalism Practice*, Advance Online Publication, 2016. doi:10.1080/17512786.2016.1205954 (Chen and Pain 2016).

75. Steffen Albrecht, "Whose Voice is Heard in Online Deliberation? A Study of Participation and Representation in Political Debates on the Internet," *Information, Communication & Society* 8, no. 1 (2006): 62–82; Papacharissi, "Democracy Online: Civility, Politeness, and Democratic Potential of Online Political Discussion Groups," 259; Edith Manosevitch and Dana Walker, "Reader Comments to Online Opinion Journalism: A Space of Public Deliberation," *International Symposium of Online Journalism* 10 (2009): 10–30 (Albrecht 2006; Manosevitch and Walker 2009).

76. Gastil, *Political Communication and Deliberation.*

77. Fishkin, *Democracy and Deliberation*; Gastil, *Political Communication and Deliberation*; Gastil and Black, "Public Deliberation as the Organizing Principle of Political Communication Research"; Jacobs, Cook, and Delli Carpini, *Talking Together: Public Deliberation and Political Participation in America*; Gutmann and Thompson, *Democracy and Disagreement*; Landemore, "Democratic Reason: The Mechanism of Collective Intelligence in Politics."

78. Lindita Camaj and Arthur D. Santana, "Political Deliberation on Facebook During Electoral Campaigns: Exploring the Relevance of the Moderator's Technical Role and Political Ideology," *Journal of Information, Technology & Politics* 12, no. 4 (2015): 325–341; Jennifer Stomer-Galley, "Diversity of Political Conversation on the Internet: Users' Perspectives," *Journal of Computer-Mediated Communication* 8, no. 3 (2003): n.p.; Carlos Ruiz, David Domingo, Josep Lluís Micó, Javier Díaz-Noci, Koldo Meso, and Pere Maship, "Public Sphere 2.0:? The Democratic Qualities of Citizen Debates in Online Newspapers," *The International Journal of Press/Politics* 16, no. 4 (2011): 463–487; Santana, "Online Readers' Comments Represent New Opinion Pipeline." (Camaj and Santana 2015; Stomer-Galley 2003; Ruiz et al. 2011).

79. Elihu Katz, "Back to the Street: When Media and Opinion Leaves Home," *Mass Communication and Society* 17 (2014): 454–463; Gabriel De Tarde, *On Communication and Social Influence*, ed. Terry N. Clark, (Chicago, IL: University of Chicago Press, 1889/1969) (Katz 2014; Tarde 1889).
80. Russell Spears, Tom Postmes, and Martin Le, and Anka Wolbert, "When Are Net Effects Gross Products? The Power of Influence and Influence of Power in Computer-Mediated Communication," *Journal of Social Issues* 58, no. 1 (2002): 91–107 (Spears et al. 2002).
81. Ori Tenenboim and Akiba A. Cohen, "What Prompts Users to Click and Comment: A Longitudinal Study of Online News," *Journalism* 16, no. 2 (2015): 198–217; Patrick Weber, "Discussions in the Comments Sections: Factors Influencing Participation and Interactivity in Online Newspapers' Reader Comments," *New Media & Society* 10, no. 6 (2013): 941–957; Stroud et al., "Changing Deliberative Norms on News Organizations' Facebook Sites." (Tenenboim and Cohen 2015; Weber 2013).

References

Akpan, Nsikan. 2016. The Very Real Consequences of Fake News Stories and Why Our Brain Can't Ignore Them. *PBS News Hour*, December 5. http://www.pbs.org/newshour/updates/real-consequences-fake-news-stories-brain-cant-ignore/. Accessed 6 Dec 2016.

Albrecht, Steffen. 2006. Whose Voice is Heard in Online Deliberation? A Study of Participation and Representation in Political Debates on the Internet. *Information, Communication & Society* 8 (1): 62–82.

Andersson, Lynne M., and Christine M. Pearson. 1999. Tit for Tat? The Spiraling Effect of Incivility in the Workplace. *Academy of Management Review* 24 (3): 452–471.

Bai, Qiyu, Weipeng Lin, and Lei Wang. 2016. Family Incivility and Counterproductive Work Behavior: A Moderated Mediation Model of Self-Esteem and Emotional Regulation. *Journal of Vocational Behavior* 94: 11–19.

Baumeister, Roy F., and Mark R. Leary. 1995. The Need to Belong: Desire for Interpersonal Attachments as a Fundamental Human Need. *Psychological Bulletin* 117 (3): 497–529.

Berry, Jeffrey M., and Sarah Sobieraj. 2014. *The Outrage Industry: Politics and the New Incivility*. New York: Oxford University Press.

Braithwaite, Andrea. 2016. It's About Ethics in Games Journalism? Gamergaters and Geek Masculinity. *Social Media + Society* 4: 1–10.

Brett, Jeanne M., Mara Olekains, Ray Friedman, Nathan Goates, Cameron Anderson, and Cara Cherry Lisco. 2007. Sticks and Stones: Language, Face, and Online Dispute Resolution. *Academy of Management Journal* 50 (1): 85–99.

Buckels, Erin E., Paul D. Trapnell, and Delroy L. Paulhus. 2014. Trolls Just Want to Have Fun. *Personality and Individual Differences* 62: 97–102.

Burns, Alexander, Maggie Haberman, and Jonathan Martin. 2016. Donald Trump Apology Caps Day of Outrage Over Lewd Tape. *The New York Times*, October 7. http://www.nytimes.com/2016/10/08/us/politics/donald-trump-women.html. Accessed 12 Dec 2016.

Camaj, Lindita, and Arthur D. Santana. 2015. Political Deliberation on Facebook During Electoral Campaigns: Exploring the Relevance of Moderator's Technical Role and Political Ideology. *Journal of Information, Technology & Politics* 12 (4): 325–341.

Chen, Gina Masullo, and Paromita Pain. 2016. Normalizing Online Comments. *Journalism Practice*. doi:10.1080/17512786.2016.1205954.

Chen, Gina Masullo, and Shuning Lu. 2017. Online Political Discourse: Exploring Differences in Effects of Civil and Uncivil Disagreement in News Website Comments. *Journal of Broadcasting & Electronic Media* 61 (1). doi:10.1080/08838151/2016/1273922.

Chess, Shira, and Adrienne Shaw. 2015. A Conspiracy of Fishes, or, How we Learned to Stop Worrying About #GamerGate and Embrace Hegemonic Masculinity. *Journal of Broadcasting & Electronic Media* 59 (1): 208–220.

Chozik, Amy. 2016. Hillary Clinton Calls Many Trump Backers 'Deplorables,' and GOP Pounces. *The New York Times*, September 10. http://www.nytimes.com/2016/09/11/us/politics/hillary-clinton-basket-of-deplorables.html. Accessed 12 Dec 2016.

Clayton, Cornell W. 2012. Historical Perspectives on the Role of Civility in American Democracy. In *Civility and Democracy in America: A Reasoned Understanding*, eds. Cornell W. Clayton and Richard Elgar, 1–4. Pullman, WA: Washington University Press.

Coe, Kevin, Kate Kenski, and Stephen A. Rains. 2014. Online and Uncivil? Patterns and Determinants of Incivility in Newspaper Website Comments. *Journal of Communication* 64: 658–679.

Cole, Kristi K. 2015. It's Like She's Eager to be Verbally Abused: Twitter, Trolls, and (En)Gendering Disciplinary Rhetoric. *Feminist Media Studies* 15 (2): 356–358.

De Tarde, Gabriel. 1889/1969. *On Communication and Social Influence*, ed. Terry N. Clark. Chicago: University of Chicago Press.

Dehue, Francine, Catherine Bolman, and Trinjntje Völlink. 2008. Cyberbullying: Youngsters' Experiences and Parental Perception. *Cyberpsychology & Behavior* 11 (2): 217–223.

Diakopoulos Nicholas, and Mor Naaman. 2011. Towards Quality Discourse in Online News Comments. In *Proceedings of the CSCW*, March 19–23, Hangzhou, China.

Ellis, Justin. 2015. What Happened When 7 News Sites Got Rid of Reader Comments. *Nieman Journalism Lab*, September 15. http://www.niemanlab.org/2015/09/what-happened-after-7-news-sites-got-rid-of-reader-comments/. Accessed 23 Aug 2016.

Entous, Adam, Ellen Nakashima, and Greg Miller. 2016. Secret CIA Assessment says Russia was Trying to Help Trump Win White House. The Washington Post, December 9. https://www.washingtonpost.com/world/national-security/obama-orders-review-of-russian-hacking-during-presidential-campaign/2016/12/09/31d6b300-be2a-11e6-94ac-3d324840106c_story.html?utm_term=.e589066144fe. Accessed 12 Dec 2016.

Fishkin, James S. 1991. *Democracy and Deliberation*. New Haven, CT: Yale University Press.

Forni, P.M. 2008. *The Civility Solution: What to Do When People are Rude*. New York: St. Martin's Press.

Gastil, John. 2008. *Political communication and deliberation*. Thousand Oaks, CA: Sage.

Gastil, John, and Laura W. Black. 2008. Public Deliberation as the Organizing Principle of Political Communication Research. *Journal of Public Deliberation* 4 (1): Article 3.

Geer, John G. 2006. *In Defense of Negativity: Attack Ads in Presidential Campaigns*, 2006. Chicago: University of Chicago Press.

Gini, Gianluca, and Dorothy L. Espelage. 2014. Peer Victimization, Cyberbullying, and Suicide Risk in Children and Adolescents. *Journal of the American Medical Association* 312 (5): 545–546.

Grice, H.P. 1969. Utterer's meaning and intention. *The Philosophical Review* 78 (2): 147–177.

Gutmann, Amy, and Dennis Thompson. 1996. *Democracy and Disagreement*. Cambridge, MA: Harvard University Press.

Herschcovis, M.Sandy. 2011. 'Incivility, Social Undermining, Bullying ... Oh My!': A Call to Reconcile Constructs Within Workplace Aggression Research. *Journal of Organizational Communication* 32 (3): 499–519.

Hwang, Hyunseo, Zhondang Pan, and Ye Sun. 2008. Influence of Hostile Media Perceptions on Willingness to Engage in Discursive Activities: An Examination of Mediating Role of Media Indignation. *Media Psychology* 11 (1): 76–97.

Jacobs, Lawrence R., Fay Lomax Cook, and Michael X. Delli Carpini. 2009. *Talking Together: Public Deliberation and Political Participation in America*. Chicago: University of Chicago Press.

Jamieson, Kathleen Hall, and Joseph N. Cappella. 2008. *Echo Chamber: Rush Limbaugh and the Conservative Media Establishment.* New York: Oxford University Press.
Jensen, Elizabeth. 2016. NPR Website to Get Rid of Comments. *NPR.org*, August 17. http://www.npr.org/sections/ombudsman/2016/08/17/489516952/npr-website-to-get-rid-of-comments. Accessed 23 Aug 2016.
Katz, Elihu. 2014. Back to the Street: When Media and Opinion Leaves Home. *Mass Communication and Society* 17: 454–463.
Khaldarova, Irina, and Mervi Pantti. 2016. Fake News. *Journalism Practice* 10 (7): 891–901.
Klofstad, Casey A., Anand Edward Sokhey, and Scott D. McClurg. 2013. Disagreeing About Disagreement: How Conflict in Social Networks Affects Political Behavior. *American Journal of Political Science* 57: 120–134.
Landemore, Hélène. 2012. Democratic Reason: The Mechanism of Collective Intelligence in Politics. In *Collective Wisdom: Principles and Mechanisms*, ed. Hélène Landemore, and John Elster, 251–289. New York: Cambridge University Press.
Leary, Mark R., and Roy F. Baumeister. 2000. The Nature and Function of Self-esteem: Sociometer Theory. *Advances in Experimental Social Psychology* 32: 1–62.
Leary, Mark R. 2010. Affiliation, Belonging, and Acceptance: The Pursuit of Interpersonal Connection. In *Handbook of Social Psychology*, ed. Susan T. Fiske, Daniel T. Gilbert, and Gardner Lindzey, 864–897. Hoboken, NJ: Wiley.
Lee, Michelle Ye Hee. 2015. Donald Trump's False Comments Connecting Mexican Immigrants and Crime. *The Washington Post*, July 18. https://www.washingtonpost.com/news/fact-checker/wp/2015/07/08/donald-trumps-false-comments-connecting-mexican-immigrants-and-crime/?utm_term=.ccfc38734c56. Accessed 7 Dec 2016.
Levendusky, Matthew. 2013. *How Partisan Media Polarize America.* Chicago: University of Chicago Press.
Logevall, Fredrik. 2012. The Paradox of Civility. In *Civility and Democracy in America: A Reasoned Understanding*, ed. Cornell W. Clayton and Richard Elgar. 5–12. Pullman: Washington University Press.
Maheshwari, Sapna. 2016. How Fake News Goes Viral: A Case Study. *The New York Times*, November 20. http://www.nytimes.com/2016/11/20/business/media/how-fake-news-spreads.html. Accessed 12 Dec 2016.
Manosevitch, Edith, and Dana Walker. 2009. Reader Comments to Online Opinion Journalism: A Space of Public Deliberation. *International Symposium of Online Journalism* 10: 10–30.
Marchi, Regina. 2012. With Facebook, Blogs, and Fake News, Teens Reject Journalistic 'Objectivity'. *Journal of Communication Inquiry* 36 (3): 246–262.

Matsunaga, Masaki. 2011. Underlying Circuits of Social Support for Bullied Victims: An Appraisal-Based Perspective on Supportive Communication and Postbullying Adjustment. *Human Communication Research* 37: 174–206.

Mohan, Geoffrey. 2016. Facebook's Zuckerberg Offers Plan to Counter Fake News Sites. *Los Angeles Times*, November 19. http://www.latimes.com/business/la-fi-fakenews-facebook-20161119-story.html. Accessed 21 Dec 2016.

Montgomery, Scott. 2016. Beyond Comments: Finding Better Ways to Connect with You. *NPR.org*, August 23. http://www.npr.org/sections/thisisnpr/2016/08/17/490208179/beyond-comments-finding-better-ways-to-connect-with-you. Accessed 23 Aug 2016.

Mutz, Diana C. 2002. Cross-Cutting Social Networks: Testing Democratic Theory in Practice. *American Political Science Review* 96 (1): 111–126.

Mutz, Diana C. 2015. *In-Your-Face Politics: The Consequences of Uncivil Media*. Princeton, NJ: Princeton University Press.

O'Keefe, Ed, and Paul Kane. 2016. McConnell Announces Senate Probe of Suspected Russian Election Interference: 'The Russians Are Not Our Friends.' *The Washington Post*, December 12. https://www.washingtonpost.com/news/powerpost/wp/2016/12/12/schumer-on-congressional-probe-of-russia-i-dont-want-this-to-turn-into-a-benghazi-investigation/?utm_term=.880d5944b09b. Accessed 12 Dec 2016.

O'Sullivan, Patrick B., and Andrew J. Flanagin. 2003. Reconceptualizing 'Flaming' and Other Problematic Messages. *New Media & Society* 5 (1): 69–94.

Ohlheiser, Abby. 2016. Just How Offensive Did Milo Yiannopoulos Have to Be to Get Banned From Twitter? *The Washington Post*, July 21. https://www.washingtonpost.com/news/the-intersect/wp/2016/07/21/what-it-takes-to-get-banned-from-twitter/?utm_term=.27ca27d651fa. Accessed 9 Dec 2016.

Olweus, Dan. 1993. *Bullying at School: What we Know and What We can Do*. Oxford, UK: Blackwell.

Papacharissi, Zizi. 2004. Democracy Online: Civility, Politeness, and the Democratic Potential of Online Political Discussion. *New Media & Society* 6 (2): 259–283.

Podsiadly, Adrzej, and Malgorzata Gamain-Wilk. 2016. Personality Traits As Predictors or Outcomes of Being Exposed to Bullying in the Workplace. *Personality and Individual Differences*, Advance Online Publication. http://dx.doi.org/10.1016/j.paid.2016.08.001. Accessed 7 Dec 2016.

Putnam, Linda L., and Dennis K. Mumby. 2014. *The Sage Handbook of Organizational Communication*. Thousand Oaks, CA: Sage.

Rappeport, Alan. 2016. Who Won the Debate? Hillary Clinton, the 'Nasty Woman.' *The New York Times*, October 20. http://www.nytimes.com/2016/10/21/us/politics/who-won-the-third-debate.html. Accessed 12 December 2016.

Rosenberry, Jack. 2011. Users Support Anonymity Despite Increasing Negativity. *Newspaper Research Journal* 32 (1): 6–19.
Rösner, Leonie, Stephan Winter, and Nicole C. Krämer. 2016. Dangerous Minds? Effects of Online Comments on Aggressive Cognitions, Emotions, and Behavior. *Computers in Human Behavior* 58: 461–470.
Ruiz, Carlos, David Domingo, Josep Lluís Micó, Javier Díaz-Noci, Koldo Meso, and Pere Maship. 2011. Public Sphere 2.0? The Democratic Qualities of Citizen Debates in Online Newspapers. *The International Journal of Press/Politics* 16 (4): 463–487.
Santana, Arthur D. 2011. Online Readers' Comments Represent New Opinion Pipeline. *Newspaper Research Journal* 32 (3): 66–88.
Santana, Arthur D. 2014. Virtuous or Vitriolic. *Journalism Practice* 8 (1): 18–33.
Shoemaker, Pamela J. 1982. The Perceived Legitimacy of Deviant Political Groups: Two Experiments on Media Effects. *Communication Research* 9 (2): 249–286.
Shoemaker, Pamela J. 1984. Media Treatment of Deviant Groups. *Journalism Quarterly* 61 (1): 66–82.
Slater, Michael D. 2007. Reinforcing Spirals: The Mutual Influence of Media Selectivity and Media Effects and Their Impact on Individual Behavior and Society Identity. *Communication Theory* 17: 281–303.
Spears, Russell, Tom Postmes, Martin Le, and Anka Wolbert. 2002. When are Net Effects Gross Products? The Power of Influence and Influence of Power in Computer-Mediated Communication. *Journal of Social Issues* 58 (1): 91–107.
Stromer-Galley, Jennifer. 2003. Diversity of Political Conversation on the Internet: Users' Perspectives. *Journal of Computer-Mediated Communication* 8 (3): n.p.
Stroud, Natalie J. 2008. Media Use and Political Dispositions: Revisiting the Concept of Selective Exposure. *Political Behavior* 30: 341–366.
Stroud, Natalie J. 2010. Polarization and Partisan Selective Exposure. *Journal of Communication* 60: 556–576.
Stroud, Natalie J., Joshua M. Scacco, Ashley Muddiman, and Alexander L. Curry. 2015. Changing Deliberative Norms on News Organizations' Facebook Sites. *Journal of Computer-Mediated Communication* 20: 188–203.
Tenenboim, Ori, and Akiba A. Cohen. 2015. What Prompts Users to Click and Comment? A Longitudinal Study of Online News. *Journalism* 16 (2): 198–217.
Weber, Patrick. 2013. Discussions in the Comments Sections: Factors Influencing Participation And Interactivity in Online Newspapers' Reader Comments. *New Media & Society* 10 (6): 941–957.
Williams, Sherri. 2015. Digital Defense: Black Feminists Resist Violence and Hashtag Activism. *Feminist Media Studies* 15 (2): 341–344.

Yourish, Karen, Larry Buchanan, and Alicia Parlapiano. 2016. More Than 160 Republican Leaders Don't Support Donald Trump. Here's When They Reached Their Breaking Point. *The New York Times*, August 28. http://www.nytimes.com/interactive/2016/08/29/us/politics/at-least-110-republican-leaders-wont-vote-for-donald-trump-heres-when-they-reached-their-breaking-point.html. Accessed Dec 2016.

Zadro, Lisa, Kipling D. Williams, and Rick Richardson. 2005. Riding the 'O' Train: Comparing the Effects of Ostracism and Verbal Dispute on Targets and Sources. *Group Processes and Intergroup Relations* 8 (2): 125–143.

Zukin, Cliff, Scott Keeter, Molly Andolina, Krista Jenkins, and Michael X. Delli Carpini. 2006. *A New Engagement? Political Participation, Civic Life and the Changing American Citizen*. New York: Oxford University Press.

CHAPTER 2

Online Incivility and Public Discourse

When newspaper reporter Marnie Eisenstadt[1] posted her story online about poverty in an Upstate New York community, predictably it received a slew of comments. Within a day, more than 500 people commented on the April 2016 story about poverty in the mid-sized city of Syracuse. They shared opinions, raised questions, and criticized the piece. Eisenstadt jumped into the fray frequently, answering questions and offering additional information all in a rational manner. For example, when ColdColdGoAway wrote: "How about finding the poor jobs?????????? So they won't be poor!"[2] Eisenstadt offered a reasoned response: "@ColdColdGoAway: We have examined this, as well, in our series, The Cost of Poverty."[3] Then she provided a link to the previous story. When ColdColdGoAway persisted, writing: "I remember that story. That was one person's story,"[4] Eisenstadt was undaunted. "It was the beginning of an examination of a program that helped more than 100 people find and keep employment,"[5] she explained and again provided a link to the rest of the series on poverty. When another poster, kayak, criticized a premise of the story that one way to solve the community's poverty crisis was to build public housing within suburbs, Eisenstadt joined the conversation again. "There is not simple, easy one-size fits all answers to Syracuse's complex poverty. There are many small answers, ways of doing things differently that might work. Here, the suggestion is not vast development of public housing in the suburbs. It is mixed income housing in places of opportunity. It's not an answer for everyone, but data shows it could substantially change the lives of some."[6]

What is notable about Eisenstadt's actions is that she is demonstrating a "deliberative moment"[7] in the public talk of a comment stream on an online news site. She is rational and clear, and she bolsters her view with evidence. She is reciprocal, meaning she leaves room for other views and even disagreement. She comes across as understanding what others are saying, not just spouting off her own ideas.[8] Certainly, the commenters she is responding to are pointed—but not uncivil. Also, she is not necessarily solving a public problem or fostering consensus,[9] as deliberation aims to do, but she is trying to inform. Even if she does not intend to, she is claiming the comment stream as the "broader deliberative arena to which journalism contributes."[10] She is fostering an environment in the virtual public sphere that is hospitable to the robust give-and-take of public debate that is vital to a healthy democracy.[11] She is creating a climate that offers the hope for the online space to "revive the public sphere"[12] as a place of "deliberative democracy" that sociologist and social psychologist Gabriel de Tarde envisioned in the salons and cafés of eighteenth century Paris.[13] In his day, de Tarde saw what he called "dispersed crowds,"[14] which were brought together by the newspaper to debate important issues of the day.[15] Eisenstadt, in her small way, is creating that experience in her newspaper's online space.

This chapter focuses on the virtual versions of these cafés and salons, the comment streams of American newspapers where today's dispersed crowds gather to debate and banter and talk. I will explore the concept of deliberative democracy, specifically within the context of online discussions. I will argue that this deliberation—including disagreement—is essential to the vigorous public debate that is the hallmark of a democratic society.[16] Disagreement—both civil and uncivil—involves a challenge to one's views.[17] This challenge can create feelings of uneasiness or internal conflict called cognitive dissonance[18] as people reconcile their views with others' opinions. This deliberation is essential to the democratic process because it allows all people to take part in the decisions that may highlight what topics are most urgent in our society. This form of communication takes on increased urgency online because the computer-mediated sphere offers more opportunity for people to speak out, so more informed voices might be drowned out. Or, as in the case of Eisenstadt, more rational voices may set a tone of deliberation. Deliberation is often associated with political talk,[19] but in this chapter I explore the concept more broadly to topics outside of politics that are important to air publicly. For example, clearly an online debate about the merits of presidential contenders is political talk that is improved if it is deliberative. However, an online discussion about the benefits of composting or growing one's own vegetables is not political per se, but it also offers more value to society as a whole if it also follows the guidelines of public deliberation. I will begin by explaining the concept of public deliberation in greater detail, and then I will explore specifically how disagreement fits into deliberation. Next I will explain how deliberation may operate online by synthesizing prior research.

Public Deliberation

At its core, public deliberation is about giving people room to speak out. The idea encompasses the value of equality that is embedded in American culture, although not always lived out. For deliberation to occur everyone must be allowed a voice and what those voices express should be rooted in reason.[20] The goal is to promote consensus, but deliberation provides room for people to disagree and debate. Deliberation also should be reciprocal, meaning it embraces different views.[21] It should be conducted publicly, and it requires that people offer some sort of evidence to justify their viewpoints.[22] In the best case, it offers solutions, not just problems, and it allows people to retain their own dignity throughout the debate.[23] As political communication scholars John Gastil and Laura W. Black explain: "When people deliberate, they carefully examine a problem and arrive at a well-reasoned solution after a period of inclusive, respectful consideration of diverse points of view."[24] Some scholars include participation in public forums or even contrasting media messages as forms of deliberation. Most theorists agree that public deliberation includes some type of "public talking"[25] that contributes to public opinion. Deliberation is about the discussion, the conversation, the exchange of ideas. It is about speaking out, so that others can hear, understand, and respond to what one is saying. It provides a sense of voice that is pivotal to how a free society should operate. People can form their own opinions and tell others, contributing to public good in society. Deliberation is not just a benefit of a free society but essential to maintaining that freedom. People must be part of the decision-making of government if a nation is to be of the people and for the people. As political scientist Harold D. Lasswell explained years ago: "Democratic governments act upon public opinion and public opinion acts openly and continually upon government. This open interplay of opinion and policy is the distinguishing mark of popular rule."[26]

The concept of public deliberation grew out of political thought. In fact, Gastil and Black argue it is the organizing principle of all political communication.[27] Theorist Hannah Arendt suggested that to be political means that decisions are made through discussion and persuasion not fights. "Everyone sees and hears from a different position,"[28] she explained. This give and take is at the heart of the type of debate that generates the "communicative power"[29] to influence political elections and legislation. Deliberation relies on the idea that a group may have knowledge greater than the individuals who comprise that group.[30] As a result, sharing ideas might improve decision-making. Deliberation happens or should happen in Congress, the courts, the media, and in the "land of middle democracy,"[31] which is any place where people gather. James Madison considered deliberation so vital to America's democracy that he included it as one of the nation's core values, along with equality and the absence of tyranny, when he penned *The Federalist Papers*.[32] Of course, talking about a problem may give those in power a sense of what the public thinks and feels, and thereby, inform the political process,[33] but that does not mean change will occur. True deliberation requires that people listen, not just speak,[34] that people act, not just listen.

Critics of the concept of public deliberation worry that speaking is not enough. Journalism scholar Michael Schudson, for instance, argues that the emphasis on spontaneous conversation is misplaced because the real goal should be talk that is not just public, but egalitarian—encompassing the ideas of many with different values and backgrounds.[35] Others view public deliberation as too idealistic because it assumes small efforts can bring about large changes, or they suggest deliberation is impossible in a complicated democratic system.[36] Public deliberation also has been criticized for being too narrow and perpetuating the same voices that always get heard and leaving out socially marginalized groups, such as women, people of color, and other minorities.[37] I embrace these criticisms, and suggest that public deliberation is not perfect. It is merely a start. We are a better society if we foster reciprocal conversations from a diversity of viewpoints about important issues, but deliberation alone cannot solve all our ills. I discuss these criticisms later in this chapter and in Part II.

In this book, I take a broad view of public deliberation. It is not reserved just for political talk. In fact, I argue that the concepts of public deliberation apply as well to discussion about almost any important issues, as they do to political topics. Part of the reason for my belief is that many topics, even those that are not overtly political, may offer political undertones. A debate over whether climate change is caused by how people have abused the environment or a natural process is not overtly political on the face of it. It becomes political as people take partisan sides on the issue, and different viewpoints become aligned with particular parties. But the important part of the issue is the discussion that may or may not bring about understanding and change.

Deliberation Beyond Politics

I submit that even topics without political undertones may be ripe for public deliberation. For example, online sites proliferate, on which people talk about all types of issues, from stories in that day's newspaper to the basics of child rearing or even ratings of the best restaurant in town. When people are recommending the best spot for barbecue on a foodie Facebook page, the discourse is improved if people state their beliefs rationally, are open to others' opinions, and offer evidence for their point of view. In the realm of interpersonal communication, these concepts suggest a form of discussion that makes communication more open and more valuable. In that sense, deliberative qualities in any type of speech offer benefits for society as a whole. It is always best to listen, not just talk; to be open to other's ideas; to offer a grounded rationale for one's thinking. The topics that are examined in this book—the 2016 U.S. presidential campaign, the debate over removing vestiges of the Confederacy from government spaces, and the continuing fight for marriage equality—certainly have political ramifications. However, I believe the principles outlined in this chapter and throughout the book apply more broadly. It is better for democracy when people can publicly deliberate about politics. Similarly, it is good for society when people can publicly deliberate about any subject. As such, deliberation cuts across a wide swatch of fields beyond political science, including interpersonal communication, mass communication, public affairs, social psychology, and sociology.[38] Yes, public deliberation is important for democracy. It is also important for life.

For example, consider what erupted on Twitter after a Texas school district decided not to cancel classes on a particularly rain-soaked day in May 2016.[39] The district tweeted that classes remained in session, and urged people to stay safe getting to school. People challenged the decision somewhat politely on Twitter, joking they would enjoy swimming through school hallways or needed a sailboat to get to class. Then they turned to memes, which are "socially constructed public discourses"[40] circulated online to make a point. One meme used an animated image file called a gif to show President Barack Obama, shaking his head and saying, "No," as if the president were disagreeing with the school district's decision to keep classes open. Another meme used a gif of a baby clenching his hands in disgust, apparently at the district's ruling. While this is certainly not the public deliberation that Madison, the Father of the Constitution, likely imagined, I submit these tweets follow much of the conventions of public deliberation. They allowed a variety of people from a cross-section of the community to speak directly to the government and challenge a government decision. These tweets did not offer much evidence or seek to solve a problem through consensus, but they did make a rational point: It is flooding too much for school to remain in session. Certainly, it would be an overstatement to label this public deliberation. But it offers a deliberative moment; deliberation light, if you will. Society gains because the school district learns what the public thinks about its actions. People gain because they have a chance to speak, to air their grievances publicly. In a very real sense, this online exchange demonstrates the ideals of democratic deliberation, a belief that the public use of arguments and reasoning among free and equal individuals is vital to society.[41]

Deliberative Disagreement

Of course, true deliberation often may be "profoundly uncomfortable"[42] because it requires talk among people who are different from each other. As a result, exposure to disagreement is a key aspect of much deliberation.[43] In fact, political scientists Amy Gutmann and Dennis Thompson assert that "moral disagreement"[44]—conflict about fundamental issues—is the root of deliberation. This is not disagreement just to be disagreeable. This is not taking an alternative view only to be contrary. In this type of disagreement, people feel an intense moral rightness deep in their beings. So when people challenge their view,[45] it hurts. In this sense, the online discussions about barbecue or a school closing lack the potential for true deliberation because the stakes are not high enough. These issues certainly can offer deliberative moments, and society is improved by those discourses. But for deliberation writ large, people must care enough about their viewpoint to feel a sense of loss when it is threatened. It requires morally loaded topics, such as abortion, immigration, or the #BlackLivesMatter movement that rose up in response to the shooting deaths of unarmed black men at the hands of police.[46] These are also the type of issues most likely to elicit strong opinions[47] and generate online comments.[48] Our need to speak out is strongest when we feel the most passionate about a topic. In addition, society benefits the most from deliberation on topics that elicit this passion.

Emotion and Reason

This also suggests that while deliberation should be rational, it cannot be divorced from emotion. While some assert that deliberation requires a lack of emotion, I support the view of affective intelligence theory,[49] which argues that emotions and reason can and should co-exist and actually complement each other. Theories differ regarding whether emotions are automatic responses to an experience[50] or if they only occur if people have thought about how they feel.[51] My intent is not to resolve this debate, which has raged for decades. However, it seems clear that emotions by their very nature help people evaluate stimuli and make decisions about what to do.[52] Emotions are temporary states that can range from positive to negative in response to a specific situation.[53] The very nature of emotions is to help in people's survival by providing clues about how they should proceed.[54] So when people are deciding their opinion on important issues, it seems natural that emotions—their responses to those issues—would be part of how they make up their minds. This is the heart of affective intelligence theory,[55] which proposes that cognitive processes—the thinking about things—are not separate from the emotional processes—the feeling about things. So how can one be rational while still emotional? The paradox relies on balance between the two. Often, we assign a negative connotation to emotion ("thinking with one's heart rather than one's head," for example). Or we see emotions as dichotomous—either bad or good—rather than merely spontaneous, natural human responses to stimuli. However, the word emotion actually stems from the Latin root of the word "to move."[56] Emotions are what move us to act in many cases. These emotional responses may help us understand important issues more fully than reason alone. Consider abortion. A person may reach a decision to support abortion rights after much thought and research but also by being emotionally moved by the story of woman impregnated during rape who seeks the freedom to end the pregnancy. Similarly, someone who opposes abortion may reach that decision through careful analysis but may also influenced by an emotional response to seeing a premature baby live outside the womb. The moment when emotion and reason depart from any potential for deliberation is when emotion takes over completely: "To be passionate is to be gripped, seized, or possessed by primordial forces beyond one's rational control."[57] When emotion and reason remain in balance, deliberation can occur. In fact, it seems unlikely that people could make a reasoned argument, supported by fact, and open to others' viewpoints without feeling some passion on the subject. I certainly would not want to spend much time with a person who only thought but never felt. Nor would I appreciate a person who only felt but never thought. Balance is the key here.

Pros and Cons of Disagreement

A great deal of research suggests that exposing people to viewpoints that differ from their own opinions has merit. These so-called crosscutting arguments help people become more familiar with others' viewpoints and the reasons they may hold these opinions.[58] This may not persuade people to change their outlook, but it may help them at least see where those who disagree with them are coming from. It may make people see the legitimate reasons for others holding divergent views, even if they still passionately disagree. "What makes opinion deliberative is not merely that is has been built upon careful contemplation, evidence, and supportive arguments, but also that it has grasped and taken into consideration the opposing views of others,"[59] as several political communication scholars put it. Exposure to disagreement may increase tolerance for difference[60] and could create a more informed populace, as people reflect on why they hold their own beliefs when those opinions are challenged.[61] Here is how this works: As people try to justify their own beliefs, they may turn to factual information or concrete arguments, which increase their own knowledge[62] even if it does not change their opinions. This is the cognitive dissonance[63] explanation for disagreement, which argues that people try to relieve the discomfort they feel because other people see things differently than they do. People employ interpersonal strategies, such as changing their own viewpoint or trying to convert others, to relieve this discomfort.[64] There is also some evidence that exposure to disagreement leads to less political polarization.[65]

However, other research suggests that exposure to crosscutting viewpoints does not deepen people's knowledge of their own position[66] but merely makes people more entrenched. In this scenario, people dig in their heels and become more certain of their opinions when they are challenged. Another negative consequence of disagreement is that it may foster ambivalence or make people less sure of their own beliefs.[67] As a result, people may withdraw from participating in the democratic process by shunning such as activities as voting, handing out leaflets for a cause, or protesting at an event. The reasoning is that people step back as they are trying to resolve their internal conflict about how they feel regarding the issue. For some, it may seem easier to withdraw than to resolve this conflict. This is the heart of the cross-pressures hypothesis,[68] which posits that exposure to disagreement in one's social group demobilizes people from participating politically. Sometimes this is termed the "deliberation–participation paradox"[69] because exposure to diverse views is a core tenet of deliberation but it may actually lead to less participation, which is the opposite of deliberation's goal to increase societal participation. This puts deliberation and political participation at cross-purposes. Increasing one decreases the other. Disagreement also may "thwart self-expression" because people are afraid of social rejection if they speak out, leading to a "silencing effect."[70] Another negative effect of disagreement is that people perceive those who disagree with them as biased. This creates the potential for a "bias-perception conflict spiral,"[71] where people perceive those who disagree with them as biased and that leads them to take conflict-escalating actions against them, which reinforce this sense of bias.[72] These conflict-escalation actions could include some of the common aspects of uncivil online debate, such as name-calling, insults, profanity, or an outright accusation of bias. No one is left better by such an exchange.

Much depends on how people encounter disagreement. People who are in the political minority in their community may be less likely to vote or get involved politically because they feel unsupported in their viewpoints, but disagreement has little effect on those in the political majority.[73] For those in the political minority, the principles of deliberation and participatory democracy are at cross-purposes.[74] If you encourage one, you decrease the likelihood of the other. It is worth pointing out that this is also an unlikely scenario because most people cannot sustain a social network where they feel so isolated without joining a more hospitable group.[75] The more common scenario is to be in a group where most people think like you or where you are confronted with a mixture of viewpoints. Research has shown in these cases that disagreement does not hamper political participation.[76] In fact, when people are faced with a mix of opinions, exposure to opposing viewpoints may speed the process toward participation: "Cross-pressures may actually help some voters make up their minds, rather than hinder the crystallization of their voting preferences."[77] If political participation is defined as more than just voting, people may be more likely to volunteer for a cause or get involved with their political party when they encounter disagreement. Another study found that encouraging uncivil—but not civil—disagreement initiated a chain reaction that lead to increased aggressive intentions and then greater likelihood to get politically involved in an issue.[78] So in that sense the incivility actually sparks an emotional response that boosts intention to participate politically.

Digital Deliberation

Public deliberation started in face-to-face communication, through collective discussion groups, such as formal meetings or informal meetings in salons and cafés.[79] However, in this book I am focusing solely on deliberation in the digital sphere. In the early days of the Internet, two competing ideals surfaced about whether the web would be a more egalitarian space for public debate. The "cybertopia" viewpoint saw the web as an anonymous space that muted differences between people, fostered cohesion, and gave the power to speak out to groups who did not have that opportunity offline.[80] A cartoon by Peter Steiner that appeared in *The New Yorker* magazine in 1993 and became an icon of the early Internet age exemplifies this view. The cartoon depicts a dog sitting at a computer with the caption: "On the Internet, nobody knows you're a dog."[81] The idea was that anyone could speak out online, so more voices would get heard. Also, online communication fosters *weak ties* between people,[82] and these weak ties were thought to encourage diversity in digital connections.[83] In contrast, critics of this utopian view espoused the "cyberghetto"[84] philosophy. This viewpoint held that the Internet reinforced the biases in the offline world because it retained "vestiges of traditional communities with similar hierarchical social linkages and class-structured relationships."[85] In other words, the same people who got heard in the offline world, largely white men, continued to have the greatest voice online because the same societal structures are in place in both spheres. In fact, the digital divide, a term used to describe the fact that some people cannot afford Internet access or computers, may have exacerbated the problem. People who had little voice offline may have had even less online because they could not even afford to join the conversation.

What really happened was a mixture of both. In the earliest days, voices of the marginalized groups, such as women or people of color, were largely absent online. But that changed in time. Blogging in particular offered a promise of digital equality because people could do it for free.[86] For example, the mommy blogging movement of the late 1990s and early 2000s gave women by the millions a voice, and these women saw the web as a tangible means to express themselves in ways they could not before.[87] The web became empowering for marginalized groups, such as African-American women, low-income families, and sexual minorities,[88] in part because people could more easily find others like them online.

Social media also opened up opportunities to speak out for women and people of color. For example, after police shot an unarmed black man in Ferguson, MO, in 2014, social media gave African-Americans a format to challenge what traditional media were reporting about the shooting.[89] In addition, hashtags—keywords signified with a pound or hash sign—started being used on Twitter, Facebook, Instagram, and YouTube as a potent, although limited, tool to give voice to the silenced and to galvanize activism efforts. For example, #BlackLivesMatter was used to highlight challenges to the discourse surrounding marginalization of African-Americans. #YesAllWomen was used to speak out against female subjugation after a man in California went on a killing spree in 2014, motivated by his revenge against females for rejecting his advances.[90] However, a digital inequality that mirrored the inequities based on race, class, gender, and education perpetuated offline also held sway online. For example, while men and women were equally likely to blog, male blogs gained greater attention from the media.[91] Even as women's numbers online are soaring, research has shown their voices are often muted, as they are offline,[92] or they get verbally attacked for what they say.[93] Also, the idea that people would gather with people different from them online largely failed to materialize. In fact, online groups tend to be as homogenous online as off.[94] If anything, the web may amplify the tendency people have to interact with those like them because people have more power to find out others' beliefs before choosing discussion partners through online platforms than they would in their own neighborhoods.[95] So they can continually expose themselves to people who think as they do.

In the context of public deliberation, experts are also divided on the potential for it online. Some argue that if people communicate with people different from them online, the potential for deliberation is limited because people are more likely to argue than deliberate.[96] However, liked-minded people may not deliberate either because they are just repeating what others say, creating an echo chamber of ideas. Some scholars have found evidence of deliberation online, through comments streams and other forms of engagement. For example, a content analysis of 2,107 comments posted on the Facebook walls of presidential candidates in 2008 and 2012 showed that sites like Facebook "represent spaces that accommodate a new public sphere,"[97] with 40% of the commenters offering some rationale for their views, and another 11% providing concrete evidence, such as links to other sites, statistics, or data. In-depth interviews with 69 people in a separate study found that people felt more comfortable sharing their views online, compared with discussing them with a neighbor who might not agree.[98] Another study found that comments posted on news stories of *The New York Times* and *The Guardian* websites demonstrated attributes of deliberation, including respectfulness, diversity of ideas, and disagreement.[99] The same study, however, found that comments posted on stories from other news organizations expressed little diversity, were often derogatory, and did not express openness to others' ideas. Similarly, in a survey of 435 newspaper journalists,[100] 65% of the sample reported that they did not see comment streams as promoting the civil discourse that makes up deliberation. Some argue that the online context is less valuable for deliberation because computer-mediated communication offers fewer cues for communicating the nuances of speech, such as emotion, but others suggest this weakness is a strength because true deliberation should allow for rational discussion without too much emotion.[101] Certainly, there are differences between the experiences of deliberating online versus offline. Young white males with at least a bachelor's degree are over-represented among online deliberators, compared to people who deliberate offline.[102] Online deliberators also view the digital climate to be more politically and racially diverse than those who debate only face to face.[103] Online deliberation tends to foment more negative emotions and is less likely to lead to consensus or political actions, such as working for a campaign, compared to face-to-face deliberation.[104] Both types increase people's knowledge of issues and general political understanding.[105] In summary, these studies suggest that the Internet holds potential for deliberation,[106] but how much the online space has realized that potential is not fully understood.

Conclusion

So what does all this mean for the potential for deliberation on social media or on news story comment streams? For these digital spaces to become fully realized as a deliberative space, people must act more like Eisenstadt, the journalist mentioned at the start of this chapter. These spaces hold promise, but that promise cannot be realized without a conscious effort on the part of all people, not just journalists or politicians, to actively deliberate online. The conversation space on the web developed in the freewheeling early days, back when the Internet was called the World Wide Web. It grew from the earlier forms of online conversations, such as computer-conferencing systems like the Whole Earth 'Lectronic Link (WELL), and later listservs, user groups, and chat rooms.[107] Then came news story comment streams and social-networking sites. People learned to use a pound sign to signify the topic of a tweet or add a smile emoticon to soften a message, but they did not claim the space as deliberative.

An anything-goes attitude seemed to develop online, and newspaper comment streams in particular became quickly mired in non-deliberative speech. Despite this early rocky start, I believe that some deliberation does take place in online comments, and this form of discourse is important to encourage. The goal should be to foster deliberative speech through creating a normative atmosphere for this discourse, rather than focusing on the limitations of online communication. The more people like Eisenstadt stop, listen, answer questions, provide evidence, and remain rational, the closer we will be to realizing a deliberative space online that truly rejuvenates the public sphere[108] as a spot for the discussion about politics and other important issues of the day, like the cafés and salons of an earlier time.[109] The online space can become the type of space that influences politics and elections,[110] and informs the public in way that is not imagined today.

Classroom Discussion Prompts

1. Explain the core principles of public deliberation. What attributes must communication include to be considered "deliberative"?
2. The author makes a distinction between public deliberation and "deliberative moments." Define each and provide an example.
3. Do online comments have potential to be deliberative? Explain why or why not.
4. Using a type of online communication you are familiar with (e.g. tweets, Instagram posts, SnapChat), explain its potential for deliberative discourse. What could be done to make discourse on this platform more deliberative?

Notes

1. Marnie Eisenstadt, "Syracuse's Public Housing Creates Prisons of Poverty; What If They Could Move to Suburbs?" *Syracuse.com*, April 14, 2016. http://www.syracuse.com/poverty/2016/04/syracuses_public_housing_creat.html (Eisenstadt 2016).
2. ColdColdGoAway, April 14, 2016, comment posted on Eisenstadt, "Syracuse's Public Housing Creates Prisons of Poverty; What If They Could Move to Suburbs?"
3. Eisenstadt, April 14, 2016, comment posted on Eisenstadt, "Syracuse's Public Housing Creates Prisons of Poverty; What If They Could Move to Suburbs?"
4. ColdColdGoAway, April 14, 2016, comment posted on Eisenstadt, "Syracuse's Public Housing Creates Prisons of Poverty; What If They Could Move to Suburbs?"
5. Eisenstadt, April 14, 2016, comment posted on Eisenstadt, "Syracuse's Public Housing Creates Prisons of Poverty; What If They Could Move to Suburbs?"
6. Eisenstadt, April 14, 2016, comment posted on Eisenstadt, "Syracuse's Public Housing Creates Prisons of Poverty; What If They Could Move to Suburbs?"
7. John Gastil and Laura W. Black, "Public Deliberation as the Organizing Principle of Political Communication Research," *Journal of Public Deliberation* 4, no. 1 (2008): Article 3, 7 (Gastil and Black 2008).
8. James S. Fishkin, *Democracy and Deliberation*, (New Haven, CT: Yale University Press, 1991); John Gastil, *Political Communication and Deliberation*, (Thousand Oaks, CA: Sage, 2011); Amy Gutmann and Dennis Thompson, *Democracy and Disagreement*, (Cambridge, MA: Harvard University Press, 1996); Lawrence R. Jacobs, Fay Lomax Cook, and Michael X. Delli Carpini, *Talking Together: Public Deliberation and Political Participation in America*, (Chicago, IL: The University of Chicago Press, 2009); Natalie J. Stroud, Joshua M. Scacco, Ashley Muddiman, and Alexander L. Curry, "Changing Deliberative Norms on News Organizations' Facebook Sites," *Journal of Computer-Mediated Communication* 20 (2015): 188–203 (Fishkin 1991; Gastil 2011; Gutmann and Thompson 1996; Jacobs et al. 2009; Stroud et al. 2015).
9. Gastil and Black, "Public Deliberation as the Organizing Principle of Political Communication Research"; Jacobs, Cook, and Delli Carpini, *Talking Together: Public Deliberation and Political Participation in America*.
10. Stephen D. Reese, "The New Geography of Journalism Research," *Digital Journalism* 4, no. 7 (2016): 818–826 (Reese 2016).

11. Hannah Arendt, *The Human Condition* (Chicago, IL: University of Chicago Press, 1958); Hélène Landemore, "Democratic Reason: The Mechanism of Collective Intelligence in Politics," in *Collective Wisdom: Principles and Mechanisms*, eds. Hélène Landemore and John Elster (New York, NY: Cambridge University Press, 2012): 251–289 (Arendt 1958; Landemore 2012).
12. Zizi Papacharissi, "Democracy Online: Civility, Politeness, and the Democratic Potential of Online Political Discussion," *New Media & Society* 6, no. 2 (2004): 259 (Papacharissi 2004).
13. Elihu Katz, "Back to the Street: When Media and Opinion Leaves Home," *Mass Communication and Society* 17 (2014): 454–463; Gabriel de Tarde, *On Communication and Social Influence*, ed. Terry N. Clark (Chicago, IL: University of Chicago Press, 1889/1969) (Katz 2014; de Tarde 1889).
14. De Tarde, *On Communication and Social Influence*, 318.
15. Katz, "Back to the Street: When Media and Opinion Leaves Home."
16. Fishkin, *Democracy and Deliberation*; Gastil, *Political Communication and Deliberation*; Gutmann and Thompson, *Democracy and Disagreement*; Jacobs, Cook, and Delli Carpini, *Talking Together: Public Deliberation and Political Participation in America*; Landemore, "Democratic Reason: The Mechanism of Collective Intelligence in Politics."
17. Casey A. Klofstad, Anand Edward Sokhey, and Scott D. McClurg, "Disagreeing About Disagreement: How Conflict in Social Networks Affects Political Behavior," *American Journal of Political Science* 57 (2013): 120–134; Lilach Nir, "Ambivalent Social Networks and Their Consequences for Participation," *International Journal of Public Opinion Research* 17 (2005): 422–442 (Klofstad et al. 2013; Nir 2005).
18. Leon Festinger, *A Theory of Cognitive Dissonance*, (Palo Alto, CA: Stanford University Press, 1957) (Festinger 1957).
19. Gastil and Black, "Public Deliberation as the Organizing Principle of Political Communication Research."
20. Jacobs, Cook, and Delli Carpini, *Talking Together: Public Deliberation and Political Participation in America*.
21. Gutmann and Thompson, *Democracy and Disagreement*.
22. Gutmann and Thompson, *Democracy and Disagreement*.
23. Ulrike Klinger and Uta Russmann, "The Sociodemographics of Political Public Deliberation: Measuring Deliberative Quality in Different User Groups," *Communications* 40, no. 4 (2015): 471–484 (Klinger and Russmann 2015).
24. Gastil and Black, "Public Deliberation as the Organizing Principle of Political Communication Research," 2.

25. Jacobs, Cook, and Delli Carpini, *Talking Together: Public Deliberation and Political Participation in America*, 4.
26. Harold D. Lasswell, *Democracy Through Public Opinion*, (Menasha, WI: George Banta Publishing Co., 1941): 15 (Lasswell 1941).
27. Gastil and Black, "Public Deliberation as the Organizing Principle of Political Communication Research."
28. Arendt, *The Human Condition*, 57.
29. Jürgen Habermas, "Three Normative Models of Democracy," *Democratic and Constitutional Theory Today* 1, no. 1 (1994): 1–10 (Habermas 1994).
30. Landemore, "Democratic Reason: The Mechanism of Collective Intelligence in Politics."
31. Gutmann and Thompson, *Democracy and Disagreement*, 12.
32. Fishkin, *Democracy and Deliberation*.
33. Jacobs, Cook, and Delli Carpini, *Talking Together: Public Deliberation and Political Participation in America*.
34. Vincent Price, Joseph N. Cappella, and Lilach Nir, "Does Disagreement Contribute to More Deliberative Opinion?" *Political Communication* 19 (2002): 95–112 (Price et al. 2002).
35. Michael Schudson, "Why Conversation is Not the Soul of Democracy," *Critical Studies in Mass Communication* 14 (1997): 297–309 (Schudson 1997).
36. Seong-Jae Min, "Online Vs. Face-To-Face Deliberation: Effects on Civic Engagement," *Journal of Computer-Mediated Communication* 12 (2007): 1369–1387 (Min 2007).
37. Steffen Albrecht, "Whose Voice is Heard in Online Deliberation? A Study of Participation and Representation in Political Debates on the Internet," *Information, Communication & Society* 8, no.1 (2006): 62–82; Min, "Online Vs. Face-To-Face Deliberation: Effects on Civic Engagement"; Klinger and Russmann, "The Sociodemographics of Political Public Deliberation: Measuring Deliberative Quality in Different User Groups" (Albrecht 2006).
38. Klinger and Russmann, "The Sociodemographics of Political Public Deliberation: Measuring Deliberative Quality in Different User Groups."
39. Maribel Molina, "Twitter Users React to Austin ISD Not Cancelling, Delaying Classes," *Austin American-Statesman*, May 19, 2016. http://austin.blog.statesman.com/2016/05/19/twitter-users-react-to-austin-isd-not-cancelling-delaying-classes/ (Molina 2016).
40. Limor Shifman, *Memes in Digital Culture*, (Cambridge, MA: MIT Press, 2014) (Shifman 2014).
41. Landemore, "Democratic Reason: The Mechanism of Collective Intelligence in Politics."

42. Schudson, "Why Conversation is Not the Soul of Democracy," 299.
43. Scott D. McClurg, "The Electoral Relevance of Political Talk: Examining Disagreement and Expertise in Social Networks on Political Participation," *American Journal of Political Science* 50, no. 3 (2006): 737–754 (McClurg 2006a).
44. Gutmann and Thompson, *Democracy and Disagreement*, 1.
45. Klofstad, Sokhey, and McClurg, "Disagreeing About Disagreement: How Conflict in Social Networks Affects Political Behavior."
46. Gina Masullo Chen, "Social Media: From Digital Divide to Empowerment," in *The Routledge Companion to Media and Race*, ed. Christopher P. Campbell (New York, NY: Routledge, 2016) (Chen 2016).
47. Gi Woong Yun and Sun-Yeon Park, "Selective Posting: Willingness to Post a Message Online. *Journal of Computer-Mediated Communication* 16, no. 2 (2011): 201–277 (Yun and Park 2011).
48. Stroud et al., "Changing Deliberative Norms on News Organizations' Facebook Sites."
49. George E. Marcus, W. Russell Neuman, and Michael MacKuen, *Affective Intelligence and Political Judgment*, (Chicago, IL: The University of Chicago Press, 2000) (Marcus et al. 2000).
50. Robert B. Zajonc, "Feeling and Thinking: Preferences Need No Inferences," *American Psychologist* 35 (1980): 151–175; Robert B. Zajonc, "On the Primacy of Affect," *American Psychologist* 39, no. 2 (1984): 117–123 (Zajonc 1980, 1984).
51. Nico H. Frijda, *The Emotions*, (New York, NY: Cambridge University Press, 1984); Richard S. Lazarus, "On the Primacy of Cognition," *American Psychologist* 39, no. 2 (1984): 124–129 (Frijda 1984; Lazarus 1984).
52. Marcus, Neuman, and MacKuen, *Affective Intelligence and Political Judgment*.
53. Paul D. Bolls, "Understanding Emotion from a Superordinate Dimensional Perspective: A Productive Way Forward for Communication Processes and Effects," *Communication Monographs* 77, no. 2 (2010): 146–152 (Bolls 2010).
54. Tori Rodriguez, "Negative Emotions are Key to Well-Being," *Scientific American*, May 1, 2013. http://www.scientificamerican.com/article/negative-emotions-key-well-being/?WT.mc_id=SA_FB_MB_EG (Rodriguez 2013).
55. Marcus, Neuman, and MacKuen, *Affective Intelligence and Political Judgment*.
56. Marcus, Neuman, and MacKuen, *Affective Intelligence and Political Judgment*.

57. Marcus, Neuman, and MacKuen, *Affective Intelligence and Political Judgment*, 14.
58. Diana C. Mutz, "Cross-Cutting Social Networks: Testing Democratic Theory in Practice," *American Political Science Review* 96, no. 1 (2002): 111–126; Price, Cappella, and Nir, "Does Disagreement Contribute to More Deliberative Opinion?" (Mutz 2002a).
59. Price, Cappella, and Nir, "Does Disagreement Contribute to More Deliberative Opinion?"
60. Mutz, "Cross-Cutting Social Networks: Testing Democratic Theory in Practice."
61. McClurg, "The Electoral Relevance of Political Talk: Examining Disagreement and Expertise in Social Networks on Political Participation"; Robert Huckfeldt, Jeannette Morehouse Mendez, and Tracy Osborn, "Disagreement, Ambivalence, and Engagement: The Political Consequences of Heterogeneous Networks," *Political Psychology* 25, no. 1 (2004): 65–95; Robert Huckfeldt, Ken'Ichi Ikeda, and Franz Urban Pappi, "Patterns of Disagreement in Democratic Politics; Comparing Germany, Japan, and the United States," *American Journal of Political Science* 49, no. 3 (2005): 497–514; Nir, "Ambivalent Social Networks and Their Consequences for Participation" (Huckfeldt et al. 2004, 2005).
62. Francis L.F. Lee, "The Impact of Political Discussion in a Democratizing society: The Moderating Role of Disagreement and Support for Democracy," *Communication Research* 36, no. 3 (2009): 379–399 (Lee 2009).
63. Festinger, *A Theory of Cognitive Dissonance*.
64. David C. Matz and Wendy Wood, "Cognitive Dissonance in Groups: The Consequences of Disagreement," *Journal of Personality and Social Psychology* 88, no. 1 (2005): 22–37 (Matz and Wood 2005).
65. Younghwan Kim, "Does Disagreement Mitigate Polarization? How Selective Exposure and Disagreement Affect Political Polarization," *Journalism & Mass Communication Quarterly* 92, no. 4 (2015): 915–937 (Kim 2015).
66. Mutz, "Cross-Cutting Social Networks: Testing Democratic Theory in Practice."
67. Mutz, "Cross-Cutting Social Networks: Testing Democratic Theory in Practice"; Nir, "Ambivalent Social Networks and Their Consequences for Participation"; Lilach Nir, "Disagreement and Opposition in Social Networks: Does Disagreement Discourage Turnout," *Political Studies* 59 (2011): 674–692 (Nir 2011).

68. Scott D. McClurg, "Political Disagreement in Context: The Conditional Effect of Neighborhood Context, Disagreement and Political Talk in Electoral Participation," *Political Behavior* 28 (2006): 349–366; Mutz, "Cross-Cutting Social Networks: Testing Democratic Theory in Practice"; Diana C. Mutz, "The Consequences of Cross-Cutting Networks for Political Participation," *American Journal of Political Science* 46, no. 4 (2002): 838–855; Nir, "Ambivalent Social Networks and Their Consequences for Participation"; Nir, "Disagreement and Opposition in Social Networks: Does Disagreement Discourage Turnout" (McClurg 2006b; Mutz 2002b).
69. Francis L.F. Lee, "Does Discussion With Disagreement Discourage All Types of Political Participation? Survey Evidence from Hong Kong," *Communication Research* 39, no. 4 (2012): 543–562 (Lee 2012).
70. Magdalena E. Wojcieszak and Vincent Price, "Perceived Versus Actual Disagreement: Which Influences Deliberative Experiences?" *Journal of Communication* 62 (2012): 431 (Wojcieszak and Price 2012).
71. Kathleen A. Kennedy and Emily Pronim, "When Disagreement Gets Ugly: Perceptions of Bias and the Escalation of Conflict," *Personality and Social Psychology Bulletin* 34, no. 6 (2008): 835 (Kennedy and Pronim 2008).
72. Myojung Chung, Greg J. Munno, and Brian Moritz, "Triggering Participation: Exploring the Effects of Third-Person and Hostile Media Perceptions on Online Participation," *Computers in Human Behavior* 53 (2015): 452–461 (Chung et al. 2015).
73. McClurg, "Political Disagreement in Context: The Conditional Effect of Neighborhood Context, Disagreement and Political Talk on Electoral Participation"; Nir, "Disagreement and Opposition in Social Networks: Does Disagreement Discourage Turnout"; Nir, "Ambivalent Social Networks and Their Consequences for Participation."
74. Nir, "Disagreement and Opposition in Social Networks: Does Disagreement Discourage Turnout."
75. Nir, "Disagreement and Opposition in Social Networks: Does Disagreement Discourage Turnout"; see also Elisabeth Noelle-Neumann, "The Spiral of Silence: A Theory of Public Opinion," *Journal of Communication* 24, no. 2 (1974): 43–51 (Noelle-Neumann 1974).
76. C.J. Pattie and R.J. Johnson, "Conversation, Disagreement and Political Participation," *Political Behavior* 31(2009): 261–285 (Pattie and Johnson 2009).
77. Nir, "Ambivalent Social Networks and Their Consequences for Participation," 438.

78. Gina Masullo Chen and Shuning Lu, "Online Political Discourse: Exploring Differences in Effects of Civil and Uncivil Disagreement in News Website Comments," *Journal of Broadcasting & Electronic Media* 61, no. 1 (2017). doi:10.1080/08838151/2016/1273922 (Chen and Lu 2017).
79. Jacobs, Cook, and Delli Carpini, *Talking Together: Public Deliberation and Political Participation in America*.
80. Albrecht, "Whose Voice is Heard in Online Deliberation? A Study of Participation and Representation in Political Debates on the Internet"; Bosah Ebo, *Cyberghetto or Cybertopia? Race, Class and Gender on the Internet*, ed., (Westport, CT: Praeger, 1998): 2 (Bosah 1998).
81. Michael Cavna, "'Nobody Knows You're a Dog': As Iconic Internet Cartoon Turns 20, Creator Peter Steiner Knows the Idea is as Relevant as Ever," *The Washington Post*, July 13, 2013. https://www.washingtonpost.com/blogs/comic-riffs/post/nobody-knows-youre-a-dog-as-iconic-internet-cartoon-turns-20-creator-peter-steiner-knows-the-joke-rings-as-relevant-as-ever/2013/07/31/73372600-f98d-11e2-8e84-c56731a202fb_blog.html (Cavna 2013).
82. Gina Masullo Chen, "Tweet This: A Uses and Gratifications Perspective on How Active Twitter Use Gratifies a Need to Connect with Others," *Computers in Human Behavior* 27 (2011): 755–762; Mark Granovetter, "The Strength of Weak Ties," *American Journal of Sociology* 78, no. 6 (1973): 1360–1380 (Chen 2011; Granovetter 1973).
83. Howard Rheingold, *The Virtual Community: Homesteading on the Electronic Frontier*, (Cambridge, MA: MIT Press, 2000) (Rheingold 2000).
84. Ebo, *Cyberghetto or Cybertopia? Race, Class and Gender on the Internet*, 2.
85. Ebo, *Cyberghetto or Cybertopia? Race, Class and Gender on the Internet*, 2.
86. Dan Gillmor, *We the Media*, (Santa Rosa, CA: O'Reilly Media, 2004); J. Schradie, "The Trend of Class, Race, and Ethnicity in Social Media Inequality: Who Still Cannot Afford to Blog," *Information, Communication & Society* 15, no. 4 (2012): 555–571 (Gillmor 2004; Schradie 2012).
87. Gina Masullo Chen, "Why Do Women Write Personal Blogs? Satisfying Needs for Self-Disclosure and Affiliation Tell Part of the Story," *Computers in Human Behavior* 28 (2012): 171–180; Bonnie A. Nardi, Diane J. Schiano, Michelle Gumbrecht, and Luke Swartz, "Why We Blog," *Communications of the ACM* 47, no. 2 (2004): 41–46; Lori Kido Lopez, "The Radical Act of 'Mommy Blogging': Refining Motherhood Through the Blogosphere," *New Media & Society* 11, no. 5 (2009): 729–747; Sarah Pedersen and Caroline Macafee, "Gender Differences in British Blogging," *Journal of Computer-Mediated Communication* 12

(2007): 1471–1492 (Chen 2012; Nardi et al. 2004; Lopez 2009; Pedersen and Macafee 2007).
88. Bharat Mehra, Cecelia Merkel, and Ann Peterson Bishop, "The Internet for Empowerment of Minority and Marginalized Groups," *New Media & Society* 6, no. 6 (2004): 781–802 (Mehra et al. 2004).
89. Chen, "Social Media."
90. Bernadette Barker-Plummer and Dave Barker-Plummer, "Hashtag Feminism, Digital Media, and New Dynamics of Social Change: A Case Study of #YesAllWomen," in *Social Media and Politics: A New Way to Participate in the Political Process*, ed. Glenn W. Richardson Jr., (Santa Barbara, CA: Praeger, 2017): 79–96; Samantha C. Thrift, "#YesAllWomen As Feminist Meme Event," *Feminist Media Studies* 14, no. 6 (2014): 1090–1092 (Barker-Plummer and Barker-Plummer 2017; Thrift 2014).
91. Gina Masullo Chen, "Don't Call Me That: A Techno-Feminist Critique of the Term *Mommy Blogger*," *Mass Communication and* Society 16, no. 4 (2013): 510–532; Dustin Harp and Mark Tremayne, "The Gendered Blogosphere: Examining Inequality Using Network and Feminist Theory," *Journalism & Mass Communication Quarterly* 32, no. 2 (2006): 247–264 (Chen 2013; Harp and Tremayne 2006).
92. Susan C. Herring, Inna Kouper, Lois Ann Scheidt, and Elijah Wright, "Women and Children Last: The Discursive Construction of Weblogs," in *Into the Blogosphere: Rhetoric, Community and Culture Weblogs*, eds. Laura Gurak, Smilijana Antonijevic, Laurie Johnson, Clancy Ratcliff, and Jennifer Reyman, (Minneapolis, MN: University of Minnesota, 2004) (Herring et al. 2004).
93. Kristi K. Cole, "'It's Like She's Eager to Be Verbally Abuse': Twitter, Trolls, and (En)Gendering Disciplinary Rhetoric," *Feminist Media Studies*, 15, no. 2 (2015): 356–358 (Cole 2015).
94. Elanor Colleoni, Alessandro Rozza, and Adam Arvidsson, "Echo Chamber or Public Sphere? Predicting Political Orientation and Measuring Political Homophily in Twitter Using Big Data," *Journal of Communication* 64, no. 2 (2014): 317–332; Itai Himelboim, Stephen McCreery, and Marc Smith, "Birds of a Feather Tweet Together: Integrating Network and Content Analyses to Examine Cross-Ideology Exposure on Twitter," *Journal of Computer-Mediated Communication* 18, no. 2 (2013): 40–60 (Colleoni et al. 2014; Himelboim et al. 2013).
95. Hai Lang, "The Organizational Principles of Online Political Discussion: A Relational Event Stream Model for Analysis of Web Forum Deliberation," *Human Communication Research* 40 (2014): 483–507 (Lang 2014).

96. Jennifer Stromer-Galley, "Diversity of Political Conversation on the Internet: Users' Perspectives," *Journal of Computer-Mediated Communication* 8, no. 3 (2003): n.p. (Stromer-Galley 2003).
97. Lindita Camaj and Arthur D. Santana, "Political Deliberation on Facebook During Electoral Campaigns: Exploring the Relevance of Moderator's Technical Role and Political Ideology," *Journal of Information, Technology & Politics* 12, no. 4 (2015): 325 (Camaj and Santana 2015).
98. Stromer-Galley, "Diversity of Political Conversation on the Internet: Users' Perspectives."
99. Carlos Ruiz, David Domingo, Josep Lluís Micó, Javier Díaz-Noci, Koldo Meso, and Pere Maship, "Public Sphere 2.0? The Democratic Qualities of Citizen Debates in Online Newspapers." *The International Journal of Press/Politics* 16, no. 4 (2011): 463–487 (Ruiz et al. 2011).
100. Arthur D. Santana, "Online Readers' Comments Represent New Opinion Pipeline," *Newspaper Research Journal* 32, no. 3 (2011): 66–88 (Santana 2011).
101. Min, "Online Vs. Face-To-Face Deliberation: Effects on Civic Engagement."
102. Baek et al., "Online Versus Face-to-Face Deliberation? Who? Why? What? With What Effects?" (Baek et al. 2011).
103. Baek et al., "Online Versus Face-to-Face Deliberation? Who? Why? What? With What Effects?"
104. Min, "Online Vs. Face-To-Face Deliberation: Effects on Civic Engagement"; Lincoln Dahlberg, "Re-Constructing Digital Democracy: an Outline of Four Positions," *New Media & Society* 13, no. 6 (2011): 855–872; Papacharissi, "Democracy Online: Civility, Impoliteness, and the Democratic Potential of Online Political Discussion Groups." (Dahlberg 2011).
105. Min, "Online Vs. Face-To-Face Deliberation: Effects on Civic Engagement."
106. Todd Graham and Tamara Witschge, "In Search of Online Deliberation: Towards a New Method of Examining the Quality of Online Discussions," *Communications* 28 (2003): 173–204 (Graham and Witschge 2003).
107. Rheingold, *The Virtual Community: Homesteading on the Electronic Frontier*.
108. Papacharissi, "Democracy Online: Civility, Politeness, and the Democratic Potential of Online Political Discussion."
109. De Tarde, *On Communication and Social Influence*; Katz, "Back to the Street: When Media and Opinion Leaves Home."
110. Habermas, "Three Normative Models of Democracy." *Democratic and Constitutional Theory Today*.

REFERENCES

Albrecht, Steffen. 2006. Whose Voice Is Heard in Online Deliberation? A Study of Participation and Representation in Political Debates on the Internet. *Information, Communication & Society* 8 (1): 62–82.
Arendt, Hannah. 1958. *The Human Condition*. Chicago: The University of Chicago Press.
Barker-Plummer, Bernadette, and Dave Barker-Plummer. 2017. Hashtag Feminism, Digital Media, and New Dynamics of Social Change: A Case Study of #YesAllWomen. In *Social Media and Politics: A New Way to Participate in the Political Process*, ed. Glenn W. Richardson Jr., 79–96. Santa Barbara, CA: Praeger.
Bolls, Paul D. 2010. Understanding Emotion from a Superordinate Dimensional Perspective: A Productive Way Forward for Communication Processes and Effects. *Communication Monographs* 77 (2): 146–152.
Camaj, Lindita, and Arthur D. Santana. 2015. Political Deliberation on Facebook During Electoral Campaigns: Exploring the Relevance of Moderator's Technical Role and Political Ideology. *Journal of Information, Technology & Politics* 12 (4): 325–341.
Cavna, Michael. 2013. 'Nobody Knows You're a Dog': As Iconic Internet Cartoon Turns 20, Creator Peter Steiner Knows the Idea is as Relevant as Ever. *The Washington Post*, July 13. https://www.washingtonpost.com/blogs/comic-riffs/post/nobody-knows-youre-a-dog-as-iconic-internet-cartoon-turns-20-creator-peter-steiner-knows-the-joke-rings-as-relevant-as-ever/2013/07/31/73372600-f98d-11e2-8e84-c56731a202fb_blog.html. Accessed 23 May 2016.
Chen, Gina Masullo. 2011. Tweet This: A Uses and Gratifications Perspective on How Active Twitter Use Gratifies a Need to Connect with Others. *Computers in Human Behavior* 27: 755–762.
Chen, Gina Masullo. 2012. Why Do Women Write Personal Blogs? Satisfying Needs for Self-Disclosure and Affiliation Tell Part of the Story. *Computers in Human Behavior* 28: 171–180.
Chen, Gina Masullo. 2013. Don't Call Me That: A Techno-Feminist Critique of the Term *Mommy Blogger*. *Mass Communication and Society* 16 (4): 510–532.
Chen, Gina Masullo. 2016. Social Media: From Digital Divide to Empowerment. In *The Routledge Companion to Media and Race*, ed. Christopher P. Campbell. New York: Routledge.
Chen, Gina Masullo, and Shuning Lu. 2017. Online Political Discourse: Exploring Differences in Effects of Civil and Uncivil Disagreement in News Website Comments. *Journal of Broadcasting & Electronic Media* 61 (1). doi:10.1080/08838151/2016/1273922.
Chung, Myojung, Greg J. Munno, and Brian Moritz. 2015. Triggering Participation: Exploring the Effects of Third-Person and Hostile Media

Perceptions on Online Participation. *Computers in Human Behavior* 53: 452–461.
Cole, Kristi K. 2015. It's Like She's Eager to Be Verbally Abused: Twitter, Trolls, and (En)Gendering Disciplinary Rhetoric. *Feminist Media Studies* 15 (2): 356–358.
Colleoni, Elanor, Alessandro Rozza, and Adam Arvidsson. 2014. Echo Chamber or Public Sphere? Predicting Political Orientation and Measuring Political Homophily in Twitter Using Big Data. *Journal of Communication* 64 (2): 317–332.
Dahlberg, Lincoln. 2011. Re-Constructing Digital Democracy: An Outline of Four Positions. *New Media & Society* 13 (6): 855–872.
De Tarde, Gabriel. 1889/1969. *On Communication and Social Influence*, ed. Terry N. Clark. Chicago: University of Chicago Press.
Ebo, Bosah. 1998. *Cyberghetto or Cybertopia? Race, Class and Gender on the Internet*, ed. Bosah Ebo. Wesport, CT: Praeger.
Eisenstadt, Marnie. 2016. Syracuse's Public Housing Creates Prisons of Poverty; What If They Could Move to Suburbs? *Syracuse.com*, April 14. http://www.syracuse.com/poverty/2016/04/syracuses_public_housing_creat.html. Accessed 13 May 2016.
Fishkin, James S. 1991. *Democracy and Deliberation*. New Haven, CT: Yale University Press.
Festinger, Leon. 1957. *A Theory of Cognitive Dissonance*. Palo Alto, CA: Stanford University Press.
Frijda, Nico H. 1984. *The Emotions*. New York: Cambridge University Press.
Gastil, John. 2011. *Political Communicationand Deliberation*. Thousand Oaks, CA: Sage.
Gastil, John, and Laura W. Black. 2008. Public Deliberation as the Organizing Principle of Political Communication Research. *Journal of Public Deliberation* 4 (1): Article 3.
Gillmor, Dan. 2004. *We the Media*. Santa Rosa, CA: O'Reilly Media.
Graham, Todd, and Tamara Witschge. 2003. In Search of Online Deliberation: Towards a New Method of Examining the Quality of Online Discussions. *Communications* 28: 173–204.
Granovetter, Mark. 1973. The Strength of Weak Ties. *American Journal of Sociology* 78 (6): 1360–1380.
Gutmann, Amy, and Dennis Thompson. 1996. *Democracy and Disagreement*. Cambridge, MA: Harvard University Press.
Habermas, Jürgen. 1994. Three Normative Models of Democracy. *Democratic and Constitutional Theory Today* 1 (1): 1–10.
Harp, Dustin, and Mark Tremayne. 2006. The Gendered Blogosphere: Examining Inequality Using Network and Feminist Theory. *Journalism & Mass Communication Quarterly* 32 (2): 247–264.

Herring, Susan C., Inna Kouper, Lois Ann Scheidt, and Elijah Wright. 2004. Women and Children Last: The Discursive Construction of Weblogs. In *Into the Blogsphere: Rhetoric, Community and Culture Weblogs*, ed. Laura Gurak, Smilijana Antonijevic, Laurie Johnson, Clancy Ratcliff, and Jennifer Reyman. Minneapolis, MN: University of Minnesota.

Himelboim, Itai, Stephen McCreery, and Marc Smith. 2013. Birds of a Feather Tweet Together: Integrating Network and Content Analyses to Examine Cross-Ideology Exposure on Twitter. *Journal of Computer-Mediated Communication* 18 (2): 40–60.

Huckfeldt, Robert, Jeannette Morehouse Mendez, and Tracy Osborn. 2004. Disagreement, Ambivalence, and Engagement: The Political Consequences of Heterogeneous Networks. *Political Psychology* 25 (1): 65–95.

Huckfeldt, Robert, Ken'Ichi Ikeda, and Franz Urban Pappi. 2005. Patterns of Disagreement in Democratic Politics: Comparing Germany, Japan, and the United States. *American Journal of Political* Science 49 (3): 497–514.

Jacobs, Lawrence R., Fay Lomax Cook, and Michael X. Delli Carpini. 2009. *Talking Together: Public Deliberation and Political Participation in America*. Chicago: University of Chicago Press.

Katz, Elihu. 2014. Back to the Street: When Media and Opinion Leaves Home. *Mass Communication and Society* 17: 454–463.

Kennedy, Kathleen A., and Emily Pronim. 2008. When Disagreement Gets Ugly: Perceptions of Bias and the Escalation of Conflict. *Personality and Social Psychology Bulletin* 34 (6): 833–848.

Kim, Younghwan. 2015. Does Disagreement Mitigate Polarization? How Selective Exposure and Disagreement Affect Political Polarization. *Journalism & Mass Communication Quarterly* 92 (4): 915–937.

Klinger, Ulrike, and Uta Russmann. 2015. The Sociodemographics of Political Public Deliberation: Measuring Deliberative Quality in Different User Groups. *Communications* 40 (4): 471–484.

Klofstad, Casey A., Anand Edward Sokhey, and Scott D. McClurg. 2013. Disagreeing about Disagreement: How Conflict in Social Networks Affects Political Behavior. *American Journal of Political Science* 57: 120–134.

Landemore, Hélène. 2012. Democratic Reason: The Mechanism of Collective Intelligence in Politics. In *Collective Wisdom: Principles and Mechanisms*, ed. Hélène Landemore, and John Elster, 251–289. New York: Cambridge University Press.

Lang, Hai. 2014. The Organizational Principles of Online Political Discussion: A Relational Event Stream Model for Analysis of Web Forum Deliberation. *Human Communication Research* 40: 483–507.

Lasswell, Harold D. 1941. *Democracy Through Public Opinion*. Menasha, WI: George Banta Publishing.

Lazarus, Richard S. 1984. On the Primacy of Cognition. *American Psychologist* 39 (2): 124–129.

Lee, Francis L.F. 2009. The Impact of Political Discussion in a Democratizing Society: The Moderating Role of Disagreement and Support for Democracy. *Communication Research* 36 (3): 379–399.

Lee, Francis L.F. 2012. Does Discussion With Disagreement Discourage All Types of Political Participation? Survey Evidence from Hong Kong. *Communication Research* 39 (4): 543–562.

Lopez, Lori Kido. 2009. The Radical Act of 'Mommy Blogging': Refining Motherhood Through the Blogosphere. *New Media & Society* 11 (5): 729–747.

Marcus, George E., W. Russell Neuman, and Michael MacKuen. 2000. *Affective Intelligence and Political Judgment*. Chicago: The University of Chicago Press.

Matz, David C., and Wendy Wood. 2005. Cognitive Dissonance in Groups: The Consequences of Disagreement. *Journal of Personality and Social Psychology* 88: 22–37.

McClurg, Scott D. 2006a. The Electoral Relevance of Political Talk: Examining Disagreement and Expertise in Social Networks on Political Participation. *American Journal of Political Science* 50 (3): 737–754.

McClurg, Scott D. 2006b. Political Disagreement in Context: The Conditional Effect of Neighborhood Context, Disagreement and Political Talk on Electoral Participation. *Political Behavior* 28: 349–366.

Mehra, Bharat, Cecelia Merkel, and Ann Peterson Bishop. 2004. The Internet for Empowerment of Minority and Marginalized Groups. *New Media & Society* 6 (6): 781–802.

Min, Seong-Jae. 2007. Online Vs. Face-To-Face Deliberation: Effects on Civic Engagement. *Journal of Computer-Mediated Communication* 12: 1369–1387.

Molina, Maribel. 2016. Twitter Users React to Austin ISD Not Cancelling, Delaying Classes. *Austin American-Statesman*, May 19. http://austin.blog.statesman.com/2016/05/19/twitter-users-react-to-austin-isd-not-cancelling-delaying-classes/. Accessed 19 May 2016.

Mutz, Diana C. 2002a. Cross-Cutting Social Networks: Testing Democratic Theory in Practice. *American Political Science Review* 96 (1): 111–126.

Mutz, Diana C. 2002b. The Consequences of Cross-Cutting Networks for Political Participation. *American Journal of Political Science* 46 (4): 838–855.

Nardi, Bonnie A., Diane J. Schiano, Michelle Gumbrecht, and Luke Swartz. 2004. Why We Blog. *Communications of the ACM* 47 (2): 41–46.

Nir, Lilach. 2005. Ambivalent Social Networks and Their Consequences for Participation. *International Journal of Public Opinion Research* 17: 422–442.

Nir, Lilach. 2011. Disagreement and Opposition in Social Networks: Does Disagreement Discourage Turnout? *Political Studies* 59: 674–692.

Noelle-Neumann, Elisabeth. 1974. The Spiral of Silence: A Theory of Public Opinion. *Journal of Communication* 24 (2): 43–51.

Papacharissi, Zizi. 2004. Democracy Online: Civility, Politeness, and the Democratic Potential of Online Political Discussion. *New Media & Society* 6 (2): 259–283.
Pattie, C.J., and R.J. Johnson. 2009. Conversation, Disagreement and Political Participation. *Political Behavior* 31: 261–285.
Pedersen, Sarah, and Caroline Macafee. 2007. Gender Differences in British Blogging. *Journal of Computer-Mediated Communication* 12: 1471–1492.
Price, Vincent, Joseph N. Cappella, and Lilach Nir. 2002. Does Disagreement Contribution to More Deliberative Opinion? *Political Communication* 19: 95–112.
Reese, Stephen D. 2016. The New Geography of Journalism Research. *Digital Journalism* 4 (7): 818–826.
Rheingold, Howard. 2000. *The Virtual Community: Homesteading on the Electronic Frontier.* Cambridge, MA: MIT Press.
Rodriguez, Tori. 2013. Negative Emotions are Key to Well-Being. *Scientific American*, May 1. http://www.scientificamerican.com/article/negative-emotions-key-well-being/?WT.mc_id=SA_FB_MB_EG. Accessed 21 June 2016.
Ruiz, Carlos, David Domingo, Josep Lluís Micó, Javier Díaz-Noci, Koldo Meso, and Pere Maship. 2011. Public Sphere 2.0? The Democratic Qualities of Citizen Debates in Online Newspapers. *The International Journal of Press/Politics* 16 (4): 463–487.
Santana, Arthur D. 2011. Online Readers' Comments Represent New Opinion Pipeline. *Newspaper Research Journal* 32 (3): 66–88.
Schudson, Michael. 1997. Why Conversation Is Not the Soul of Democracy. *Critical Studies in Mass Communication* 14: 297–309.
Schradie, Jen. 2012. The Trend of Class, Race, and Ethnicity in Social Media Inequality: Who Still Cannot Afford to Blog. *Information, Communication & Society* 15 (4): 555–571.
Shifman, Limor. 2014. *Memes in Digital Culture.* Cambridge, MA: MIT Press.
Stromer-Galley, Jennifer. 2003. Diversity of Political Conversation on the Internet: Users' Perspectives. *Journal of Computer-Mediated Communication* 8 (3).
Stroud, Natalie J., Joshua M. Scacco, Ashley Muddiman, and Alexander L. Curry. 2015. Changing Deliberative Norms on News Organizations' Facebook Sites. *Journal of Computer-Mediated Communication* 20: 188–203.
Thrift, Samantha C. 2014. #YesAllWomen as Feminist Meme Event. *Feminist Media Studies* 14 (6): 1090–1092.
Wojcieszak, Magdalena E., and Vincent Price. 2012. Perceived Versus Actual Disagreement: Which Influences Deliberative Experiences? *Journal of Communication* 62: 418–436.

Yun, Gi Woong, and Sun-Yeon Park. 2011. Selective Posting: Willingness to Post a Message Online. *Journal of Computer-Mediated Communication* 16 (2): 201–277.

Zajonc, Robert B. 1980. Feeling and Thinking: Preferences Need No Inferences. *American Psychologist* 35: 151–175.

Zajonc, Robert B. 1984. On the Primacy of Affect. *American Psychologist* 39 (2): 117–123.

CHAPTER 3

Nasty Talk Online

Over Memorial Day weekend in 2016, a three-year-old boy entered the gorilla enclosure at an Ohio zoo, and zoo workers killed the rare gorilla to save the boy.[1] Predictably, the Internet erupted. Comments on the *Cincinnati Enquirer*'s online story started out calm enough, with questions about what happened. But by comment number four out of 1,327 posted on the story, things started to unravel. "My sympathy is for the gorilla only,"[2] one poster wrote, prompting support as well as outrage at the poster's lack of empathy for the family. By the eighth comment, profanity had joined the conversation. Posters blamed the child's parents for not watching him well enough. Some comments were heartless and mean, yet did not rise to the level of uncivil speech—defined as exhibiting profanity; name-calling; or homophobia, racism, sexism, xenophobia, or bigotry.[3] For example, one commenter suggested the parents "were probably taking selfies,"[4] rather than overseeing their child as they should. The parents were labeled over-indulgent, lazy, and neglectful. The child was dubbed a brat. One poster suggested the parents should "rot in hell."[5]

Soon the conversation shifted from a heated and uncomfortable discussion about who was responsible for the incident—the parents or the zoo—to a verbal free-for-all, replete with name-calling and personal attacks. The discourse grew bigoted. One poster noted that the voice of the African-American boy's mother could be heard on a video that accompanied the news story:[6] "The mom can clearly be heard calling to the boy, saying 'I'm right here'. Typical black mom. She probably has ten other kids."[7] Commenters began to turn on each. One poster told another to "go kill urself and do everyone a favor."[8] Posters called each other racist and stupid. The story became a national debate, gaining widespread coverage, spawning a #GorillaLivesMatter[9] hashtag on Twitter, and generating memes[10] that spread across Facebook. The uncivil racist undercurrent of the discourse continued. One of the most virulent memes compared the dead gorilla to Adam Goodes, an Aboriginal who is retired from playing for the Australian Football League (AFL) and was infamously called an ape in 2013.[11] One meme showed a picture of the gorilla, named Harambe, with the little boy, but the description read: "RIP Adam Goodes." The memes were later removed from the "AFL Memes" Facebook page.[12]

This chapter explores what sets apart the type of public discourse exemplified by the debate after the gorilla's death from earlier forms of incivility. I argue that while certainly a lack of civility in public debate is nothing new,[13] today's online discussions across social media and news site comment streams are marked by a particularly unbridled vitriol. Attributes of these digital platforms that make them so hospitable for engaging with other people also offer fertile ground for a legitimate topic of debate to turn into a violent, verbal melee with a lightning speed unknown in earlier days. I will begin by explaining how the attributes of computer-mediated communication make it so conducive to incivility. Then I will examine what influence this online incivility has on those exposed to it and how that affects the larger public discourse.

ONLINE INCIVILITY

Certainly, our current age is not the first to encounter incivility. The U.S.A. has a long history of divisive political campaigns; duels and fights took place in Congress in the days before the Civil War; the Civil Rights Movement was fraught with violence.[14] Historian Fredrik Logevall argues that the "halcyon days of political geniality and decorum in the United States never really existed."[15] Democratic decision-making requires "vigorous contestation of ideas and interests,"[16] and too much civility could stifle that. However, today's nasty online conversations are marked by two attributes that set them apart from those in the past: They are more public, and they can go viral in seconds. These online conversations are not the "uninhibited, robust, and wide open" discourses that the U.S. Supreme Court urged in *New York Times v. Sullivan* in 1964,[17] ruling that free debate trumps damage to public officials' reputations. It is more to akin to discourse that marks outrage media, an emerging genre of opinion-based cable news shows, blogs, and talk radio that feature "incivility writ large" with "vilification of opponents and fear mongering."[18] It also mimics "in-your-face-politics,"[19] the type of up-close-and-personal political battles on television that violate any conversational norms.

For a prime example of in-your-face politics, look no farther than Presidential Donald Trump's 2016 campaign. As Tom Leonard, a U.S. correspondent for the *Daily Mail*, writes, "Trump is a ferocious user of Twitter, his favorite medium in that it is short, sharp and—in his hands—shocking."[20] And when Trump tweets, his startling thoughts ricochet around the world in mere minutes. To a lesser extent, even the average person can harness some of that power. In today's always-on media culture, people can comment on what's happening in the news in real time at speeds unrivaled in any other time period. They are typing their opinions in the privacy of their own homes, shielded from public view, but what they say becomes public immediately in today's new town square—social media and comment streams. As political scientist Diana C. Mutz notes,[21] when Vice President Aaron Burr fatally shot his rival Alexander Hamilton during a duel in 1804,[22] the public did not witness it firsthand but learned about it later through newspapers and word of mouth. If the duel were to happen today, someone would be lurking nearby, cell phone in hand to tweet it and live stream it. Within seconds, potentially millions of people could watch, comment, and argue with each other about the shooting, likely even before Hamilton was officially pronounced dead. Part of this shift certainly may be due to changes in what people consider news and our own sensibilities about what is appropriate. But much of the shift is due to technology. Technology is not the demon here, of course. It is merely a tool. However, technological advances have created the potential for the type of instantaneous response that fuels our current uncivil discourse.

Why Is Computer-Mediated Communication Susceptible to Incivility?

So what makes online communication so hospitable to incivility? In the early days of the Internet, many scholars believed computer-mediated communication was too impersonal, or "lean,"[23] for effective social connection. Online discourse lacks the nonverbal cues, such as tone of voice and body language, of face-to-face encounters, this thinking went. As a result, online conversation was seen as best for rational tasks, not for communicating emotions or forming relationships. Based on information richness theory and the cues-filtered-out approach, online communication was viewed as having less potential for social connecting, compared to "richer" forms of communication, such as face to face.[24] As online communication evolved, however, this view was seen as limited. Communication scholar Joseph B. Walther suggested that digital discussions have the potential to be just as personal as face-to-face communication or even to be "hyperpersonal."[25] Computer-mediated discussions may blur boundaries between people[26] and can foster a sense of camaraderie between people[27] or "we-ness"[28] through weak ties,[29] which are connections based on a shared interest or hobby. Online discourse may make people feel more connected through these weak ties than they really are, as explained by the Social Identification Model of Deindividuation Effect (SIDE).[30] Deindividuation is when people feel as if their individual identity becomes less important because they see themselves as part of a group. Without facial cues, subtle paralinguistic cues take on greater meaning online, and social groups become more important. People have a sense of "deindividuation"[31] online even when their real names are visible because it appears as if their actions cannot be traced to them. As a result, they may feel more comfortable connecting with others, freed from the obstacles of physical appearance. They feel hidden by the group online in a sense, so they can build relationships with others more quickly, based on only a limited shared identity. For example, I recently joined a Weight Watchers online group for people to support each other in losing weight. On the group's app, I posted about my excitement and trepidation about embarking on what I know will be an arduous task. I immediately got a rush of supportive comments to my post that made me feel a connection to these people whom I will never meet, and with whom I likely share few commonalities except a desire to shed a few pounds. I would likely be less open with my real-life friends about my weight-loss journey than I would with these new virtual acquaintances because I would feel too vulnerable. I feel comfortable sharing within this group, solidified through our common goal. That is the kind of hyperpersonal relationship computer-mediated communication offers based on our sense of deindividuation online.

Darker Side of Deindividuation

However, this deindividuation also offers a darker side. When people's group identity is more salient than their individual identity, they also may feel freer to act out in socially undesirable ways. Consider spectators at a football game who jump on seats, scream, or even break things when they are frenzied by their team's win or loss. These people have lost themselves in the group identity of fandom and no longer see their actions as traceable to them. Similarly, when people communicate online sometimes they feel more uninhibited, so they say things they would likely not say to someone's face. The fact that comment streams on news sites developed in a way that allowed anonymity exacerbates this effect. In the pre-digital days, newspapers generally printed only signed letters to the editor. Yet, when online commenting started in the late 1990s on online news sites,[32] anonymity became the norm. Some researchers have found links between anonymity and incivility. In a study of news site comments about immigration, for example, 65% of the 359 uncivil comments were from anonymous posters, while named posters contributed 35% of the incivility.[33] News organizations have taken steps to curb the incivility by requiring posters to register before commenting[34] or to link their comments to their own identities on social media sites, such as Facebook or LinkedIn.[35] News sites also allow readers to flag offensive comments. Sites can monitor, hide, or delete comments or even ban users in attempts to control the incivility.[36] News organizations also have created methods for commenters to rank each other and prioritize commenters who rank highly.[37] These actions have led to more civil and less hostile comment streams,[38] but they do not eliminate nasty talk online.

Even when people must use their own name, they may still feel a sense of deindividuation, perhaps because the Internet feels like such a big place. It is similar to comparing small-town America to a big city. When people live in a small town, it is easy for others to connect their behavior back to them because so many other people know them or their relatives and friends. Bad behavior could easily get back to them. But when people from a small town move to a big city, they may feel emboldened because initially they may never see another person they know. So even when using their own names, they feel a sense of anonymity. I suggest the Internet works like that. At some level people figure that amid the millions of people using the web at any given moment, they are hidden in plain sight. After a while, however, even people living in a big city get to know their neighborhood. The clerk at the corner store knows their names. They pass the same people from their building in the hallways each day, and nod "hello." The sense of deindividuation decreases, although perhaps not to the extent that they would feel in a small town. This explains why news organizations' attempt to foster a sense of community on their news sites[39] that mimics this neighborhood feel and why journalists engaging in comment streams may foster a more civil environment.[40] These efforts emphasize a sense of group identity on a site, so people want to follow the normal practices of that group. When journalists or other people set a tone of civility on a site, other people are more likely to be civil as well, so they fit into the group.[41] It also explains why uncivil commenters tend to be infrequent commenters on a site.[42] Those who feel least part of online community on the site feel more deindividuated, so they are liberated to act inappropriately. Thus, even a few proverbial rotten apples can turn a comment stream into the cesspools of trash talk that both journalists and the public bemoan.[43]

Casualties of Nasty Talk

Of course, all this nasty talk online is not a victimless crime. While the general public may be initially drawn to the titillation of watching online arguments—much as they cannot take their eyes off a train derailment—incivility makes comment streams less hospitable places for public engagement. Research has shown that readers have greater tolerance than journalists do for some vitriol in comment streams if it means they get a chance to engage.[44] But even readers report that angry and insulting posts get in the way of productive online conversations[45] and may make them less likely to comment or even read comments.[46] Journalists often see it as their job to police the conversation to keep it civil[47]—although some eschew this function[48]—through moderating comments, deleting them, or engaging with commenters.[49] So the first casualty of online incivility is the death of the utopian dream of the Internet's potential[50] to foster an unfettered space for discussion and debate, a virtual version of the public sphere that social psychologist Gabriel de Tarde[51] and sociologist Jürgen Habermas[52] imagined. The cost to society is we have this enormous, global network that is uniquely suited for fostering engagement between people, but it does not work as well as it might. Only a fraction of the public engages in comment streams, and a fraction of those who do engage spew such filth that the rest of the population flees the space or ignores it. People who try to debate and discuss are frustrated. The chance to discuss topics that are relevant and important to society is lost at least in this virtual space, and the opportunity to provide a voice to those who have less chance to speak out offline[53] are squashed. The potential of fruitful computer-mediated public talk[54] that builds bridges and draws people together while airing grievances and stirring interest in politics goes unrealized. One arena for the interplay of opinion and policy that distinguishes democracy[55] is gone at least from this digital space. Instead the dystopian horror has been realized of comment streams that have become what Pulitzer-Prize-winning journalist Leonard Pitts Jr. called "havens for a level of crudity, bigotry, meanness and plain nastiness that shocks the tattered remnants of our propriety."[56]

The costs of incivility online are also psychological and social. The belongingness hypothesis proposes that people are evolutionarily hardwired to gather with other people and form connections.[57] This stems from our primitive days when being completely separate from a group meant greater risk of danger or death at the hands of predators. So the humans who survived were those who learned how to attract and remain with other people, and these humans passed on their genes, feeding our predilection today to gather in groups. Sociometer theory[58] builds on this notion by proposing that people's self-esteem—how they feel about themselves in general—acts as a thermostat of how valuable they are to others. When people believe others value them, they feel in balance. But depressions in self-esteem spark a warning that their goal of being part of the group is at risk. So being social online is more than just a fun way for people to communicate. It is intrinsic to our very humanity. Studies have shown that the human body responds to mediated messages much the same as it does to face-to-face messages[59] because our physiology has not evolved enough to know the difference, even if our intellect does. So our natural need to affiliate with others easily translates to the online sphere. When incivility challenges people's sense that they are valued as relationship partners in that digital space, they feel an emotional pain similar to what they would experience from a physical assault.[60] These hurt feelings act like a warning system to people, sounding an alarm to change behavior much like physical pain would spark a child to remove her hand from a hot stove. Brain scans have shown that this type of social pain activates the brain similarly to physical pain.[61] So when one poster called another a "vile bigot" in the aftermath of the mass shooting at a gay nightclub in Florida in June 2016,[62] the target's body senses this as a physical threat, triggering a primal instinct to fight or flee.[63]

People figure out how to respond somewhat automatically, often driven by emotions that may or may not be tempered by thinking before they act.[64] Face and politeness theories[65] explain this response by suggesting that incivility harms people's constructed sense of their public identity called *face* that symbolizes their relational value to others.[66] So in essence, at some level, when a person is insulted or attacked by words online, they feel less valuable as a social partner because they lose *face*. This results in negative emotions[67] and triggers a primal urge to restore their relational value by regaining *face*.[68] How people respond at this point depends on their personality, their upbringing, and how much the words really hurt them. Some may attempt to restore their *face* by diminishing the *face* of their attacker by shooting back with uncivil words, becoming verbally aggressive, or even retaliating.[69] Others may simply ignore it. Indeed, research has found that people who are attacked online are not more likely to respond than those who are not attacked, but if they do respond, their response is more likely to be nasty.[70] This means that one uncivil barb can taint the tone of a whole comment thread rather quickly. One troll who disrupts the discourse with "no apparent instrumental purpose"[71] except to cause trouble can quickly lead to escalating incivility if not stopped. Here again, the causality is that a dynamic discourse is lost, and people feel angry and upset or even rejected at some level.

Thus, the deindividuation of online discourse along with the lack of conversational cues plus the speed with which a comment can go public and viral online foments a perfect storm of sorts for incivility to flourish and cause harm. Unlike the offline world, where a nasty remark in relative private will sting but then diffuse, a biting online taunt lasts longer and potentially exposes the target to embarrassment on a larger scale. Instead of a handful of people seeing a person's pain from incivility offline, an online assault may produce hundreds, thousands, or even millions of witnesses. As a result, the same words may hurt more in a populated online space than in a sparse offline one. Therefore, the likelihood that the injured party will attack grows, particularly because people feel somewhat deindividuated online. For example, few us of would snarl back at a rude clerk at the supermarket, even if we mutter a few choice words under our breath. We do not want to cause a scene or look like the crazy person in the grocery store where our friends and neighbors might see us. But the cost to our reputations does not seem so great if we nastily respond to an uncivil comment in the seeming anonymity of the web. Plus, gripped by the intensity of our own emotions and the ease at which we can type a response, biting back may become too tempting to resist.

So when a commenter on the gorilla story that started this chapter wrote something offensive, a handful of other people blasted him for being a "racist,"[72] and "idiot,"[73] or even implying he was in the Ku Klux Klan.[74]

Whether these commenters would have been so strident face to face is not known, but it seems very likely at least some of them would have curbed their tongues or merely walked away. Their forthrightness, of course, has value. They challenged the initial poster for writing something inappropriate. But the words they chose as they did this could merely have enflamed the debate further.

Classroom Discussion Prompts

1. Explain the concept of deindividuation and how it applies to computer-mediated communication.
2. Discuss how the reduced social cues in online communication influence how people form social relationships online.
3. What are the major casualties of online incivility?
4. Explain why a digital environment is so hospitable to incivility?

Notes

1. Cameron Knight and Mallorie Sullivan, "Gorilla Killed After 3-Year-Old Falls Into Zoo Enclosure," *Cincinnati* (Ohio) *Enquirer*, May 28, 2016. http://www.cincinnati.com/story/news/2016/05/28/police child-taken-hospital-after-falling-into-gorilla-pen/85095094/ (Knight and Sullivan 2016).
2. Elizabeth McMahon, May 28, 2016, comment posted on Knight and Sullivan, "Gorilla Killed After 3-Year-Old Falls Into Zoo Enclosure."
3. Sarah Sobieraj and Jeffrey M. Berry, "From Incivility to Outrage: Political Discourse in Blogs, Talk Radio, and Cable News," *Political Communication* 28, no. 1 (2011): 19–41; Gina Masullo Chen and Shuning Lu, "Online Political Discourse: Exploring Differences in Effects of Civil and Uncivil Disagreement in News Website Comments," *Journal of Broadcasting & Electronic Media*, 61, no. 1 (2017). doi:10.1080/08838151/2016/1273922; Zizi Papacharissi, "Democracy Online: Civility, Politeness, and Democratic Potential of Online Political Discussion Groups," *New Media & Society* 7, no. 2 (2004): 259–283; Natalie J. Stroud, Joshua M. Scacco, Ashley Muddiman, and Alexander L. Curry, "Changing Deliberative Norms on News Organizations' Facebook Sites," *Journal of Computer-Mediated Communication* 20 (2015): 188–203 (Sobieraj and Berry 2011; Chen and Lu 2017; Papacharissi 2004; Stroud et al. 2015).

4. Mike Steele, May 29, 2016, comment posted on Knight and Sullivan, "Gorilla Killed After 3-Year-Old Falls Into Zoo Enclosure."
5. Jack Straw, May 28, 2016, comment posted on Knight and Sullivan, "Gorilla Killed After 3-Year-Old Falls Into Zoo Enclosure."
6. The video has since been taken down from the *Cincinnati Enquirer* site but can be accessed at the *Daily Mail*'s website: http://www.dailymail.co.uk/news/article-3616453/New-video-footage-Harambe-shows-400-pound-gorilla-HOLDING-HANDS-four-year-old-boy-fell-zoo-enclosure-witnesses-say-animal-acting-protectively.html.
7. Bobbie White, May 29, 2016, comment posted on Knight and Sullivan, "Gorilla Killed After 3-Year-Old Falls Into Zoo Enclosure."
8. Jorge Cajamarca, May 28, 2016, comment posted on Knight and Sullivan, "Gorilla Killed After 3-Year-Old Falls Into Zoo Enclosure."
9. Accessed June 23, 2016 at: https://twitter.com/search?q=%23gorillalivesmatter&src=tyah.
10. Limor Shifman, *Memes in Digital Culture*, (Cambridge, MA: MIT Press, 2014) (Shifman 2014).
11. Allan Clarke, "Facebook Memes Compare Aboriginal Athlete to Gorilla That Was Fatally Shot," *BuzzFeed*, June 1, 2016. https://www.buzzfeed.com/allanclarke/facebook-memes-compare-adam-goodes-to-the-gorilla-that-was-f?utm_term=.vcqRN7Mqa#.lb6zDXZAV; Leith Huffadine, "'Utterly appalling': Racist Memes Comparing Retired Star Adam Goodes to Shot Gorilla Harambe Pulled From Facebook," June 2, 2016. http://www.dailymail.co.uk/news/article-3621232/Shocking-racist-memes-compared-retired-indigenous-AFL-star-Adam-Goodes-gorilla.html (Clarke 2016; Huffadine 2016).
12. Huffadine, "'Utterly appalling': Racist Memes Comparing Retired Star Adam Goodes to Shot Gorilla Harambe Pulled From Facebook."
13. Cornell W. Clayton, "Historical Perspectives on the Role of Civility in American Democracy," in *Civility and Democracy in America: A Reasonable Understanding*, eds. Cornell W. Clayton and Richard Elgar, (Pullman, WA: Washington State University Press, 2012); Diana C. Mutz *In-Your-Face-Politics: The Consequences of Uncivil Media*, (Princeton, NJ: Princeton University Press, 2015) (Clayton 2012; Mutz 2015).
14. Clayton, "Historical Perspectives on the Role of Civility in American Democracy."
15. Fredrik Logevall, "The Paradox of Civility," in *Civility and Democracy in America: A Reasonable Understanding*, eds. Cornell W. Clayton and Richard Elgar, (Pullman, WA: Washington State University Press, 2012) (Logevall 2012).

16. Cornell W. Clayton and Richard Elgar, "Civility and American Democracy," in *Civility and Democracy in America: A Reasonable Understanding*.
17. John G. Geer, *In Defense of Negativity: Attack Ads in Presidential Campaigns*, (Chicago, IL: Chicago University Press, 2006) (Geer 2006).
18. Jerry M. Berry and Sarah Sobieraj, *The Outrage Industry: Political Opinion Media and the New Incivility*, (New York, NY: Oxford University Press, 2014): 6, 7 (Berry and Sarah Sobieraj 2014).
19. Mutz, *In-Your-Face-Politics: The Consequences of Uncivil Media*.
20. Tom Leonard, "They Should Have Seen Him Coming," *British Journalism Review* 27, no. 2 (2016): 16–21 (Leonard 2016).
21. Mutz, *In-Your-Face-Politics: The Consequences of Uncivil Media*.
22. Aaron Burr Biography, Bio.com. http://www.biography.com/people/aaron-burr-9232241.
23. Joseph B. Walther, "Computer-Mediated Communication: Impersonal, Interpersonal, and Hyperpersonal Interaction," *Communication Research* 23, no. 1 (1996): 3 (Walther 1996).
24. Richard L. Daft and Robert H. Lengel, "Information Richness: A New Approach to Managerial Behavior and Organizational Design," in *Research in Organizational Behavior*, eds. Barry M. Staw and Larry L. Cummings, (Greenwich, CT: Jai, 1986): 554–571; Walther, "Computer-Mediated Communication: Impersonal, Interpersonal, and Hyperpersonal Interaction" (Daft and Lengel 1986).
25. Walther, "Computer-Mediated Communication: Impersonal, Interpersonal, and Hyperpersonal Interaction," 17.
26. Nancy K. Baym and danah boyd, "Socially Mediated Publicness: An Introduction," *Journal of Broadcasting & Electronic Media* 56, no. 3 (2012): 320–329 (Baym and boyd 2012).
27. Gina Masullo Chen, "Tweet This: A Uses and Gratifications Perspective on How Active Twitter Use Gratifies a Need to Connect With Others," *Computers in Human Behavior* 27 (2011): 755–762 (Chen 2011).
28. Leda Cooks, Mari Castañeda Paredes, and Erica Scharrer, "There's 'O Place' Like Home: Searching For Community on Oprah.com," in *Women & Everyday Uses of the Internet: Agency & Identity*, eds. Mia Consalvo and Susanna Paasonen, (New York, NY: Peter Lang, 2002): 133–167 (Cooks et al. 2002).
29. Mark A. Granovetter, "The Strength of Weak Ties," *American Journal of Sociology* 78, no. 6 (1973): 1360–1380 (Granovetter 1973).
30. Russell Spears, Tom Postmes, and Martin Le, and Anka Wolbert, "When Are Net Effects Gross Products? The Power of Influence and Influence of Power in Computer-Mediated Communication," *Journal of Social Issues*

58, no. 1 (2002): 91–107; John Suler, "The Online Disinhibition Effect," *CyberPsychology & Behavior* 7, no. 3 (2004): 321–326 (Spears et al. 2002; Suler 2004).
31. Spears et al., "When Are Net Effects Gross Products? The Power of Influence and Influence of Power in Computer-Mediated Communication," 91.
32. Arthur D. Santana, "Online Readers' Comments Represent New Opinion Pipeline," *Newspaper Research Journal* 32, no. 3 (2011): 66–81 (Santana 2011).
33. Arthur D. Santana, "Virtuous or Vitriolic," *Journalism Practice* 8, no. 1 (2014): 18–33 (Santana 2014).
34. Thomas B. Ksiazek, "Civil Interactivity: How News Organizations' Commenting Policies Explain Civility and Hostility in User Comments," *Journal of Broadcasting & Electronic Media* 59, 4 (2015): 556–573; Ian Rowe, "Civility 2.0: A Comparative Analysis of Incivility in Online Political Discussion," *Information, Communication & Society* 18, no. 2 (2015): 121–138 (Ksiazek 2015; Rowe 2015).
35. Kimberly Meltzer, "Journalistic Concern About Uncivil Political Talk in Digital News Media: Responsibility, Credibility, and Academic Influence," *The International Journal of Press/Politics* 20, no. 1 (2015): 85–107 (Meltzer 2015).
36. Lori Brost, "Editors Have Mixed Feelings on User-Generated Comments," *Newspaper Research Journal* 34, no. 3 (2013): 101–115; Gina Masullo Chen and Paromita Pain, "Normalizing Online Comments," *Journalism Practice*, Advance Online Publication: 10.1080/17512786.2016.1205954; John A. Hatcher and Mary Currin-Percival, "Does the Structural Pluralism Model Predict Differences in Journalists' Perceptions of Online Comments?" *Digital Journalism* 4, no. 3 (2016): 302–320; Ksiazek, "Civil Interactivity: How News Organizations' Commenting Policies Explain Civility and Hostility in User Comments"; Jaime Loke, "Old Turf, New Neighbors," *Journalism Practice* 6, no. 2 (2012); 233–249; Jack Rosenberry, "Users Support Anonymity Despite Increasing Negativity," *Newspaper Research Journal* 32, no. 1 (2011): 6–19 (Brost 2013; Chen and Pain 2016; Hatcher and Currin-Percival 2016; Loke 2012; Rosenberry 2011).
37. Richard Pérez-Peña, "News Sites Rethink Anonymous Online Comments," *The New York Times*, 2010, April 11. http://www.nytimes.com/2010/04/12/technology/12comments.html?_r=0 (Pérez-Peña 2010).
38. Ksiazek, "Civil Interactivity: How News Organizations' Commenting Policies Explain Civility and Hostility in User Comments."
39. Gina Masullo Chen et al., "Personalizing News Websites Attracts Young Readers," *Newspaper Research Journal* 32, no. 4 (2011): 22–38 (Chen et al. 2011).

40. Chen and Pain, "Normalizing Online Comments"; Stroud et al., "Changing Deliberative Norms on News Organizations' Facebook Sites."
41. Soo-Hye Han and LeAnn M. Brazeal, "Playing Nice: Modeling Civility in Online Political Discussions," *Communication Research Reports* 32, no. 1 (2015): 20–28; Abhay Sukumaran, Stephanie Vezich, Melanie McHugh, and Clifford Nass, "Normative Influences on Thoughtful Online Participation," *Proceedings of the CHI 2011 Session: Incentives & User Generated Content*, Vancouver, British Columbia, (2011): 3401–3410 (Han and Brazeal 2015; Sukumaran et al. 2011).
42. Kevin Coe, Kate Kenski, and Stephen A. Rains, "Online and Uncivil? Patterns and Determinants of Incivility in Newspaper Website Comments," *Journal of Communication* 64 (2014): 658–679 (Coe et al. 2014).
43. Chen and Pain, "Normalizing Online Comments"; Bill Reader, "Free Press Vs. Free Speech? The Rhetoric of 'Civility' in Regard to Anonymous Online Comments," *Journalism & Mass Communication Quarterly* 89, no. 3 (2012): 495–512; Rosenberry, "Users Support Anonymity Despite Increasing Negativity" (Reader 2012).
44. Reader, "Free Press Vs. Free Speech? The Rhetoric of 'Civility' in Regard to Anonymous Online Comments."
45. Rosenberry, "Users Support Anonymity Despite Increasing Negativity."
46. Nicholas Diakopoulos and Mor Naaman, "Towards Quality Discourse in Online News Comments," *Proceedings of the CSCW*, (Hangzhou, China, March 19–23, 2011) (Diakopoulos and Naaman 2011).
47. Meltzer, "Journalistic Concern About Uncivil Political Talk in Digital News Media: Responsibility, Credibility, and Academic Influence."
48. Chen and Pain, "Normalizing Online Comments."
49. Brost, "Editors Have Mixed Feelings on User-Generated Comments"; Chen and Pain, "Normalizing Online Comments"; Hatcher and Currin-Percival, "Does the Structural Pluralism Model Predict Differences in Journalists' Perceptions of Online Comments?" Ksiazek, "Civil Interactivity: How News Organizations' Commenting Policies Explain Civility and Hostility in User Comments"; Loke, "Old Turf, New Neighbors"; and Rosenberry, "Users Support Anonymity Despite Increasing Negativity."
50. Steffen Albrecht, "Whose Voice is Heard in Online Deliberation? A Study of Participation and Representation in Political Debates on the Internet," *Information, Communication & Society* 8, no.1 (2006): 62–82; Bosah Ebo, *Cyberghetto or Cybertopia? Race, Class and Gender on the Internet*, ed., (Wesport, CT: Praeger, 1998), 2; Papacharissi, "Democracy Online: Civility, Politeness, and Democratic Potential of Online Political Discussion Groups," 259 (Albrecht 2006; Ebo 1998).

51. Gabriel de Tarde, *On Communication and Social Influence*, ed. Terry N. Clark, (Chicago, IL: University of Chicago Press, 1889/1969) (Tarde 1889/1969).
52. Jürgen Habermas, "Three Normative Models of Democracy," *Democratic and Constitutional Theory Today* 1, no. 1 (1994): 1–10 (Habermas 1994).
53. Ebo, *Cyberghetto or Cybertopia? Race, Class and Gender on the Internet*; Gina Masullo Chen, "Why Do Women Write Personal Blogs? Satisfying Needs for Self-Disclosure and Affiliation Tell Part of the Story," *Computers in Human Behavior* 28 (2012): 171–180; Ananda Mitra, "Marginal Voices in Cyberspace," *New Media & Society* 3, no. 1 (2001): 29–48 (Chen 2012; Mitra 2001).
54. John Gastil and Laura W. Black, "Public Deliberation as the Organizing Principle of Political Communication Research," *Journal of Public Deliberation* 4, no. 1 (2008): Article 3, 7; Lawrence R. Jacobs, Fay Lomax Cook, and Michael X. Delli Carpini, *Talking Together: Public Deliberation and Political Participation in America*, (Chicago, IL: The University of Chicago Press, 2009) (Gastil and Black 2008; Jacobs et al. 2009).
55. Harold D. Lasswell, *Democracy Through Public Opinion*, (Menasha, WI: George Banta Publishing Co., 1941) (Lasswell 1941).
56. Leonard Pitts, "Anonymity Brings Out the Worst in Expression," *The Gazette.com*, April 1, 2010. http://gazette.com/anonymity-brings-out-the-worst-in-expression/article/96545; this piece was originally published on the *Miami Herald*'s website but has since been removed; see also Reader, "Free Press Vs. Free Speech? The Rhetoric of 'Civility' in Regard to Anonymous Online Comments," 500–501 (Pitts 2010).
57. Roy F. Baumeister and Mark R. Leary, "The Need to Belong: Desire for Interpersonal Attachments as a Fundamental Human Need," *Psychological Bulletin* 117, no. 3 (1995): 497–529 (Baumeister and Leary 1995).
58. Mark R. Leary and Roy F. Baumeister, "The Nature and Function of Self-Esteem: Sociometer Theory," *Advances in Experimental Social Psychology* 32 (2000): 1–62 (Baumeister and Leary 2000).
59. Byron Reeves and Clifford Nass, *The Media Equation*, (Cambridge, MA: Cambridge University Press, 1996) (Reeves and Nass 1996).
60. Naomi I. Eisenberger, Matthew D. Lieberman, and Kipling D. Williams, "Does Rejection Hurt? An fMRI Study of Social Exclusion," *Science*, 203 (2003): 290–292; Geoff MacDonald and Mark R. Leary, "Why Does Social Exclusion Hurt? The Relationship Between Social and Physical Pain," *Psychological Bulletin* 131, no. 2 (2005): 202–223; Kipling D. Williams, Joseph P. Forgas, and William von Hippel, *The Social Outcast*, (New York, NY: Psychology Press, 2005) (Eisenberger et al. 2003; MacDonald and Leary 2005; Williams et al. 2005).

61. Eisenberger, Lieberman, and Williams, "Does Rejection Hurt? An fMRI Study of Social Exclusion."
62. Samuel 1974, June 14, 2016, comment posted on Matthew Grimson, David Wyllie, and Elisha Fieldstadt, "Orlando Nightclub Shooting: Mass Casualties After Gunman Opens Fire in Gay Club," *NBCNews.com*, June 13, 2016. http://www.nbcnews.com/storyline/orlando-nightclub-massacre/orlando-nightclub-shooting-emergency-services-respond-reports-gunman-n590446.
63. Annie Lang, "The Limited Capacity Model of Mediated Message Processing," *Journal of Communication* 50, no. 1 (2000): 46–70 Lang (2000).
64. George E. Marcus, W. Russell Neuman, and Michael MacKuen, *Affective Intelligence and Political Judgment*, (Chicago, IL: University of Chicago Press, 2000) (Marcus et al. 2000).
65. Erving Goffman, *Presentation of the Self in Everyday Life*, (Garden City, NY: Doubleday, 1959); Penelope Brown and Stephen C. Levinson, *Politeness: Some Universals in Language Usage*, (New York, NY: Cambridge Press, 1987); Sandra Metts and William R. Cupach, "Face Theory: Goffman's Dramatist Approach to Interpersonal Interaction," in *Engaging Theories in Interpersonal Communication*, eds. Dawn O. Braithwaite and Paul Schrodt, (Thousand Oaks, CA: Sage, 2015): 203–214 (Goffman 1959; Brown and Levinson 1987; Metts and Cupach 2015).
66. John G. Oetzel and Stella Ting-Toomey, "Face Concerns in Interpersonal Conflict: A Cross-Cultural Empirical Test of Face Negotiation Theory," *Communication Research* 30, no. 6 (2003): 599–624; Metts and. Cupach, "Face Theory: Goffman's Dramatist Approach to Interpersonal Interaction" (Oetzel and Ting-Toomey 2003).
67. Gina Masullo Chen, "Losing *Face* on Social Media: Threats to *Positive Face* Lead to an Indirect Effect on Retaliatory Aggression Through Negative Affect," *Communication Research* 42, no. 6 (2015): 819–838; Gina Masullo Chen and Zainul Abedin, "Exploring Differences in How Men and Women Respond to Threats to *Positive Face* on Social Media," *Computers in Human Behavior* 38 (2014): 118–126; Gina Masullo Chen and Pei Zheng, *Online Public Discourse: Exploring Differences in Responses to Civil and Uncivil Disagreement in News Story Comments*, presented to the Mass Communication and Society Division of the Association for Education in Journalism and Mass Communication annual conference in Minneapolis, MN, in August 2016; Gina Masullo Chen and Pei Zheng, *The "Defensive Effect": Uncivil Comments Indirectly Increase Intention to Participate Politically, Through Negative Affect*, presented to the Mass Communication Division of the International Communication Association annual

conference in Fukuoka, Japan, in June 2016; Chen and Lu, "Online Political Discourse: Exploring Differences in Effects of Civil and Uncivil Disagreement in News Website Comments"; Bryan T. Gervais, "Incivility Online: Affective and Behavioral Reactions to Uncivil Political Posts in a Web-Based Experiment," *Journal of Information, Technology & Politics* 12 (2015): 167–185; Jeanne M. Brett, Mara Olekains, Ray Friedman, Nathan Goates, Cameron Anderson, and Cara Cherry Lisco, "Sticks and Stones: Language, Face, and Online Dispute Resolution," *Academy of Management Journal* 50, no. 1 (2007): 85–99; Leonie Rösner, Stephan Winter, and Nicole C. Krämer, "Dangerous Minds? Effects of Online Comments on Aggressive Cognitions, Emotions, and Behavior," *Computers in Human Behavior* 58 (2016): 461–470 (Chen 2015; Chen and Abedin 2014; Chen and Zheng 2016a, b; Chen and Lu 2015; Gervais (2015); Brett et al. 2007; Rösner et al. 2016).

68. Brett et al., "Sticks and Stones: Language, Face, and Online Dispute Resolution"; Metts and Cupach, "Face Theory: Goffman's Dramatist Approach to Interpersonal Interaction."
69. Brett et al., "Sticks and Stones: Language, Face, and Online Dispute Resolution"; Chen, "Losing *Face* on Social Media"; Chen and Abedin, "Exploring Differences in How Men and Women Respond to Threats to *Positive Face* on Social Media"; Chen and Lu, "Online Political Discourse: Exploring Differences in Effects of Civil and Uncivil Disagreement in News Website Comments"; Rösner, Winter, and Krämer, "Dangerous Minds? Effects of Online Comments on Aggressive Cognitions, Emotions, and Behavior"; Metts and Cupach, "Face Theory: Goffman's Dramatist Approach to Interpersonal Interaction."
70. Chen and Lu, "Online Political Discourse: Exploring Differences in Effects of Civil and Uncivil Disagreement in News Website Comments."
71. Erin E. Buckels, Paul D. Trapnell, and Delroy L. Paulhus, "Trolls Just Want to Have Fun," *Personality and Individual Differences* 62 (2014): 97 (Buckels et al. 2014).
72. Jerry Hutchins, May 28, 2016, comment posted on Knight and Sullivan, "Gorilla Killed After 3-Year-Old Falls Into Zoo Enclosure."
73. Robert Lloyd Sr., May 28, 2016, comment posted on Knight and Sullivan, "Gorilla Killed After 3-Year-Old Falls Into Zoo Enclosure."
74. Brett Vrendenburg, May 28, 2016, comment posted on Knight and Sullivan, "Gorilla Killed After 3-Year-Old Falls Into Zoo Enclosure."

REFERENCES

Albrecht, Steffen. 2006. Whose Voice is Heard in Online Deliberation? A Study of Participation and Representation in Political Debates on the Internet. *Information, Communication & Society* 8 (1): 62–82.

Baumeister, Roy F., and Mark R. Leary. 1995. The Need to Belong: Desire for Interpersonal Attachments as a Fundamental Human Need. *Psychological Bulletin* 117 (3): 497–529.

Baym, Nancy K., and danah boyd. 2012. Socially Mediated Publicness: An Introduction. *Journal of Broadcasting & Electronic Media* 56 (3): 320–329.

Berry, Jerrey M., and Sarah Sobieraj. 2014. *The Outrage Industry: Politics and the New Incivility.* New York: Oxford University Press.

Brett, Jeanne M., Mara Olekains, Ray Friedman, Nathan Goates, Cameron Anderson, and Cara Cherry Lisco. 2007. Sticks and Stones: Language, Face, and Online Dispute Resolution. *Academy of Management Journal* 50 (1): 85–99.

Brost, Lori. 2013. Editors Have Mixed Feelings on User-Generated Comments. *Newspaper Research Journal* 34 (3): 101–115.

Brown, Penelope, and Stephen C. Levinson. 1987. *Politeness: Some Universals in Language Usage.* New York: Cambridge University Press.

Buckels, Erin E., Paul D. Trapnell, and Delroy L. Paulhus. 2014. Trolls Just Want to have fun. *Personality and Individual Differences* 62: 97–102.

Chen, Gina Masullo. 2011. Tweet this: A Uses and Gratifications Perspective on How Active Twitter Use Gratifies a Need to Connect with Others. *Computers in Human Behavior* 27: 755–762.

Chen, Gina Masullo. 2012. Why do Women Write Personal Blogs? Satisfying Needs for Self-Disclosure and Affiliation Tell Part of the Story. *Computers in Human Behavior* 28: 171–180.

Chen, Gina Masullo. 2015. Losing *Face* on Social Media: Threats to *Positive Face* Lead to an Indirect Effect on Retaliatory Aggression Through Negative Affect. *Communication Research* 42 (6): 819–838.

Chen, Gina Masullo, and Zainul Abedin. 2014. Exploring Differences in How Men and Women Respond to Threats to *Positive Face* on Social Media. *Computers in Human Behavior* 38: 118–126.

Chen, Gina Masullo, and Paromita Pain. 2016. Normalizing Online Comments. *Journalism Practice.* doi:10.1080/17512786.2016.1205954.

Chen, Gina Masullo, and Pei Zheng. 2016, August. *Online Public Discourse: Exploring Differences in Responses to Civil and Uncivil Disagreement in News Story Comments.* Presented to the Mass Communication and Society Division of the Association for Education in Journalism and Mass Communication Annual Conference in Minneapolis, MN.

Chen, Gina Masullo, and Pei Zheng. 2016, June. *The "Defensive Effect": Uncivil Comments Indirectly Increase Intention to Participate Politically, Through*

Negative Affect. Presented to the Mass Communication Division of the International Communication Association Annual Conference in Fukuoka, Japan.

Chen, Gina Masullo, and Shuning Lu. 2017. Online Political Discourse: Exploring Differences in Effects of Civil and Uncivil Disagreement in News Website Comments. *Journal of Broadcasting & Electronic Media* 61 (1). doi:10.1080/08838151/2016/1273922.

Clarke, Allan. 2016. Facebook Memes Compare Aboriginal Athlete to Gorilla That Was Fatally Shot. *BuzzFeed*, June 1 2016. https://www.buzzfeed.com/allanclarke/facebook-memes-compare-adam-goodes-to-the-gorilla-that-was-f?utm_term=.vcqRN7Mqa#.lb6zDXZAV.

Clayton, Cornell W. 2012. Historical Perspectives on the Role of Civility in American Democracy. In *Civility and Democracy in America: A Reasoned Understanding*, ed. Cornell W. Clayton and Richard Elgar, 1–4. Pullman, WA: Washington University Press.

Coe, Kevin, Kate Kenski, and Stephen A. Rains. 2014. Online and Uncivil? Patterns and Determinants of Incivility in Newspaper Website Comments. *Journal of Communication* 64: 658–679.

Cooks, Leda, Mari Castañeda Paredes, and Erica Scharrer. 2002. There's 'O Place' Like Home: Searching for Community on Oprah.com. In *Women & Everyday Uses of the Internet: Agency & Identity*, ed. Mia Consalvo, and Susanna Paasonen, 133–167. New York: Peter Lang.

Daft, Richard L, and Robert H. Lengel. 1986. Information Richness: A New Approach To Managerial Behavior And Organizational Design. In *Research in Organizational Behavior*, ed. Barry M. Staw, and Larry L. Cummings, 554–571. Greenwich, CT: Jai.

De Tarde, Gabriel. 1889/1969. *On Communication and Social Influence*, ed. Terry N. Clark. Chicago: University of Chicago Press.

Diakopoulos, Nicholas, and Mor Naaman. 2011. Towards Quality Discourse in Online News Comments. In *Proceedings of the CSCW*, March 19–23. Hangzhou, China.

Ebo, Bosah. 1998. *Cyberghetto or Cybertopia? Race, Class and Gender on the Internet*, ed., Wesport, CT: Praeger.

Eisenberger, Naomi I., Matthew D. Lieberman, and Kipling D. Williams. 2003. Does Rejection Hurt? An fMRI Study of Social Exclusion. *Science* 203: 290–292.

Gastil, John, and Laura W. Black. 2008. Public Deliberation as the Organizing Principle of Political Communication Research. *Journal of Public Deliberation* 4 (1): Article 3.

Geer, John G. 2006. *In Defense of Negativity: Attack ads in Presidential Campaigns*, 2006. Chicago: University of Chicago Press.

Gervais, Bryan T. 2015. Incivility Online: Affective and Behavioral Reactions to Uncivil Political Posts in a Web-Based Experiment. *Journal of Information Technology & Politics* 12: 167–185.

Goffman, Erving. 1959. *Presentation of the Self in Everyday Life.* Garden City, NY: Doubleday.

Granovetter, Mark. 1973. The Strength of Weak Ties. *American Journal of Sociology* 78 (6): 1360–1380.

Habermas, Jürgen. 1994. Three Normative Models of Democracy. *Democratic and Constitutional Theory Today* 1 (1): 1–10.

Han, Soo-Hye, and LeAnn M. Brazeal. 2015. Playing Nice: Modeling Civility in Online Political Discussions. *Communication Research Reports* 32 (1): 20–28.

Hatcher, John A., and Mary Currin-Percival. 2016. Does the Structural Pluralism Model Predict Differences in Journalists' Perceptions of Online Comments? *Digital Journalism* 4 (3): 302–320.

Huffadine, Leith. 2016. 'UTTERLY appalling': Racist Memes Comparing Retired Star Adam Goodes to Shot Gorilla Harambe Pulled From Facebook. http://www.dailymail.co.uk/news/article-3621232/Shocking-racist-memes-compared-retired-indigenous-AFL-star-Adam-Goodes-gorilla.html.

Jacobs, Lawrence R., Fay Lomax Cook, and Michael X. Delli Carpini. 2009. *Talking Together: Public Deliberation and Political Participation in America*, Chicago: University of Chicago Press.

Knight, Cameron, and Mallorie Sullivan. 2016. *Gorilla Killed after 3-Year-Old Falls into Zoo Enclosure.* Cincinnati (Ohio) Enquirer, June 18. http://www.cincinnati.com/story/news/2016/05/28/police-child-taken-hospital-after-falling-into-gorilla-pen/85095094/.

Ksiazek, Thomas B. 2015. Civil Interactivity: How News Organizations' Commenting Policies Explain Civility and Hostility in User Comments. *Journal of Broadcasting & Electronic Media* 59 (4): 556–573.

Lang, Annie. 2000. The Limited Capacity Model of Mediated Message Processing. *Journal of Communication* 50 (1): 46–70.

Lasswell, Harold D. 1941. *Democracy Through Public Opinion.* Menasha, WI: George Banta Publishing Co.

Leary, Mark R., and Roy F. Baumeister. 2000. The Nature and Function of Self-Esteem: Sociometer Theory. *Advances in Experimental Social Psychology* 32: 1–62.

Leonard, Tom. 2016. They Should Have Seen Him Coming. *British Journalism Review* 27 (2): 16–21.

Logevall, Fredrik. 2012. The Paradox of Civility. In *Civility and democracy in America: A reasoned understanding*, ed. Cornell W. Clayton and Richard Elgar, 5–12. Pullman, WA: Washington University Press.

Loke, Jaime. 2012. Old Turf, New Neighbors. *Journalism Practice* 6, no. 2.

MacDonald, Geoff, and Mark R. Leary. 2005. Why does Social Exclusion Hurt? The Relationship Between Social and Physical Pain. *Psychological Bulletin* 131 (2): 202–223.

Marcus, George E., W. Russell Neuman, and Michael MacKuen. 2000. *Affective Intelligence and Political Judgment*. Chicago: The University of Chicago Press.

Meltzer, Kimberly. 2015. Journalistic Concern About Uncivil Political Talk in Digital Media: Responsibility, Credibility, and Academic Influence. *The International Journal of Press/Politics* 20 (1): 85–107.

Metts, Sandra, and William R. Cupach. 2015. Face Theory: Goffman's Dramatist Approach to Interpersonal Interaction. In *Engaging Theories in Interpersonal Communication*, ed. Leslie A. Baxter and Dawn O. Braithwaite, 203–214. Thousand Oaks, CA: Sage.

Mitra, Ananda. 2001. Marginal Voices in Cyberspace. *New Media & Society* 3 (1): 29–48.

Mutz, Diana C. 2015. *In-Your-Face Politics: The Consequences of Uncivil Media*. Princeton, NJ: Princeton University Press.

Oetzel, John G., and Stella Ting-Toomey. 2003. Face Concerns in Interpersonal Conflict: A Cross-Cultural Empirical Test of Face Negotiation Theory. *Communication Research* 30 (6): 599–624.

Papacharissi, Zizi. 2004. Democracy Online: Civility, Politeness, and the Democratic Potential of Online Political Discussion. *New Media & Society* 6 (2): 259–283.

Pérez-Peña, Richard. 2010. News Sites Rethink Anonymous Online Comments. *The New York Times*, April 1. http://www.nytimes.com/2010/04/12/technology/12comments.html?_r=0. Accessed 24 June 2016.

Pitts, Leonard. 2010. Anonymity Brings Out the Worst in Expression. *The Gazette.com*, April 1. http://gazette.com/anonymity-brings-out-the-worst-in-expression/article/96545. Accessed 20 June 2016.

Reader, Bill. 2012. Free Press Vs. Free Speech? The Rhetoric of 'Civility' in Regard to Anonymous Online Comments. *Journalism & Mass Communication Quarterly* 89 (3): 495–512.

Reeves, Byron, and Clifford Nass. 1996. *The Media Equation*. Cambridge, MA: Cambridge University Press.

Rosenberry, Jack. 2011. Users Support Anonymity Despite Increasing Negativity. *Newspaper Research Journal* 32 (1): 6–19.

Rösner, Leonie, Stephan Winter, and Nicole C. Krämer. 2016. Dangerous minds? Effects of Online Comments on Aggressive Cognitions, Emotions, and Behavior. *Computers in Human Behavior* 58: 461–470.

Rowe, Ian. 2015. Civility 2.0: A Comparative Analysis of Incivility in Online Political Discussion. *Information, Communication & Society* 18 (2): 121–138.

Santana, Arthur D. 2011. Online Readers' Comments Represent New Opinion Pipeline. *Newspaper Research Journal* 32 (3): 66–88.

Santana, Arthur D. 2014. Virtuous or vitriolic. *Journalism Practice* 8 (1): 18–33.
Shifman, Limor. 2014. *Memes in digital culture.* Cambridge, MA: MIT Press.
Sobieraj, Sarah, and Jeffrey M. Berry. 2011. From Incivility to Outrage: Political Discourse in Blogs, Talk Radio, and Cable News. *Political Communication* 28 (1): 19–41.
Spears, Russell, Tom Postmes, Martin Le, and Anka Wolbert. 2002. When are Net Effects Gross Products? The Power of Influence and Influence of Power in Computer-Mediated Communication. *Journal of Social Issues* 58 (1): 91–107.
Stroud, Natalie J., Joshua M. Scacco, Ashley Muddiman, and Alexander L. Curry. 2015. Changing Deliberative Norms on News Organizations' Facebook Sites. *Journal of Computer-Mediated Communication* 20: 188–203.
Sukumaran, Abhay, Stephanie Vezich, Melanie McHugh, and Clifford Nass. 2011. Normative Influences on Thoughtful Online Participation. In *Proceedings of the CHI 2011: Session: Incentives & User Generated Content*, 3401–3410, Vancouver, BC.
Suler, John. 2004. The Online Disinhibition Effect. *CyberPsychology & Behavior* 7 (3): 321–326.
Walther, Joseph B. 1996. Computer-Mediation Communication: Impersonal, Interpersonal, and Hyperpersonal Interaction. *Communication Research* 23 (1): 3–43.
Williams, Kipling D., Joseph P. Forgas, and William von Hippel. 2005. *The Social Outcast.* New York: Psychology Press.

PART II

Online Incivility: Three Examples in the News

CHAPTER 4

Can Incivility and Deliberation Co-exist?

In August 2016, National Public Radio (NPR) announced it was disabling commenting on its stories because less than 1% of its audience was actually commenting. "We've concluded that the comment sections on NPR.org stories are not providing a useful experience for the vast majority of our users,"[1] wrote Scott Montgomery, NPR's managing editor for digital news. NPR announced it would still engage with its audience through social media, but comments on stories had outlived their usefulness. NPR's ombuds Elizabeth Jensen wrote in a companion piece that the announcement is "sure to upset a loyal core of its audience" and noted that the decision to limit public input seems "especially jarring"[2] at a news organization dedicated to public good. But she explained NPR felt the commenters were not representative of its audience as a whole. The two stories generated 5,027 comments before comments were disabled and another 91 comments were posted about it on NPR's Facebook page.[3] The response on Twitter also was swift.

"NPR is killing off comments. That's great news!"[4] tweeted the verified Twitter account for Chris Cillizza, who covers the White House and writes a political blog for *The Washington Post*. Many other Twitter users agreed: "@NPR that's a plus. Comments are vile," tweeted @onemikeNJ.[5] On NPR's Facebook page, Josh Widup cheered the decision: "Good job, NPR. Embrace the social networking changes and adopt the more dynamic conversations as well as the engagement across other platforms."[6] Others were more critical. "@NPR—Can I comment on how I feel about the removal of comments? Hello? Is there anyone there? #TalkToTheHand," tweeted @RFLPolitics.[7] A commenter on NPR's initial story was also perplexed, seeming to see the decision as a poor cure for the problem of incivility: "NPR's decision is like sweeping the kitchen scraps under the rug. The ugliness may be out of sight and out of mind, but now it's left to rot and attract nastier pests."[8] Others expressed a sincere sense of loss at what they saw as a positive forum for discussion. "I enjoyed having intelligent discussions with like minded people, but since that's over I'm done with NPR, except for listening to podcasts while I'm in the shower or grocery shopping,"[9] commented Nicholas Wolfe. In a similar vein, Abbi Baily wrote: "I am distressed to lose contact with the most interesting, vibrantly (sometimes quirkily) intellectual community of people I'll never have chance to meet in person."[10] NPR's decision had such far-reaching effects that the London-based *Guardian* newspaper asked its readers what they thought about the shift and compiled their responses. "Without comments, the news becomes a passive experience for a reader like me," wrote rickylee369, as quoted in *The Guardian* story. "To me, it feels like censorship."[11]

This debate cuts to the heart of the focus of this chapter: Are comment streams fostering a robust and important public debate? Or are they too mired in incivility to offer a positive contribution to the larger public discourse? To answer these larger questions, I focus on one simple question: Can incivility and deliberation co-exist? If incivility and deliberation can co-exist, it may be worth the trouble it takes to monitor comments, moderate them, or even encourage journalists to jump into the comment streams to set a deliberative tone for the conversation.[12] It may be a good investment to improve the streams to make them more conducive to deliberation and to discourage virulent incivility. However, if no deliberative discussions—or even "deliberative moments," as I call them—are occurring in comment streams then, perhaps, other news organizations should follow the lead of NPR, Reuters, the *Chicago Sun-Times*, and others, and disable commenting.[13] But first, we must understand what is really happening in these freewheeling debates. That is the aim of this section. In this chapter, I begin by reviewing what I mean by incivility and deliberation and then propose why these two concepts may not be mutually exclusive, using a conceptual model to illustrate my point. Next I explore what news topics and what news organizations I focused on in my content analysis of news comments to answer the larger question about whether incivility and deliberation can co-exist. Finally I draw on prior research to explain what attributes of comments I will analyze in the next chapter.

Public Deliberation and Incivility

As I explain more fully in Chap. 2, public deliberation encompasses the idea that people should have a right to speak out about important issues, and that this discussion should be open to divergent views, rooted in reason, and should attempt to promote consensus, but also leave room for respectful disagreement.[14] It also includes "public talking"[15] about important issues to raise the profile of these topics, offering a clue to government leaders about what concerns people. Much debate has focused on whether deliberation can truly take place online.[16] Indeed, some studies have found evidence that deliberation can take place in comment streams or social media posts,[17] but others have not.[18] This chapter and the next aim to provide some clarity to this issue. Incivility, as I have defined it in Chap. 1, is not the same as impoliteness, although uncivil comments may indeed be impolite. I see incivility as part a larger spectrum of types of speech that violate norms of conversation.[19] Incivility is a broad category that includes such attributes as name-calling, insults, and profanity, as well as speech that includes stereotypes, homophobic, racist, and sexist language; and sweeping xenophobic statements, such as "All Muslims are terrorists."[20] What moves speech along the continuum is the intensity and frequency of these attributes. At the poles of this continuum are mere politeness, at the mild end, and hate speech, at the most virulent end.

Impoliteness could include mild breaches of etiquette, such as disagreeing with another or failing to use social niceties, such as "please." At the more virulent end is nasty speech intended to inflame—also known as trolling[21]—and hate speech. Hate speech is a particularly aversive form of communication that differs from the larger category of incivility because it hurls abusive or harassing language at specific groups based on their race, ethnic origin, religion, gender, sexual orientation, or other attributes.[22] In other words, "you're an effing idiot" would be uncivil, but "we must exterminate all effing Jews" would be hate speech. Trolling differs from hate speech because of intent. Trolls are fueled not by passion of their beliefs but by a desire to disrupt others with no real purpose[23] except to humiliate.[24]

So how would it be possible for these two concepts—incivility and deliberation—to overlap? For deliberation to occur there must be some type of moral disagreement.[25] A discussion does not truly become a deliberative debate unless there is more than one side of an issue to consider. The stakes also must be high. Why deliberate about something that no one cares about? But when people disagree, sometimes they grow angry or let their emotions take over their reason or they grow passionate, fueled by the fervor of their beliefs. When that happens, they may say something that upsets others. The result can be uncivil debate. So the question is not: Can we deliberate without being uncivil? Of course, we can. We should strive for that, and the best among us achieve it. They stay cool and detached and rational even when they feel impassioned. However, public deliberation also requires that we open the conversation to as many voices as we can. Is it really possible for all those voices to remain as reasonable in the heat of a debate? Perhaps, but it seems unlikely. That is why I focus on this question: Can deliberation occur even when incivility seeps in? It is not that I favor incivility. It is because I would prefer a robust debate that is a bit tainted than no debate at all. It seems the pragmatic goal is balance: Too much civility may stifle free discussion; too little may make that discussion impossible.[26]

Therefore, I propose a conceptual model that captures this continuum of non-normative speech that ranges from impoliteness to virulent hate speech. Incivility that can be deliberative would hit the midpoint on this spectrum. I call this midpoint the "deliberative moment zone," suggesting this type of speech may exhibit deliberative attributes even if it is does not meet all the requirements of public deliberation. This zone is shown as a gray circle on the model. Communication that is too polite or too nasty has no potential for deliberation. For example, the model shows agreement and not speaking at all on the far-left side, bottom half of the model, indicating they have both low incivility and low potential for deliberation. Impoliteness is closer to the center and within the zone because it is more uncivil, but it offers potential for deliberation. Making rational arguments, asking legitimate questions, and providing evidence to support one's points anchor the high deliberative top portion of the model. Meanwhile, profanity, name-calling, and insulting language straddle the "deliberative zone" indicating they may have potential for deliberation, but they are also clearly uncivil. Where they fall depends on what words are used. For example, calling someone an "idiot" while making a larger rational point, could still be deliberative yet uncivil. But telling someone they are "the biggest F-ing moron on the planet with no redeemable qualities" would make the potential for deliberation less possible. Finally, hate speech—encompassing homophobic, racist, sexist, and xenophobic statements—and trolling are at the far-right side of the model, indicating they are the most uncivil and offer no potential for deliberative moments because they are outside the gray circle. It is important to note

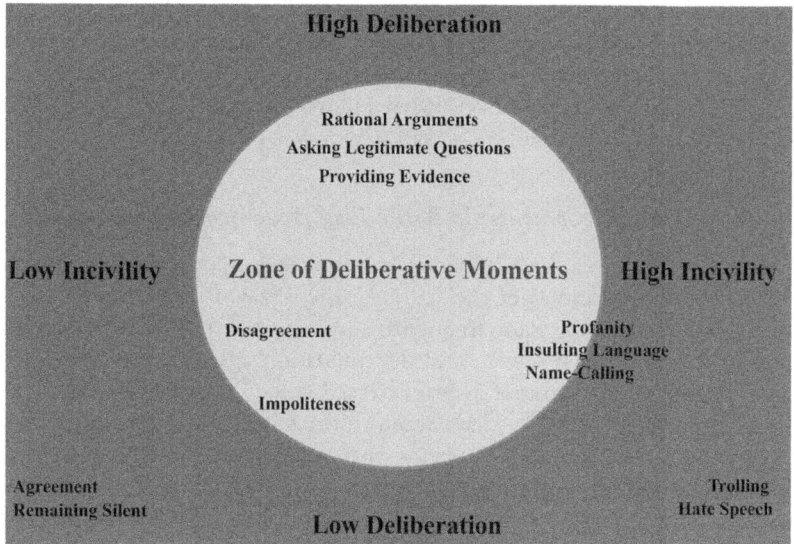

Fig. 4.1 Conceptual model of how incivility and deliberation may overlap

that this model proposes only what type of speech has potential to be deliberative, without guaranteeing that this will occur. Figure 4.1 depicts this conceptual model.

Three Topics in the News

To understand the extent and frequency of attributes of both incivility and deliberation in comment streams, I focused on three topics in the news: the efforts started in June 2015 to remove the Confederate battle flag from government spaces; the Supreme Court decision on June 26, 2015,[27] that legalized same-sex marriage throughout the United States; and the Super Tuesday U.S. presidential primaries on March 1, 2016. These were chosen because they are topics with clear sides, which are most likely to elicit debate.[28] These are also topics that tap into people's feelings about race, sexuality, politics, and religion—highly charged areas that would likely spark intense feelings that could lead to uncivil speech. These topics were appropriate to study because people can only truly debate about an issue for which they have strong feelings, and issues that connect to their core principles, moral beliefs, and emotions are topics about which people care the most.[29] To understand how incivility and deliberation may overlap in news story comments, it is vital to examine topics that offer potential for both incivility and deliberation. What follows is a brief description of the context for each of these topics, and why it was included.

Removing the Confederate Battle Flag from Government Spaces

The U.S.A. has a long history of racial tension, stemming from its turbulent history of slavery and later the battle in the 1960s for civil rights. Even today, racial tensions flare frequently over issues, such as immigration regulation, affirmative action, and discrimination against people of color. The Internet—once touted as a post-racial space[30] freed from the "confines of racial identity"[31]—has largely turned into the opposite. Digital sociologist Jessie Daniels[32] argues that rather than mute differences between people, the Internet has allowed a form of cyber racism to flourish in part because white supremacists were early adopters of the technology, and the web makes it easier for people with extremist views to hide their identities and spread their divergent ideas more readily. Certainly, the web has provided a space for a greater voice for those normally left out of the public conversation,[33] but it has also made it easier for people to lash back at them.[34] Most notably the #BlackLivesMatter movement that started after the shooting death of an unarmed black man at the hands of police has brought great attention to the issue of racial injustice, but it also has engendered virulent pushback online.[35] Online comments on news stories have become a particular place for racist vitriol,[36] as people used coded language to insert racialized speech into comments or statements based on implicit racial stereotypes.[37]

This context highlights the importance of considering comments posted on stories about the debate over the Confederate flag. The Confederacy fought the Union and lost during the U.S. Civil War in the 1860s, leading to tension that has lasted for decades. A major issue of the war was whether to allow slavery of African Americans to continue, and for many the Confederate battle flag remains a symbol of racism and hate.[38] The debate over whether to remove the flag from government spaces erupted after Dylann Roof, a white man, was identified as the suspect in a mass shooting at a black church in Charleston, South Carolina, that left nine people dead in June 2015.[39] Pictures of Roof—who was later convicted[40]—posing with the Confederate battle flag and other flags associated with white supremacy surfaced, along with a racist manifesto attributed to him.[41] In response to the massacre, then South Carolina Gov. Nikki Haley called for removal of the Confederate battle flag from the statehouse that it had adorned since 1962 largely in defiance of the expanding civil rights of blacks at the time.[42] A nationwide debate erupted through news stories and social media about the significance of the flag—whether it was a symbol of racism or a tribute to Southern history. The debate focused on whether the flag should be removed from the South Carolina statehouse or other government buildings nationwide and from its spot in the corner of Mississippi's state flag.[43] The debate took on even greater meaning throughout the year following Haley's suggestion, a period marked by multiple shootings of black men at the hands of police as well as shootings of police officers.[44] Thus, this topic proved a meaningful way to understand how online comments may deal with a racially charged issue.

Same-Sex Marriage Supreme Court Decision

As with racial bias, discrimination toward people who are gay or lesbian has a long history in the U.S.A. A protest in 1969, prompted by a police raid at the Stonewall Inn, a Greenwich Village gay bar,[45] launched the modern gay rights movement. But gay rights simmered in the background of politics before moving to the "center stage of mainstream cultural debate"[46] in the 1990s and then again in the 2000s. A series of court cases laid the groundwork for this shift. In 1996, a Hawaii court decision found that prohibiting same-sex couples from participating in marriage was unconstitutional, and the same year Congress passed a federal act defining marriage as between one man and one woman.[47] Vermont offered civil unions to same-sex couples in 2000.[48] Then in 2003 the U.S. Supreme Court overturned sodomy laws in *Lawrence v. Texas*, igniting intense reactions from supporters and opponents, and a Massachusetts court ruled that same-sex couples should have access to civil marriage.[49] While the right to marry is certainly not the only right homosexual Americans sought, these court decisions created a perfect storm that fueled a "straight panic"[50]—that homosexual marriage would "destabilize traditional heterosexual unions."[51] Other states and other countries legalized same-sex marriage, leading up to the pivotal decision in June 2015, when the U.S. Supreme Court declared bans against marriage equality unconstitutional. That decision brought the issue of gay rights to a frenzied forefront and prompted backlash across the nation as some states refused to follow the decision. Most notably, Kim Davis, a clerk in Kentucky became an icon of the movement against gay marriage for vehemently refusing to issue marriage licenses to gay couples, saying she was acting on "God's authority."[52] The debate touches on issues of sexuality and sin, as religious conservatives worried that the ruling usurped their right to practice their faith.[53] States, such as Indiana, Mississippi, and North Carolina, tried to circumvent the Court's ruling by passing "religious freedom" acts that allowed clerks to refuse to issue licenses or wedding vendors, such as bakers, to decline to serve same-sex couples.[54] In the wake, the fight for marriage equality took on a larger importance in the fight for gay civil rights. As a result, analyzing comments from stories about the 2015 Supreme Court decision seemed a viable way to understand the discourse over this controversial issue.

2016 Presidential Campaign

Like race and religion, politics is one of the polarizing topics that have both great potential for deliberation but also for incivility. Emotion, in the context of politics, is a "potent, volatile, instigator of change."[55] How people feel about candidates shapes much of how they vote and even their worldview.[56] Therefore, in any presidential election year, understanding the discourse around the campaign would seem important. And 2016 was no typical election year. Both major parties had a wide field of presidential contenders—six for the Democrats and 17 for Republicans—that narrowed over time.[57] Donald Trump, as both "a political outsider and the fringe candidate"[58] was perhaps one of the most atypical presidential contenders in U.S. history, as he vied for the GOP bid. During the primaries, Trump was causing consternation amid the Republican Party and its more traditional candidates, who were fighting to be the party's nominee. Democrat Hillary Clinton, while a more mainstream politician with experience as a U.S. senator and secretary of state, raised her own controversy. She was the first female candidate from a major party to receive her party's nomination for president, but she was also widely disliked. Super Tuesday, when more delegates were up for grabs than in any other single day of the campaign,[59] seemed a pivotal moment to understand how America talks about politics, through the lens of online commenting. As a result, I focused my analysis on comments posted on this one important day in the election cycle, to serve as an example of how incivility or deliberation may surface in discussions about presidential candidates.

News Organizations Studied

Comments that were analyzed were posted on five different news organizations' websites. These were *Fox News*, the *Huffington Post*, *NBC News Digital*, *The New York Times*, and *USA Today*. Several criteria were used to select these sites for study. First, my goal was heavily trafficked general-interest news sites that have a national reach in the U.S.A.[60] because that seemed the best route to examine comments regarding the Confederate battle flag issue, the same-sex marriage decision, and the 2016 presidential campaign. All these sites were among the top 15 news sites at the time of data collection.[61] While all three topics have regional and local relevance—particularly the story about the Confederate battle flag that originated in South Carolina—my interest in these topics is how the national societal debate evolved about them. Other content analyses of news site comments have focused on geographically specific news organizations[62] or one national site[63] and offer compelling findings about incivility in these online debates. A group of scholars from Spain, for example, examined comments posted on international newspapers and provide important findings about how the democratic qualities of online speech vary between these sites.[64] However, I wanted to examine multiple national sites in the U.S.A., so I could compare them across the three news topics. I also sought sites that draw an audience with a range of political viewpoints within mainstream U.S.A., not extremist sites. According to a Pew Research Center study, conservative Americans are tightly clustered around a single news source, *Fox News*, while the liberal audience is less unified.[65] According to that study, the audience for *The New York Times* and the *Huffington Post* skews to the left of the average American; Fox's audience skews to the right; and the audience of *USA Today* and *NBC News Digital* are typical of the average American.[66] Therefore, these five news organizations offer a varied cross section of the mainstream American audience. Because news organizations' commenting policies may play a role in comment civility,[67] variety was sought in that regard. All the sites, except *NBC News*, offered explicit commenting policies, and *Fox News*, the *Times*, and *Huffington Post* advised that some comments might be moderated before they appeared.[68] Commenting goes through a person's Facebook profile for *USA Today* and *Huffington Post*—a strategy some news sites employ to curb incivility by connecting the comment to the person's real identity.[69] The idea is that people will be more restrained if they know their friends can see what they say. However, some of those comments were still anonymous, suggesting people must have profiles that do not appear to reflect a real name. *Fox* and *NBC News* required registration, but it could be through a variety of social media platforms, including Twitter, where real names are not required.

COMMENT ATTRIBUTES STUDIED

I examined general attributes of the comments themselves—length and whether they were posted anonymously or contained words in all capital letters—as well as attributes of incivility and deliberation in the comments. Anonymity of commenters, in particular, was a focus because prior research has found a link between uncivil commenting and commenters not using their real names,[70] although another study found no connection.[71] Also, news sites have begun prohibiting anonymous commenting in an attempt to quell incivility.[72] I examined use of all capital letters for words because, in computer-mediated speech, this is considered an indicator of yelling.[73] Because people might be more likely to yell while being uncivil, I wanted to see if these two concepts would connect. Length of comments was considered because it seems likely that to express a compelling deliberative argument, one would require some space. I also examined attributes of incivility—profanity; insulting language; and homophobic, racist, sexist, xenophobic speech—and the indicators of deliberation—asking legitimate questions and providing evidence. Those concepts are defined earlier in the chapter.

CONCLUSION

In summary, this chapter provided the rationale for some of the main questions Chap. 5 will answer: Are comment streams worth saving? Or should they all be shut down, as NPR and other news organizations have done? We live in a moment where technology's rapid changes provide greater means to engage with each other virtually every day, but the swiftness of this evolution also creates a tension. The comment streams provide a telling example of this tension. They offer such potential for the type of robust and important debate that could prove valuable to society and perpetuate the importance of free speech. Yet, the very socio-technological affordances of these online platforms open the doors to the very darkest sides of human behavior as well. It is so easy to comment on a news story, but it also is so easy to say something perhaps one should not have said. The potential these digital spaces offer for public deliberation also make them hospitable to vitriol and damaging speech. Since it is a given that technology will not go backward—we cannot return to a day when online debate does not occur—it is vital to understand whether comment streams can offer more good than harm. In the next chapter, I will explain how I analyzed the news story comments about same-sex marriage, the Confederate battle flag's removal, and the 2016 presidential campaign. I will explore differences in comments across the three news topics and across the five news organizations and answer the larger question about whether incivility and deliberation can co-exist.

CLASSROOM DISCUSSION PROMPTS

1. This chapter examines three morally loaded topics in the news. If you were going to expand this study, what other topics would you consider and why?
2. This chapter proposes analyzing comments from five news organizations. Based on what you know about these news organizations, how do you think their comment streams might differ?
3. The chapter proposes that incivility and deliberation may overlap. Agree or disagree. Explain your answer.
4. The chapter explains that anonymity has been linked to incivility in comments. In your own experience, has that been true? Why or why not?

NOTES

1. Scott Montgomery, "Beyond Comments: Finding Better Ways to Connect with You," *NPR.org*, August 17, 2016. http://www.npr.org/sections/thisisnpr/2016/08/17/490208179/beyond-comments-finding-better-ways-to-connect-with-you (Montgomery 2016).
2. Elizabeth Jensen, "NPR Website to Get Rid of Comments," *NPR.org*, August 17, 2016. http://www.npr.org/sections/ombudsman/2016/08/17/489516952/npr-website-to-get-rid-of-comments (Jensen 2016a).
3. Once comments were disabled, the comments posted on the two stories announcing NPR's decision to disable comments were no longer available at those links. However, the comments remain available in links posted to Elizabeth Jensen, "Mailbag: Saying Goodbye to Comments," *NPR.org*,

August 24, 2016. http://www.npr.org/sections/ombudsman/2016/08/24/491099942/mailbag-saying-goodbye-to-comments?utm_campaign=storyshare&utm_source=twitter.com&utm_medium=social (Jensen 2016b).
4. @Chris Cillizza, August 18, 2016, "NPR is killing off comments. That's great news!" tweet on Twitter. https://twitter.com/search?src=typd&q=NPR%20comments.
5. @OnemikeNJ, August 23, 2016, "@NPR: that's a plus. Comments are vile," tweet on Twitter. https://twitter.com/search?src=typd&q=NPR%20comments.
6. Josh Widup, online comment posted on NPR's Facebook page. Retrieved at: https://disqus.com/home/discussion/thisisnpr/beyond_comments_finding_better_ways_to_connect_with_you/.
7. @RFLPolitics, August 23, 2016, "@NPR—Can I comment on how I feel about the removal of comments? Hello? Is there anyone out there? #TalkToTheHand," tweet on Twitter. https://twitter.com/search?vertical=news&q=NPR%20comments&src=typd.
8. Zach Norstedt, online comment, posted on Montgomery, "Beyond Comments: Finding Better Ways to Connect with You." Retrieved at: https://disqus.com/home/discussion/thisisnpr/beyond_comments_finding_better_ways_to_connect_with_you/.
9. Nicholas Wolfe, online comment posted on, Montgomery, "Beyond Comments: Finding Better Ways to Connect with You." Retrieved at: https://disqus.com/home/discussion/thisisnpr/beyond_comments_finding_better_ways_to_connect_with_you/.
10. Abbi Baily, posted on Jensen, "NPR Website to Get Rid of Comments," Retrieved at: https://disqus.com/home/discussion/thisisnpr/beyond_comments_finding_better_ways_to_connect_with_you/.
11. *The Guardian*, "'It feels like censorship': Guardian Readers on NPR's Decision to Close Comments," *The Guardian.com*, August 19, 2016. https://www.theguardian.com/media/2016/aug/19/npr-comments-decision-guardian-readers?CMP=twt_gu (The Guardian 2016).
12. Natalie J. Stroud, Joshua M. Scacco, Ashley Muddiman, and Alexander L. Curry, "Changing Deliberative Norms on News Organizations' Facebook Sites," *Journal of Computer-Mediated Communication* 20 (2015): 188–203 (Stroud et al. 2015).
13. Justin Ellis, "What Happened When 7 News Sites Got Rid of Reader Comments," *Nieman Journalism Lab*, September 16, 2015. http://www.niemanlab.org/2015/09/what-happened-after-7-news-sites-got-rid-of-reader-comments/ (Ellis 2015).
14. Lawrence R. Jacobs, Fay Lomax Cook, and Michael X. Delli Caprini, *Talking Together: Public Deliberation and Political Participation in America*, (Chicago, IL: The University of Chicago Press, 2009); Amy

Gutmann and Dennis Thompson, *Democracy and Disagreement* (Cambridge, MA: Harvard University Press, 1996); James S. Fishkin, Democracy and Deliberation, (New Haven, CT: Yale University Press, 1991) (Jacobs et al. 2009; Gutmann and Thompson 1996; Fishkin 1991).

15. Jacobs, Cook, and Delli Carpini, *Talking Together: Public Deliberation and Political Participation in America*.
16. Jennifer Stromer-Galley, "Diversity of Political Conversation on the Internet: Users' Perspectives," *Journal of Computer-Mediated Communication* 8, no. 3 (2003): n.p (Stromer-Galley 2003).
17. Lindita Camaj and Arthur D. Santana, "Political Deliberation on Facebook During Electoral Campaigns: Exploring the Relevance of Moderator's Technical Role and Political Ideology," *Journal of Information, Technology & Politics* 12, no. 4 (2015): 325; Carlos Ruiz, David Domingo, Josep Lluís Micó, Javier Díaz-Noci, Koldo Meso, and Pere Masiph, "Public Sphere 2.0? The Democratic Qualities of Citizen Debates in Online Newspapers," *The International Journal of Press/Politics* 16, no. 4 (2011): 463–487 (Camaj and Santana 2015; Ruiz et al. 2011).
18. Stromer-Galley, "Diversity of Political Conversation on the Internet: Users' Perspectives"; Arthur D. Santana, "Online Readers' Comments Represent New Opinion Pipeline," 32, no. 3 (2011): 66–88 (Santana 2011).
19. Zizi Papacharissi, "Democracy Online: Civility, Politeness, and Democratic Potential of Online Political Discussion Groups," *New Media & Society* 7, no. 2 (2004): 259–283; H.P. Grice, "Utterer's Meaning and Intention," *The Philosophical Review* 78, no. 2 (1969): 147–177 (Papacharissi 2004; Grice 1969).
20. Jeffrey M. Berry and Sarah Sobieraj, "From Incivility to Outrage: Political Discourse in Blogs, Talk Radio, and Cable News," *Political Communication* 28, no. 1 (2011): 19–41; Gina Masullo Chen and Shuning Lu, "Online Political Discourse: Exploring Differences in Effects of Civil and Uncivil Disagreement in News Website Comments," *Journal of Broadcasting & Electronic Media* 61, no. 1 (2017). doi:10.1080/08838151/2016/ 1273922; Papacharissi, "Democracy Online: Civility, Politeness, and Democratic Potential of Online Political Discussion Groups"; Stroud et al., "Changing Deliberative Norms on News Organizations' Facebook Sites," *Journal of Computer-Mediated Communication* (Sobieraj and Berry 2011; Chen and Lu 2017).
21. Kristi K. Cole, "'It's Like She's Eager to Be Verbally Abused': Twitter, Trolls, and (En)Gendering Disciplinary Rhetoric," *Feminist Media Studies* 15, no. 2 (2015): 356–358; Erin E. Buckels, Paul D. Trapnell, Delroy L. Paulhus, "Trolls Just Want to Have Fun," *Personality and Individual Difference* 67 (2014): 97–102; Patrick B. O'Sullivan and Andrew J. Flanagin, "Reconceptualizing 'Flaming' and Other Problematic Messages," *New Media*

& *Society* 5, no. 1 (2003): 69–94 (Cole 2015; Buckels et al. 2014; O'Sullivan and Flanagin 2003).
22. Karmen Erjavec and Melita Poler Kovačič, "'You Don't Understand, This is a New War!' Analysis of Hate Speech in News Web Sites' Comments," *Mass Communication and Society* 15 (2012): 899–920 (Erjavec and Kovačič 2012).
23. Buckels, Trapnell, Paulhus, "Trolls Just Want to Have Fun."
24. Erjavec and Kovačič, "'You Don't Understand, This is a New War!' Analysis of Hate Speech in News Web Sites' Comments."
25. Gutmann and Thompson, *Democracy and Disagreement*.
26. Papacharissi, "Democracy Online: Civility, Politeness, and Democratic Potential of Online Political Discussion Groups"; Cornell W. Clayton and Richard Elgar, "Civility and American Democracy," in *Civility and Democracy in America: A Reasonable Understanding*, eds. Cornell W. Clayton and Richard Elgar, (Pullman, WA: Washington State University Press, 2012): ix–xxii (Clayton and Elgar 2012).
27. A copy of the decision is available at: https://www.supremecourt.gov/opinions/14pdf/14-556_3204.pdf.
28. Ori Tenenboim and Akiba A. Cohen, "What Prompts Users to Click and Comment: A Longitudinal Study of Online News" *Journalism* 16, no. 2 (2015): 198–217; Patrick Weber, "Discussions in the Comments Sections: Factors Influencing Participation and Interactivity in Online Newspapers' Reader Comments," *New Media & Society* 10, on. 6 (2013): 941–957; Stroud et al., "Changing Deliberative Norms on News Organizations' Facebook Sites" (Tenenboim and Cohen 2015; Weber 2013).
29. Elmie Nekmat and William J. Gonzebach, "Multiple Opinion Climates in Online Forums: Role of Website Source Reference and Within-Forum Opinion Congruency," *Journalism & Mass Communication Quarterly* 90, no. 4 (2013): 736–756; Gutmann and Thompson, *Democracy and Disagreement* (Nekmat and Gonzebach 2013).
30. Steffen Albrecht, "Whose Voice is Heard in Online Deliberation? A Study of Participation and Representation in Political Debates on the Internet," *Information, Communication & Society* 8, no.1 (2006): 62–82; Bosah Ebo, *Cyberghetto or Cybertopia? Race, Class and Gender on the Internet*, ed., (Wesport, CT: Praeger, 1998) (Albrecht 2006; Ebo 1998).
31. Matthew W. Hughey and Jessie Daniels, "Racist Comments at Online News Sites: A Methodological Dilemma for Discourse Analysis," *Media, Culture & Society* 35, no. 3 (2013): 335 (Hughey and Daniels 2013).
32. Jessie Daniels, *Cyber Racism: White Supremacy Online and the New Attack on Civil Rights*, (Lanham, MD; Rowman and Littlefield, 2009) (Daniels 2009).

33. Bernadette Barker-Plummer and Dave Barker-Plummer, "Hashtag Feminism, Digital Media, and New Dynamics of Social Change: A Case Study of #YesAllWomen," in *Social Media and Politics: A New Way to Participate in the Political Process*, ed. Glenn W. Richardson Jr., (Santa Barbara, CA: Praeger, 2017): 79–96; Dan Gillmor, *We the Media*, (Santa Rosa, CA: O'Reilly Media, 2004); J. Schradie, "The Trend of Class, Race, and Ethnicity in Social Media Inequality: Who Still Cannot Afford to Blog," *Information, Communication & Society* 15, no. 4 (2012): 555–571; Bharat Mehra, Cecelia Merkel, and Ann Peterson Bishop, "The Internet for Empowerment of Minority and Marginalized Groups," *New Media & Society* 6, no. 6 (2004): 781–802; Samantha C. Thrift, "#YesAllWomen As Feminist Meme Event," *Feminist Media Studies* 14, no. 6 (2014): 1090–1092; Gina Masullo Chen, "Social Media: From Digital Divide to Empowerment," in *The Routledge Companion to Media and Race*, ed. Christopher P. Campbell (New York, NY: Routledge, 2016) (Barker-Plummer and Barker-Plummer 2017; Gillmor 2004; Schradie 2012; Mehra et al. 2004; Thrift 2014; Chen 2016).
34. Cole, "'It's Like She's Eager to Be Verbally Abused': Twitter, Trolls, and (En)Gendering Disciplinary Rhetoric"; Hughey and Daniels, "Racist Comments at Online News Sites: A Methodological Dilemma for Discourse Analysis."
35. Niraj Chokshi, "How #BlackLivesMatter Came to Define a Movement," *The New York Times*, August 22, 2016. http://www.nytimes.com/2016/08/23/us/how-blacklivesmatter-came-to-define-a-movement.html (Chokshi 2016).
36. Matthew W. Hughey, "Show Me Your Papers! Obama's Birth and the Whiteness of Belonging," *Qualitative Sociology* 35 (2012): 163–181 (Hughey 2012).
37. Hughey and Daniels, "Racist Comments at Online News Sites: A Methodological Dilemma for Discourse Analysis."
38. Frances Robles, Jason Horowitz, and Shaila Dewan, "Dylann Roof, Suspect in Charleston Shooting Flew the Flag of White Power," *The New York Times*, June 18, 2015. http://www.nytimes.com/2015/06/19/us/on-facebook-dylann-roof-charleston-suspect-wears-symbols-of-white-supremacy.html?_r=0 (Robles et al. 2015a).
39. Frances Robles, Jason Horowitz, and Shaila Dewan, "Dylann Roof, Suspect in Charleston Shooting Flew the Flag of White Power," *New York Times*, June 18, 2015. http://www.nytimes.com/2015/06/19/us/on-facebook-dylann-roof-charleston-suspect-wears-symbols-of-white-supremacy.html?_r=0; Mother Jones, "Here's What Appears to be Dylann Roof's Racist Manifesto," *MotherJones.com*, June 20, 2015. http://www.motherjones.com/politics/2015/06/alleged-charleston-shooter-dylann-roof-manifesto-racist; Frances Robles, Richard Fausset, and Michael

Barbaro, "Nikki Haley, South Carolina Governor, Calls for Removal of Confederate Battle Flag," *The New York Times*, June 22, 2015. http://www.nytimes.com/2015/06/23/us/south-carolina-confederate-flag-dylann-roof.html (Mother 2015; Robles et al. 2015b).
40. Dustin Waters and Mark Berman, "Dylann Roof Found Guilty on All Counts in Charleston Church Massacre Trial," The Washington Post, December 15, 2016. https://www.washingtonpost.com/news/post-nation/wp/2016/12/15/jurors-begin-deliberating-in-charleston-church-shooting-trial/?utm_term=.cb55248a9782 (Waters and Berman 2016).
41. Robes, Horowitz, and Dewan, "Dylann Roof, Suspect in Charleston Shooting Flew the Flag of White Power."
42. Robles, Fausset, and Barbaro, "Nikki Haley, South Carolina Governor, Calls for Removal of Confederate Battle Flag."
43. Emanuella Grinberg, "Battle Over Symbols Continues with Mississippi State Flag," *CNN.com*, June 19, 2016. http://www.cnn.com/2016/06/19/us/mississippi-state-flag/ (Grinberg 2016).
44. Erica Hunzinger, "Two Weeks of Shock, Tragedy," *Austin American-Statesman*, July 19, 2016, p. B4 (Hunzinger 2016).
45. Introduction: Stonewall Uprising, *PBS.org*. http://www.pbs.org/wgbh/americanexperience/features/introduction/stonewall-intro/.
46. Leigh Moscowitz, *The Battle Over Marriage: Gay Rights Activism Through the Media*, (Chicago, IL: University of Illinois Press, 2013), 125 (Moscowitz 2013).
47. Moscowitz, *The Battle Over Marriage*.
48. Moscowitz, *The Battle Over Marriage*.
49. Moscowitz, *The Battle Over Marriage*; Ron Becker, *Gay TV and Straight America*, (New Brunswick, NJ: Rutgers University Press, 2006) (Becker 2006).
50. Becker, *Gay TV and Straight America*, 214.
51. Moscowitz, *The Battle Over Marriage*, 125.
52. Alan Blinder and Richard Pérez-Peña, "Kentucky Clerk Denies Same-Sex Marriage Licenses, Defying Court," *The New York Times*, September 1, 2015. http://www.nytimes.com/2015/09/02/us/same-sex-marriage-kentucky-kim-davis.html (Blinder and Pérez-Peña 2015).
53. David Masci and Mike Lipka, "Where Christian Churches, Other Religions Stand on Gay Marriage," Pew Research, December 15, 2015. http://www.pewresearch.org/fact-tank/2015/12/21/where-christian-churches-stand-on-gay-marriage/ (Masci and Lipka 2015).
54. Jacob Gershman and Tamara Audi, "Court Rules Baker Can't Refuse to Make Wedding Cake for Gay Couple," *Wall Street Journal*, August 13, 2015. http://www.wsj.com/articles/court-rules-baker-cant-refuse-to-make-wedding-cake-for-gay-couple-1439506296; Jenny Jarvie, "Mississippi

Law Opens a New Front on the Battle Over Gay Rights," *Los Angeles Times*, April 5, 2016. http://www.latimes.com/nation/nationnow/la-na-mississippi-law-service-denial-gays-20160405-story.html (Gershman and Audi 2015; Jarvie 2016).
55. George E. Marcus, W. Russell Neuman, and Michael MacKuen, *Affective Intelligence and Political Judgment*, (Chicago, IL: The University of Chicago Press, 2000), 26 (Marcus et al. 2000).
56. Renita Coleman and H. Denis Wu, *Image & Emotion in Voter Decisions: The Affect Agenda*, (New York, NY: Lexington Books, 2015) (Coleman and Wu 2015).
57. The New York Times, "Who is Running for President," *The New York Times*, July 26, 2016. http://www.nytimes.com/interactive/2016/us/elections/2016-presidential-candidates.html (The New York Times 2016).
58. Bill Schneider, "What Makes Donald Trump a New Kind of Candidate?" *Reuters.com*, August 12, 2015. http://blogs.reuters.com/great-debate/2015/08/12/what-makes-donald-trump-a-new-kind-of-candidate/ (Schneider 2015).
59. Meet the Press, "Are You Excited About Super Tuesday?" *NBCNews.com*, March 1, 2016. http://www.nbcnews.com/meet-the-press/are-you-excited-about-super-tuesday-we-are-n529226 (Meet the Press 2016).
60. In deciding what news sites to include, my first goal was to find the most heavily trafficked news sites, which using rankings of user traffic on Alexa, Compete, and Quantcast, as reported by eBiz at: http://www.ebizmba.com/articles/news-websites. All the sites I used were in the top 15 news sites, based on user traffic at the time of data collection. News sites were chosen to provide variety of audience ideology, news type (newspaper, broadcast, online only), and commenting policies.
61. As reported by eBiz at: http://www.ebizmba.com/articles/news-websites.
62. Kevin Coe, Kate Kenski, and Stephen A. Rains, "Online and Uncivil? Patterns and Determinants of Incivility in Newspaper Website Comments," *Journal of Communication* 64 (2014): 658–679; Arthur D. Santana, "Incivility Dominates Online Comments on Immigration," *Newspaper Research Journal* 36, no. 1 (2015): 92–107 (Coe et al. 2014; Santana 2015).
63. Ian Rowe, "Civility 2.0: A Comparative Analysis of Incivility in Online Political Discussion," *Information, Communication & Society* 18, no. 2 (2015): 121–138 (Rowe 2015).
64. Carlos Ruiz, David Domingo, Josep Lluís Micó, Javier Díaz-Noci, Koldo Meso, and Pere Masiph. "Public Sphere 2.0? The Democratic Qualities of

Citizen Debates in Online Newspapers," *The International Journal of Press/Politics* 16, no. 4 (2011): 463–487 (Ruiz et al. 2011).
65. Amy Mitchell, Jeffrey Gottfried, Jocelyn Kiley, and Katerina Eva Matsa, "Political Polarization & Media Habits," Pew Research Center, October 21, 2014. http://www.journalism.org/2014/10/21/political-polarization-media-habits/ (Mitchell et al. 2014).
66. Mitchell, Gottfried, Kiley, and Matsa, "Political Polarization & Media Habits."
67. Thomas B. Ksiazek, "Civil Interactivity: How News Organizations Commenting Policies Explain Civility and Hostility in User Comments," *Journal of Broadcasting & Electronic Media* 59, no. 4 (2015): 556–573 (Ksiazek 2015).
68. Information obtained from each website: *Fox News*: http://help.foxnews.com/hc/en-us/articles/233194408-Why-aren-t-my-comments-going-through; *Huffington Post*: http://www.huffingtonpost.com/static/comment-policy; *The New York Times*: http://www.nytimes.com/content/help/site/usercontent/usercontent.html; *USA Today*: http://www.usatoday.com/conversation-guidelines/.
69. Jeff Sonderman, "News Sites Using Facebook Comments See Higher Quality Discussions, More Referrals," *Poynter.org*, August 18, 2011. http://www.poynter.org/2011/news-sites-using-facebook-comments-see-higher-quality-discussion-more-referrals/143192/ (Sonderman 2011).
70. Rowe, "Civility 2.0: A Comparative Analysis of Incivility in Online Political Discussion"; Arthur D. Santana, "Virtuous or Vitriolic," *Journalism Practice* 8, no. 1 (2014): 18–33.
71. Leonie Rösner and Nicole C. Krämer, "Verbal Venting in the Social Web: Effects of Anonymity and Group Norms on Aggressive Language Use in Online Comments," *Social Media + Society*, July/September (2016): 1–13 (Rösner and Krämer 2016).
72. Richard Pérez-Peña, "News Sites Rethink Anonymous Comments," *The New York Times*, April 11, 2010. http://www.nytimes.com/2010/04/12/technology/12comments.html?_r=2 (Pérez-Peña 2010).
73. Erika Darics, "Politeness in Computer-Mediated Discourse of a Virtual Team," *Journal of Politeness Research* 6 (2010): 129–150; Papacharissi, "Democracy Online: Civility, Politeness, and the Democratic Potential of Online Political Discussion Groups" (Darics 2010).

References

Albrecht, Steffen. 2006. Whose Voice is Heard in Online Deliberation? A Study of Participation and Representation in Political Debates on the Internet. *Information, Communication & Society* 8 (1): 62–82.

Barker-Plummer, Bernadette, and Dave Barker-Plummer. 2017. Hashtag Feminism, Digital Media, and New Dynamics of Social Change: A Case Study of #YesAllWomen. In *Social Media And Politics: A New Way to Participate in the Political Process*, ed. Glenn W. Richardson Jr., 79–96. Santa Barbara, CA: Praeger.

Becker, Ron. 2006. *Gay TV and Straight America*. New Brunswick, NJ: Rutgers University Press.

Blinder, Alan, and Richard Pérez-Peña. 2015. Kentucky Clerk Denies Same-Sex Marriage Licenses, Defying Court. *NYTimes.com*, September 1. http://www.nytimes.com/2015/09/02/us/same-sex-marriage-kentucky-kim-davis.html. Accessed 25 Aug 2016.

Buckels, Erin E., Paul D. Trapnell, and Delroy L. Paulhus. 2014. Trolls Just Want to Have Fun. *Personality and Individual Differences* 62: 97–102.

Camaj, Lindita, and Arthur D. Santana. 2015. Political Deliberation on Facebook During Electoral Campaigns: Exploring the Relevance of Moderator's Technical Role and Political Ideology. *Journal of Information, Technology & Politics* 12 (4): 325–341.

Chen, Gina Masullo. 2016. Social Media: From Digital Divide to Empowerment. In *The Routledge Companion to Media and Race*, ed. Christopher P. Campbell. New York, NY: Routledge.

Chen, Gina Masullo, and Shuning Lu. 2017. Online Political Discourse: Exploring Differences in Effects of Civil and Uncivil Disagreement in News Website Comments. *Journal of Broadcasting & Electronic Media* 61 (1). doi:10.1080/08838151/2016/1273922.

Chokshi, Niraj. 2016. How #BlackLivesMatter Came to Define a Movement. *The New York Times*, August 22. http://www.nytimes.com/2016/08/23/us/how-blacklivesmatter-came-to-define-a-movement.html. Accessed 24 Aug 2016.

Clayton, Cornell W., and Richard Elgar. 2012. Civility and American Democracy. In *Civility and Democracy in America: A Reasoned Understanding*, ed. Cornell W. Clayton and Richard Elgar. Pullman, ix–xxii. WA: Washington University Press.

Coe, Kevin, Kate Kenski, and Stephen A. Rains. 2014. Online and Uncivil? Patterns and Determinants of Incivility in Newspaper Website Comments. *Journal of Communication* 64: 658–679.

Cole, Kristi K. 2015. It's Like She's Eager to be Verbally Abused: Twitter, Trolls, and (En)Gendering Disciplinary Rhetoric. *Feminist Media Studies* 15 (2): 356–358.

Coleman, Renita, and H. Denis Wu. 2015. *Image & Emotion in Voter Decisions: The Affect Agenda*. New York, NY: Lexington Books.

Daniels, Jessie. 2009. *Cyber Racism: White Supremacy Online and the New Attack on Civil Rights*. Lanham, MD: Rowman and Littlefield.

Darics, Erika. 2010. Politeness in Computer-Mediated Discourse of a Virtual Team. *Journal of Politeness Research* 6: 129–150.

Ebo, Bosah. 1998. *Cyberghetto or Cybertopia? Race, Class and Gender on the Internet*, ed. Wesport. CT: Praeger.

Ellis, Justin. 2015. What Happened when 7 News Sites Got Rid of Reader Comments. *Nieman Journalism Lab*, September 15. http://www.niemanlab.org/2015/09/what-happened-after-7-news-sites-got-rid-of-reader-comments/. Accessed 23 Aug 2016.

Erjavec, Karmen, and Melita Poler Kovačič. 2012. 'You Don't Understand, this is a New War!' Analysis of Hate Speech in News Web Sites' Comments. *Mass Communication and Society* 15: 899–920.

Fishkin, James S. 1991. *Democracy and Deliberation*. New Haven, CT: Yale University Press.

Gershman, Jacob, and Tamara Audi. 2015. Court Rules Baker Can't Refuse to Make Wedding Cake for Gay Couple. *Wall Street Journal*, August 13. http://www.wsj.com/articles/court-rules-baker-cant-refuse-to-make-wedding-cake-for-gay-couple-1439506296. Accessed 25 Aug 2016.

Gillmor, Dan. 2004. *We the Media*. Santa Rosa, CA: O'Reilly Media.

Grice, H.P. 1969. Utterer's Meaning and Intention. *The Philosophical Review* 78 (2): 147–177.

Grinberg, Emanuella. 2016. Battle Over Symbols Continues with Mississippi State Flag. *CNN.com*, June 19. http://www.cnn.com/2016/06/19/us/mississippi-state-flag/. Accessed 25 Aug 2016.

Gutmann, Amy, and Dennis Thompson. 1996. *Democracy and Disagreement*. Cambridge, MA: Harvard University Press.

Hughey, Matthew W. 2012. Show Me Your Papers! Obama's Birth and the Whiteness of Belonging. *Qualitative Sociology* 35: 163–181.

Hughey, Matthew W., and Jessie Daniels. 2013. Racist Comments at Online News Sites: A Methodological Dilemma for Discourse Analysis. *Media, Culture and Society* 35 (3): 332–337.

Hunzinger, Erica. 2016. July 19. Two Weeks of Shock, Tragedy. *Austin American-Statesman*, B4.

Jacobs, Lawrence R., Fay Lomax Cook, and Michael X. Delli Carpini. 2009. *Talking Together: Public Deliberation and Political Participation in America*. Chicago, IL: University of Chicago Press.

Jarvie, Jenny. 2016. Mississippi Law Opens a New Front on the Battle Over Gay Rights. *Los Angeles Times*, April 5. http://www.latimes.com/nation/nationnow/la-na-mississippi-law-service-denial-gays-20160405-story.html. Accessed 25 Aug 2016.

Jensen, Elizabeth. 2016a. NPR Website to Get Rid of Comments, *NPR.org*, August 17. http://www.npr.org/sections/ombudsman/2016/08/17/489516952/npr-website-to-get-rid-of-comments. Accessed 23 Aug 2016.

Jensen, Elizabeth. 2016b. Mailbag: Saying Goodbye to Comments, *NPR.org*, August 24. http://www.npr.org/sections/ombudsman/2016/08/24/491099942/mailbag-saying-goodbye-to-comments?utm_campaign=storyshare&utm_source=twitter.com&utm_medium=social. Accessed 24 Aug 2016.

Ksiazek, Thomas B. 2015. Civil Interactivity: How News Organizations' Commenting Policies Explain Civility and Hostility in User Comments. *Journal of Broadcasting & Electronic Media* 59 (4): 556–573.

Marcus, George E., W. Russell Neuman, and Michael MacKuen. 2000. *Affective Intelligence and Political Judgment*. Chicago, IL: The University of Chicago Press.

Masci, David, and Mike Lipka. 2015. Where Christian Churches, Other Religions Stand on Gay Marriage. *Pew Research Center*, December 15. http://www.pewresearch.org/fact-tank/2015/12/21/where-christian-churches-stand-on-gay-marriage/. Accessed 25 Aug 2016.

Meet the Press. 2016. Are You Excited About Super Tuesday? *NBCNews.com*, March 1. http://www.nbcnews.com/meet-the-press/are-you-excited-about-super-tuesday-we-are-n529226. Accessed 25 Aug 2016.

Mehra, Bharat, Cecelia Merkel, and Ann Peterson Bishop. 2004. The Internet for Empowerment of Minority and Marginalized Groups. *New Media & Society* 6 (6): 781–802.

Mitchell, Amy, Jeffrey Gottfried, Jocelyn Kiley, and Katerina Eva Matsa. 2014. *Political Polarization & Media Habits*. Pew Research Center, October 21. http://www.journalism.org/2014/10/21/political-polarization-media-habits/. Accessed 1 Feb 2016.

Montgomery, Scott. 2016. Beyond Comments: Finding Better Ways to Connect with You. *NPR.org*, August 23. http://www.npr.org/sections/thisisnpr/2016/08/17/490208179/beyond-comments-finding-better-ways-to-connect-with-you. Accessed 23 Aug 2016.

Moscowitz, Leigh. 2013. *The Battle Over Marriage: Gay Rights Activism Through the Media*. Chicago, IL: University of Illinois Press.

Mother Jones. 2015. Here's what Appears to be Dylann Roof's Racist Manifesto. *MotherJones.com*, June 20. http://www.motherjones.com/politics/2015/06/alleged-charleston-shooter-dylann-roof-manifesto-racist. Accessed 25 Aug 2016.

Nekmat, Elmie, and William J. Gonzebach. 2013. Multiple Opinion Climates in Online Forums: Role of Website Source Reference and Within-Forum Opinion Congruency. *Journalism & Mass Communication Quarterly* 90 (4): 736–756.

O'Sullivan, Patrick B., and Andrew J. Flanagin. 2003. Reconceptualizing 'Flaming' and other Problematic Messages. *New Media & Society* 5 (1): 69–94.

Papacharissi, Zizi. 2004. Democracy Online: Civility, Politeness, and the Democratic Potential of Online Political Discussion. *New Media & Society* 6 (2): 259–283.

Pérez-Peña, Richard. 2010. News Sites Rethink Anonymous Online Comments. *The New York Times*, April 1. http://www.nytimes.com/2010/04/12/technology/12comments.html?_r=0. Accessed 24 June 2016.

Robles, Frances, Jason Horowitz, and Shaila Dewan. 2015a. Dylann Roof, Suspect in Charleston Shooting Flew the Flag of White Power. *The New York Times*, June 18. http://www.nytimes.com/2015/06/19/us/on-facebook-dylann-roof-charleston-suspect-wears-symbols-of-white-supremacy.html?_r=0. Accessed 25 Aug 2016.

Robles, Frances, Richard Fausset, and Michael Barbaro. 2015b. Nikki Haley, South Carolina Governor, Calls for Removal of Confederate Battle Flag. *The New York Times*, June 22. http://www.nytimes.com/2015/06/23/us/south-carolina-confederate-flag-dylann-roof.html. Accessed 25 Aug 2016.

Rösner, Leonie, and Nicole C. Krämer. 2016. "Verbal Venting in the Social Web: Effects of Anonymity and Group Norms on Aggressive Language Use in Online Comments," *Social Media+Society*. 1–13.

Rowe, Ian. 2015. Civility 2.0: A Comparative Analysis of Incivility in Online Political Discussion. *Information, Communication & Society* 18 (2): 121–138.

Ruiz, Carlos, David Domingo, Josep Lluís Micó, Javier Díaz-Noci, Koldo Meso, and Pere Maship. 2011. Public Sphere 2.0? The Democratic Qualities of Citizen Debates in Online Newspapers. *The International Journal of Press/Politics* 16 (4): 463–487.

Santana, Arthur D. 2011. Online Readers' Comments Represent New Opinion Pipeline. *Newspaper Research Journal* 32 (3): 66–88.

Santana, Arthur D. 2015. Incivility Dominates Online Comments on Immigration. *Newspaper Research Journal* 36 (1): 92–107.

Schneider, Bill. 2015. What Makes Donald Trump a New Kind of Candidate? *Reuters.com*, August 12. http://blogs.reuters.com/great-debate/2015/08/12/what-makes-donald-trump-a-new-kind-of-candidate/. Accessed 25 Aug 2016.

Schradie, Jen. 2012. The Trend of Class, Race, and Ethnicity in Social Media Inequality: Who Still Cannot Afford to Blog. *Information, Communication & Society* 15 (4): 555–571.

Sobieraj, Sarah, and Jeffrey M. Berry. 2011. From Incivility to Outrage: Political Discourse in Blogs, Talk Radio, and Cable News. *Political Communication* 28 (1): 19–41.

Sonderman, Jeff. 2011. News Sites Using Facebook Comments See Higher Quality Discussions, More Referrals, *Poynter.org*, August 11. http://www.poynter.org/2011/news-sites-using-facebook-comments-see-higher-quality-discussion-more-referrals/143192/. Accessed 9 Sep 2016.

Stromer-Galley, Jennifer. 2003. Diversity of Political Conversation on the Internet: Users' Perspectives. *Journal of Computer-Mediated Communication* 8 (3): n.p.

Stroud, Natalie J., Joshua M. Scacco, Ashley Muddiman, and Alexander L. Curry. 2015. Changing Deliberative Norms on News Organizations' Facebook Sites. *Journal of Computer-Mediated Communication* 20: 188–203.

Tenenboim, Ori, and Akiba A. Cohen. 2015. What Prompts Users to Click and Comment? A Longitudinal Study of Online News. *Journalism* 16 (2): 198–217.

The Guardian. 2016. 'It Feels Like Censorship': Guardian Readers on NPR's Decision to Close Comments. *The Guardian*, August 19. https://www.theguardian.com/media/2016/aug/19/npr-comments-decision-guardian-readers?CMP=twt_gu. Accessed 23 Aug 2016.

The New York Times. 2016. Who is Running for President. *The New York Times*, July 26. http://www.nytimes.com/interactive/2016/us/elections/2016-presidential-candidates.html. Accessed 25 Aug 2016.

Thrift, Samantha C. 2014. #YesAllWomen as Feminist Meme Event. *Feminist Media Studies* 14 (6): 1090–1092.

Waters, Dustin, and Mark Berman. 2016. Dylann Roof Found Guilty on all Counts in Charleston Church Massacre Trial. *The Washington Post*, December 15. https://www.washingtonpost.com/news/post-nation/wp/2016/12/15/jurors-begin-deliberating-in-charleston-church-shooting-trial/?utm_term=.cb55248a9782. Accessed 2 Jan 2017.

Weber, Patrick. 2013. Discussions in the Comments Sections: Factors Influencing Participation and Interactivity in Online Newspapers' Reader Comments. *New Media & Society* 10 (6): 941–957.

CHAPTER 5

Analyzing Comments in the News

This chapter aims to answer one of the over-arching questions of this book: Can incivility and deliberation co-exist in news site comment streams? I answer this question by analyzing 3508 user-generated comments on news stories about three highly charged topics in the news that were posted on five different news organizations' websites. As detailed in the previous chapter, these topics were: the Supreme Court decision on June 26, 2015,[1] that legalized same-sex marriage throughout the U.S.A.; the efforts started in June 2015 to remove the Confederate battle flag from government spaces; and the Super Tuesday presidential primaries on March 1, 2016. These issues were chosen because they were in the news at the time of this book's writing, and prior research suggests that online comments are more frequent on topics with clear sides.[2] These types of morally and emotionally loaded issues[3] connect to people's core values,[4] which provide more potential for deliberation as well as for incivility, as is explained in greater detail in Chap. 4. In essence, if we want to understand how people debate about important issues, we must focus on topics that people care deeply about, and these types of issues may divide them or elicit intemperate speech. The five news sites I studied —*Fox News*, the *Huffington Post*, *NBC News Digital*, *The New York Times*, and *USA Today*—were chosen because they are heavily trafficked national news sites in the U.S.A. with diverse audiences, as explained more fully in the previous chapter. In this chapter, I first explain how the sample of comments was collected and categorized and then answer specific research questions by analyzing these comments.

Then I situate these findings along with those of other scholars to make a larger statement about what the results of this content analysis say about incivility and deliberation in news comment streams.

CREATING THE SAMPLE OF COMMENTS

A separate sample of comments was created for each of the three topics. For all the topics, samples were created by searching for stories through a Google News search, which retrieves only news stories, not other items. All searches included the URL of the news site to narrow them and focused only on the day of the news (for example, the day of the Supreme Court decision) or several days if one day did not provide enough comments.[5] The same keywords were used in the searches for all news sites to retrieve stories about that topic.[6] About 35,000 comments were posted across the five websites' news stories about the three topics. A random sample of 3508 comments (about 10%) was drawn from the total number of comments, following accepted practices for quantitative content analysis.[7] Table 5.1 shows a breakdown of the comments in the sample by news organization and topic.

ANALYZING THE COMMENTS

I coded the comments along with a second coder after we both underwent extensive training[8] to ensure we were coding aspects of the comments the same way. After the training, we assessed whether we were coding the comments in the same manner by using a randomly selected subset of the total of about 35,000 comments that were not part of the study sample of

Table 5.1 Breakdown of comments that were analyzed by topic and news organization

	Fox News	Huffington Post	NBC News Digital	The New York Times	USA Today	
Confederate flag debate	73	352	114	183	177	899
Same-Sex Marriage	444	362	250	354	105	1515
Super Tuesday	490	243	80	261	20	1094
Total	1007	957	444	798	302	3508

3508 comments.[9] Then we moved onto coding the actual sample.[10] We coded the comments for general attributes about the comments as well as attributes of incivility and deliberation. Each code is explained below.

General Comment Attributes

All Capital Letters
Words in all capital letters were coded because this is considered yelling in computer-mediated speech.[11] We coded "yes" for this category if any words in the comment were in all capital letters, except acronyms that are usually capitalized (e.g. "You have no idea what the FBI does" would not count as all capital letters because FBI is normally written in all capital letters).

Anonymity
Based on the screen name, we coded whether a commenter was anonymous or not. Comments that appeared to have a real full name were coded as not anonymous (e.g. "Shonda Bell"), as were real names with additional characters or numbers (e.g. "ShondaBell101" or ShondaBell$"). A partial name or an initial with a surname was coded as anonymous (e.g. "S. Bell" and "Bell"), as were names that appeared made up (e.g. "Mickey Mouse").

Gender
The gender of the commenter was code 0 for male, 1 for female, and 2 for could not determine. Determination of the gender was made based on the screen name. Traditionally male screen names or those that contained words such as "dad," "dude," or "father" were coded as male, and screen names with a traditional female name or that contained words such as "mom," "mother," or "lady" were coded as female. Screen names that were unclear or were not what are generally considered names (e.g. "DuckHunter" or "TKL") were coded as undetermined.

Comment Length
Every word in the comment was counted, including "a," "the," etc. If the commenter incorrectly merged two words (e.g. "allright" instead of "all right"), words were counted as the commenter wrote them.

Deliberation

We coded for two aspects of deliberation identified in prior research: providing evidence to support one's point and asking legitimate questions.[12] These also were summed into an index of deliberation.

Evidence

We coded for the presence of evidence in accordance with prior research[13] if a comment included a hyperlink to more information (e.g. "see www.wikipedia.org"), described information from a database or other public records ("According to the Supreme Court decision...") or used numbers, percentages, or dollar amounts ("Crime has gone up 20% since Obama became president"), regardless of whether the facts were true.

Legitimate Questions

Any question posed by a commenter was coded as a legitimate question unless it contained attributes of incivility (e.g. profanity; insults; name-calling; or stereotypical, homophobic, racist, sexist, or xenophobic language) or attacked another person in anyway. (For example, "Where is the money coming from?" was considered a legitimate question, but "How can you be so stupid?" was not.)

Deliberation Index

For each comment, a yes (coded as 1) for evidence or legitimate question was totaled to form the index, for a total possible score of 2.

Incivility

We coded for three attributes of incivility from prior research.[14] These were use of profanity, insults or name-calling, and stereotypical, homophobic, racist, sexist, or xenophobic speech.

Profanity

A comment was coded as profane if any instance of profanity was included in the comment, regardless of how many times. Profane language was defined broadly[15] to include "hell," "damn," "crap" even if symbols stood in for letters (e.g. "F*CK"), common profane abbreviations were used ("STFU"), or the profanity was misspelled but understandable in context (e.g. "dam idiots").

Insults
Use of pejorative name-calling or more general insults were coded for, regardless of how many times they occurred. For example, "you idiot," "You have an IQ of 20," and "If you don't know this, you are in a coma" were all coded "yes" as insults. If an incidence of name-calling was also profane ("you motherf*cker"), it was coded as profanity only.

Stereotypical/homophobic/racist/sexist/xenophobic speech
Any comment that contained a clearly stated negative connotation[16] about a group of people based on race, class, sex/gender/religion, or sexual orientation was coded yes for this category. Examples included racial slurs and epithets, such as the "n-word," "feminazis," "wetbacks," "welfare queen," or sweeping xenophobic statements such as "All Muslims are terrorists."[17]

Incivility Index
For each comment, a yes (coded 1) for profanity, insulting language, or stereotypical speech was totaled to form the index, with a total possible score of three.

Answering Key Questions

First, I examined the attributes of the commenters who posted the commenter in our sample to answer the following questions:

What was the Gender Breakdown of Commenters Across News Organizations and Topics?

Men were more frequent commenters in the sample (38.1%) than women (15.2%), although gender could not be determined for 46.7% of commenters. When the sample was split by news organization and by topic,[18] I found statistically significant differences between men and women. For example, women were much less likely to comment on *NBC News Digital*, *USA Today*, and *Fox News* compared with men, even when the differences in their total numbers were factored in. But percentage-wise women were more likely to post on the *Huffington Post*, despite their smaller numbers. In regard to topics, the percentage of male commenters exceeded the percentage of female commenters for all three topics, although men commented most about the Confederate flag topic compared with same-sex marriage or Super Tuesday. Table 5.2 shows this.

Table 5.2 Gender of commenters by news organization and topic

News Organizations

	Fox News	Huffington Post	NBC News Digital	The New York Times	USA Today	Totals
Male commenters	169 16.8%	556 58.1%	99 22.3%	279 35%	235 77.8%	1338
Female commenters	47 4.7%	309 32.3%	17 3.8%	123 15.4%	37 12.3%	533
Could not determine gender	791 78.6%	92 9.6%	328 73.9%	396 49.6%	30 9.9%	1637

News Topics

	Confederate Flag	Same-Sex Marriage	Super Tuesday	
Male commenters	448 49.8%	602 39.7%	288 26.3%	1338
Female commenters	146 16.2%	277 18.3%	110 10.1%	533
Could not determine gender	305 33.9%	636 42%	696 63.6%	1637

Some columns of percentage do not total exactly 100% because of rounding

What was the Role of Anonymity Among the Commenters Across News Organizations and Topics?

A majority of the commenters in our sample used real names (56.8%) compared to those who were anonymous (43.2%). However, more detailed analyses[19] showed that anonymity varied by news topic and news organization even though none of the news sites studied explicitly required real names. A larger percentage of commenters were anonymous at *Fox News* (92.9%), *NBC News* (88.5%) and *The New York Times* (78.7%), compared with the other two sites. *USA Today* and *Huffington Post* had almost no anonymous commenters. This is likely because these sites require people to comment through their Facebook profiles, and Facebook requires real names, although people can get around that rule by using a name that appears to be a first name and surname but is not (e.g. "Phoebe Thedog").

Table 5.3 Anonymous comments by news organization and topic

News Organizations					
	Fox News	Huffington Post	NBC News Digital	The New York Times	USA Today
Anonymous commenters	936 92.9%	21 2.2%	393 88.5%	628 78.7%	13 4.3%
Total comments	1007	957	444	798	302

News Topics			
	Confederate Flag	Same-Sex Marriage	Super Tuesday
Anonymous commenters	325 36.2%	896 59.1%	770 70.4%
Total comments	899	1515	1094

When the topics were considered, Super Tuesday drew the most anonymous commenters (70.4%). Table 5.3 shows these numbers.

Next, I shifted my analysis to the attributes of the comments themselves, including use of all capital letters and length of comments.

How did Length of Comments and Use of All Capital Letters Compare Across News Organizations and Topics?

Overall, comments ranged in length from 1 to 615 words, with an average of 35.50 words and a median of 21 words. The distribution of words was fairly spread out.[20] Statistical analyses showed that comment length varied significantly by topic and by news organization.[21] The debate over the Confederate flag generated significantly longer comments (42.64 words on average) than comments posted about Super Tuesday (36.35 words on average) or the same-sex marriage decision (34.28 words on average).[22] Comments in *The New York Times* (59.92 words on average) were significantly longer[23] than those posted on *NBC News Digital* (42.77 words on average), *USA Today* (35.18 words on average), the *Huffington Post* (30.61 words on average), or *Fox News* (23.34 words on average). Length was significantly different between all the news organizations, except between *USA Today* and *NBC News*.[24] In addition, results showed that the relationship between comment length and news organization varied based on the topic of the news articles.[25] For example, while comments were longest overall for *The New York Times*, this was particularly true for comments posted on the Super Tuesday stories, where the average length was 60.1 words. Comment length was shortest on *Fox News*' Super Tuesday story. Figure 5.1 shows this.

All capital letters were used in 418 comments, which constitute 11.9% of the sample. Statistical tests showed that frequency of use of all capital letters was related to the topic of the comment, but not the news organization.[26] When looking at all comments that contained instances of all capital letters, 48.8% of that total was for comments posted on same-sex marriage stories, compared with 25.8% posted on Confederate flag stories or 25.6% posted on Super Tuesday news. Because use of all capital letters is considered a form of yelling in computer-mediated speech,[27] this suggests same-sex marriage provoked emotion in a way the other stories did not.

The remaining questions focus on the core of this project: examining the attributes of incivility and deliberation in the comment streams and whether these two concepts can co-exist.

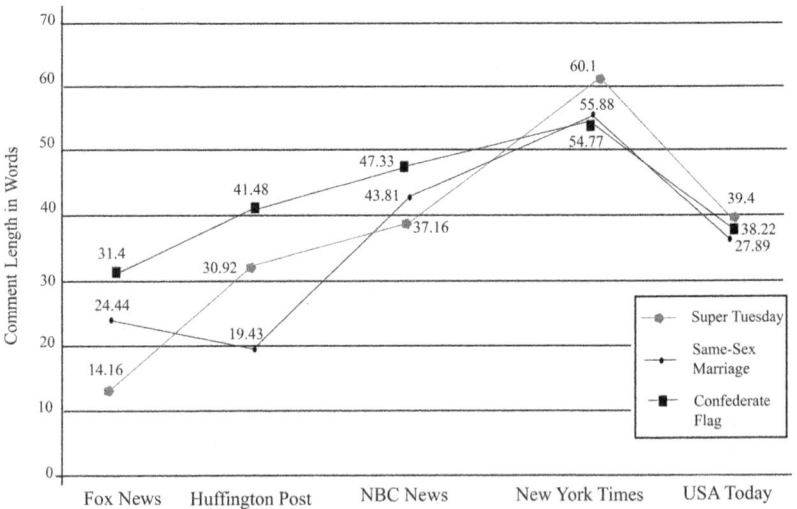

Fig. 5.1 Comment length by topic and news organization

How Much Incivility was in the Comments, Compared with Deliberation?

Overall, deliberation was more common in the comments than incivility. Deliberative attributes were in 909 comments, which constitute 25.9% of the total sample of 3508 comments. In comparison, 627 comments, or 17.8% of the sample, were uncivil. Asking legitimate questions was the most frequent deliberative attribute, while insulting language was more common for incivility. Figure 5.2 shows more detail.

What Comment Attributes Were Associated with Incivility and Deliberation?

This question aimed to understand what aspects of the comments themselves were related to the larger concepts of incivility or deliberation. As mentioned in Chap. 4, prior research had found that anonymous comments are more likely to be uncivil.[28] However, that is not what I found.

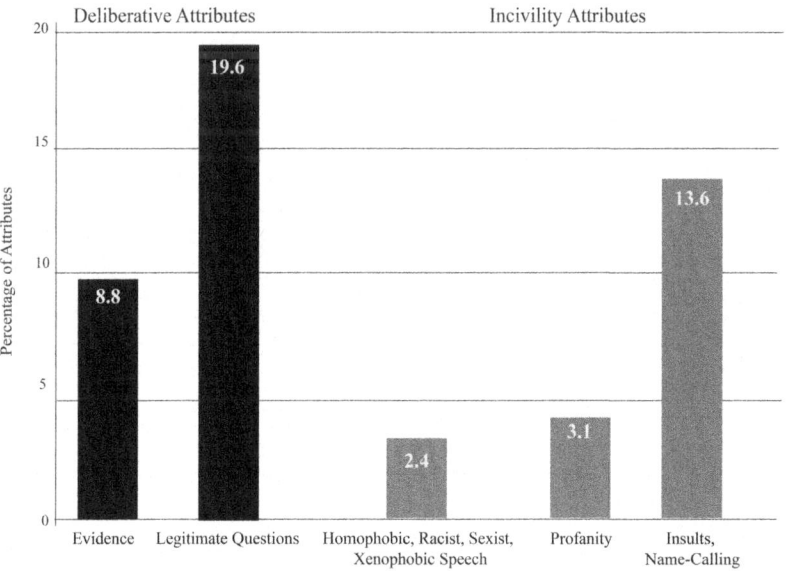

Fig. 5.2 Percentages of attributes of incivility and deliberation in 3508 comments

Comments posted anonymously were no more uncivil than comments posted with what appeared to be a real name.[29] In my data, what really explained whether comments were uncivil or not was the topic and the news site where the comment was posted.[30] On a 1 to 3 incivility scale, where 3 is most uncivil, comments posted on Super Tuesday stories on average scored 0.25 and comments posted on Confederate flag stories scored 0.24 on average, compared with the lower average score of 0.15 for comments posted on same-sex marriage stories.[31] Incivility also varied by news organization, with comments posted on *NBC News Digital* (average score of 0.36) being most uncivil, followed by *USA Today* (average score 0.28), *Fox News* (average score of 0.16), the *Huffington Post* (average score 0.13), and *The New York Times* (average score 0.12). When both news organization and topic were considered together, comments were most uncivil on the *NBC News Digital* site, and this effect was heightened for those posted on Super Tuesday and Confederate flag stories.[32] Comments were least uncivil for same-sex marriage stories, except at *Fox News*. This effect is depicted in Fig. 5.3.

Similarly, deliberative attributes were related to the topic of the story where the comment was posted, not whether the commenter posted

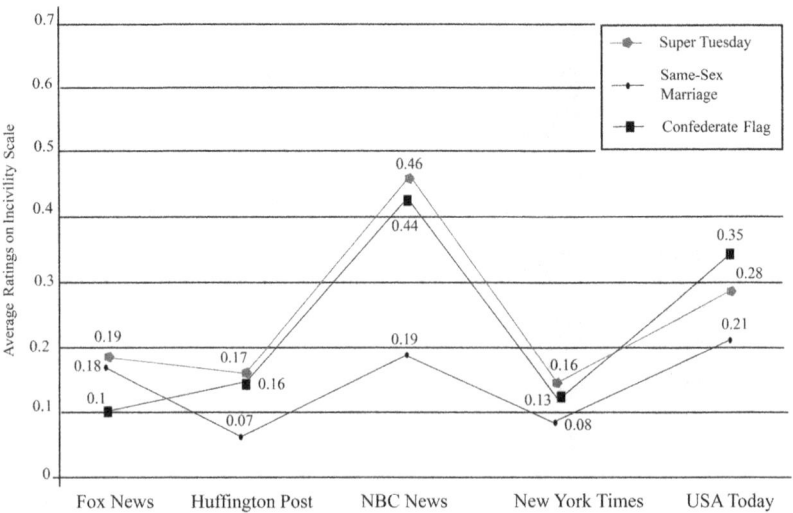

Fig. 5.3 Incivility by topic and news organization

anonymously or not.[33] On a 1 to 2 deliberation scale, where 2 is most deliberative, comments posted on the same-sex marriage stories (average score 0.26) were significantly less deliberative than those posted on either the Confederate flag stories (average score 0.33) or Super Tuesday stories (average score 0.34).[34] No significant differences in deliberation were found between Confederate and Super Tuesday comments.[35] Unlike incivility, whether comments were deliberative or not did not vary based on the news organization where the story was posted.[36] But when topic and news organization were considered together, results showed differences.[37] For example, *The New York Times* was most deliberative, particularly for comments posted on Super Tuesday stories. Same-sex marriage stories produced the least deliberative comments, especially in the *Huffington Post* and *USA Today*. See Fig. 5.4 for details.

Analyses showed that longer comments were related to both incivility and deliberation, but the relationship with deliberation was strongest.[38] Use of words in all capital letters was more frequent in uncivil comments but also showed a relationship with deliberation.[39] Among 627 uncivil comments, 101 (16.1%) contained all capital letters. In contrast, only 11% of the 2881 civil comments employed the use of all capital letters. This

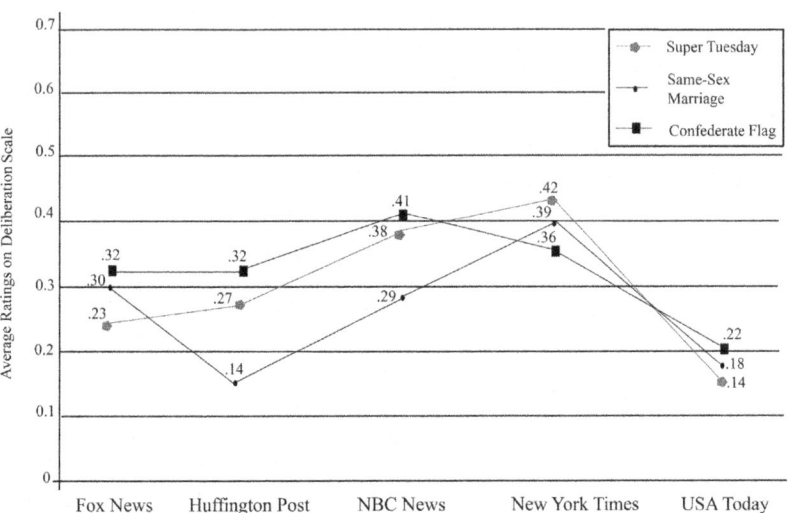

Fig. 5.4 Deliberation by topic and news organization

suggests that using all capital letters not only constitutes yelling in computer-mediated speech[40] but is also an attribute of incivility in online speech. When gender was considered, analyses found neither men nor women were more likely to be either deliberative or uncivil.[41]

CAN INCIVILITY AND DELIBERATION CO-EXIST IN THE SAME COMMENTS?

That brings us to the seminal question of this chapter: Can comments be both uncivil and deliberative? The answer is a definitive yes. I answered this question by filtering my data and considering only uncivil comments and only deliberative comments separately. When the 627 uncivil comments are considered alone, they scored on average 1.07[42] on the 0–2 deliberation scale, where a 2 is most deliberative. In addition, 21.1% of these comments contained some attribute of deliberation. Legitimate questions were most common, contained in 16.3% of these comments, compared to use of evidence in 8.1% of uncivil comments.[43] Similarly, when I considered only the 909 deliberative comments, they scored on average of 0.16[44] on the 0–3 incivility index, where 3 is most uncivil. Also, uncivil comments were significantly more uncivil than deliberative ones.[45] In addition, 18.7% of the deliberative comments contained incivility. Insulting language was most frequent (10.5%), followed by profanity (4.1%), and homophobic, racist, sexist, and xenophobic speech (1.9%).[46] As shown in Table 5.4, incivility attributes were present in 17.9% of the entire sample, but these same attributes were exhibited in 132 (14.5%) of the deliberative comments. Similarly, deliberative attributes were present in 25.9% of the entire sample, but these also were displayed in 132 (21.1%) of the uncivil comments.

WHAT THIS ALL MEANS

These findings offer three important contributions to our understanding of how incivility influences the public debate about important issues in the news. First, while incivility is certainly present in these comment streams, deliberation was more frequent. These findings mirror earlier research that incivility mars nearly 20% of comments,[47] but it also showed that deliberative attributes were present in just over a fourth of comments. That suggests that comment streams can indeed be a place of public deliberation —or at least offer "deliberative moments"—that scholars since the 1800s

Table 5.4 Frequency of incivility and deliberation attributes

	Whole Sample, N = 3508	Uncivil Comments, n = 627	Deliberative Comments, n = 909
Incivility Attributes			
Profanity	109 (3.1%)		37 (4.1%)
Insulting Language	478 (13.6%)		95 (10.5%)
Racist, Sexist, Xenophobic Speech	83 (2.4%)		17 (1.9%)
Total	627 (17.9%)		132 (14.5%)
Deliberative Attributes			
Evidence	307 (8.8%)	51 (8.1%)	
Legitimate Questions	686 (19.6%)	102 (16.3%)	
Total	909 (25.9%)	132 (21.1%)	

Total number of attributes does not equal the total number of comments because some comments lacked any attributes of deliberation or incivility, and some included more than one attribute

Percentages are in reference to the whole sample in the left-hand column, uncivil comments only in the middle column, and deliberative comments only in the right-hand column

have imagined for public debate.[48] This is not, however, the sanitized public sphere of sociologist Jürgen Habermas,[49] who favored past forms of civic engagement and rational discourse.[50] This is a more freewheeling public debate that is inclusive but often leaves us concerned. It is debate unvarnished, exposing a jaundiced underbelly of emotion peppered with moments of rationality. Political scientist John G. Geer argues that negativity and criticism in politics is a vital part of democracy,[51] and I suggest these findings suggest the same is true for public debate. This is also not to say that incivility should be trumpeted. It should not. There is no doubt in my mind that a deliberative comment would be improved if it did not include an insult or profanity. Yet, as a pragmatist, I would rather the comment contain some incivility than that deliberative thought not get aired in the public sphere.

Another strongly positive finding from this analysis is that deliberation and incivility can live in the same comments. Certainly a world where people are never nasty may be a goal. But we do not live in that world. It is encouraging to me that people can still make cogent arguments, supported by evidence and enhanced by legitimate questions, even when their fervor is incited. In fact, if we value free speech and we value discourse about topics of "moral disagreement,"[52] it seems some incivility may be an evil we need to tolerate. I have argued elsewhere[53] that a discussion about politics or societal ills that is so benign that nobody feels anything, and nobody cares, is pointless. These findings provide further evidence of this. We can debate online, and that debate can raise important points, even if it is somewhat mired by aspects of speech we wish were not there. In fact, these findings underscore the notion of affective intelligence theory [54]—that emotions and rationality need not be diametrically opposed. Feeling intense passion or emotions about an issue, in fact, can lead to rational arguments about that issue[55] or at least efforts to make these arguments. Communication scholar Zizi Papacharissi explains that emotions are a "key part of how people internalize and act on everyday experiences,"[56] and eastern philosophy suggests emotions and rationality can be reconciled.[57] I agree, and I submit that this combination is what we are seeing in at least some of these comments—a mix of emotion-laden incivility with rational thoughts.

A third important contribution these data provide is to expand our understanding of the relationship between anonymity of commenters and incivility. While prior research links anonymity and incivility,[58] these findings suggest a more complex explanation. I did not find a significant relationship between anonymity and incivility. Instead, incivility emerged based on the topic or the news site where the comment was posted. I would submit this does not necessarily conflict with earlier findings that found a relationship between anonymity and incivility because those studies were conducted differently. For example, two studies compared comment streams that allow anonymity to those that require real names and both found incivility more frequent in the anonymous streams.[59] In contrast, this chapter compared anonymous commenters to those with real names on five sites that had some of both and found incivility differed by news organization and topic, but not by anonymity of commenter. In fact, the site with the most anonymous commenters, the *Times*, was the most civil. However, anonymity may play some role that is too small to be detected by a main effect. The *Huffington Post*, which requires people to comment through their Facebook profiles, in an apparent effort to foster accountability,[60] had comments that were significantly less uncivil than *NBC News*, which allows commenting through any social media site profile, including those that do not require real names. But the reason for the *Huffington Post*'s milder comments may also be because it sometimes pre-moderates comments, as do the *Times* and *Fox News*. Comments at *USA Today*, which also requires Facebook profile commenting but does not pre-moderate comments, were more civil than those at *NBC News*, except in regard to same-sex marriage.

My findings coincide more with an experimental study that found social norms on a site regarding aggressiveness, not anonymity, predicted whether people would be uncivil.[61] There are several plausible explanations for these differing results. It may be that that different types of people comment on streams that allow anonymity and those that do not. It is also possible that a cultural norm that is less hospitable to incivility develops on sites that require real names, as prior research has found that commenters can set a tone for a conversation.[62] Both of these theories could explain why those previous studies found a link between anonymity and incivility, and I did not. It is also plausible that anonymity has an effect at some news organizations or in regard to some topics, but that effect is not necessarily consistent. In addition, other research has found that certain topics—such as immigration—provoke particularly heated incivility.[63] This jibes with my findings that particular topics incited more incivility than others. For all the news organizations, except *Fox News*, Super Tuesday and the debate over the Confederate flag generated the most uncivil comments. At *Fox*, same-sex marriage and Super Tuesday elicited about the same levels of incivility, but more than the flag debate. Clearly, we do not completely understand what provokes online incivility, but these findings strongly suggest that examining anonymity alone cannot capture the full picture. I proposed in Chap. 3 that people may feel a sense of deindividuation amid the millions of people online even if they use their real names, so they feel freer to act out their hostility. These results support this viewpoint and suggest requiring real names in comment streams alone will not cure incivility.

In summary, these findings offer encouraging promise for the potential for online debate. It would be foolish to be too naïve and suggest that it is not a worthy goal to aim to tame some of the incivility in comment streams. I think it is. However, it is also clear that online debates are not always the cesspools of hate that some bemoan. Deliberation is happening, amid the incivility. It is also important to point out that these findings show that the discourse varies widely based on the news organization that hosts the site. Comment streams at *The New York Times* and *NBC News Digital* offered the most deliberation, while *USA Today* offered the least, and the other news sites were between these poles. Our challenge for the future is to learn how to harness the deliberative qualities exhibited at some news organizations' comment streams and mute the incivility that dominates at others.

Classroom Discussion Prompts

1. Explain the role of anonymity in online comments and propose whether you think commenters should be required to use real names. Defend your answer.
2. Differences in incivility were found across news organizations and across topics. Why do you think that occurred?
3. A main finding of this chapter is that incivility and deliberation can co-exist. Explain how that is possible.
4. Even though this chapter offers hope for comments streams, what do you think can be done to make them more deliberative and less uncivil?

Notes

1. A copy of the decision is available at: https://www.supremecourt.gov/opinions/14pdf/14-556_3204.pdf.
2. Ori Tenenboim and Akiba A. Cohen, "What Prompts Users to Click and Comment? A Longitudinal Study of Online News," *Journalism* 16, no. 2 (2015): 198–217; Patrick Weber, "Discussions in the Comments Sections: Factors Influencing Participation and Interactivity in Online Newspapers' Reader Comments," *New Media & Society* 10, no. 6 (2013): 941–957; Natalie J. Stroud, Joshua M. Scacco, Ashley Muddiman, and Alexander L. Curry, "Changing Deliberative Norms on News Organizations' Facebook Site," *Journal of Computer-Mediated Communication* 20 (2015): 188–203 (Tenenboim and Cohen 2015; Stroud et al. 2015).
3. Elmie Nekmat and William J. Gonzebach, "Multiple Opinion Climates in Online Forums: Role of Website Source Reference and Within-Forum Opinion Congruency," *Journalism & Mass Communication Quarterly* 90, no. 4 (2013): 736–756 (Nekmat and Gonzebach 2013).
4. Amy Gutmann and Dennis Thompson, *Democracy and Disagreement*, (Cambridge, MA: Harvard University Press, 1996) (Gutmann and Thompson 1996).
5. It should be noted that comments were collected in spring 2016, months after the Supreme Court decision and the debate over removing the Confederate flag from public places occurred. It is possible, therefore, that some comments had been deleted through news organizations' moderation efforts before we retrieved our sample. This is a limitation, but not a fatal flaw, because we analyzed comment streams that appear the

way an average person might see them, as moderation of comments happens regularly.
6. Keywords were derived by testing out several different keywords and then assessing whether these words were generating stories about the topic. Keywords were adjusted as necessary. For the same-sex marriage decision, I sought articles that covered the actual decision on June 26, 2015. Using a Google News search narrowed only to June 26 through June 27, 2015, I used the keywords "gay marriage" and "same-sex marriage." Only one news story per news organization was used because each story generated thousands of comments. For the debate over removing the Confederate flag from government spaces, I used a Google News Search from June 21, 2015, to July 6, 2015, because the news developed over a series of time. The keywords were "Confederate flag" or "rebel flag" and "South Carolina." Super Tuesday was March 1, 2016, so I delimited the Google News search to that day and used the keyword "Super Tuesday" and "results." For both the Confederate flag and Super Tuesday topics, multiple stories were analyzed to generate enough comments to be comparable to the large number of comments generated by the same-sex marriage decision.
7. Stephen Lacy, Brendan R. Watson, Daniel Riffe, and Jennette Lovejoy, "Issues and Best Practices in Content Analysis," *Journalism & Mass Communication Quarterly* 92, no. 4 (2015): 791–811. The procedure of creating the sample was as follows: For four of the sites, the commenting software indicated how many comments were posted, providing an estimate of how many comments we needed to collect to reach 10% of that number. I used a random number generator to pick a random start for the first comment to include in the sample for each topic and each news site. For example, for *The New York Times*' story on the same-sex marriage decision, I started with the fifth comment to begin the random sample, but for *Huffington Post*'s same-sex marriage story, I used the eighth comment. Starting with this initial comment, I then counted every tenth comment to include in the sample, as I aimed to include approximately 10% of the universe in our sample. The *Fox News* commenting system was different from the others, as it does not provide a number of commenters. In addition, the page refreshes every 20 to 30s, adding new commenters, so it is impossible to get an accurate count of comments manually. As a result, we used a random start and selected every tenth comment until we reached a significant corpus of comments (Lacy et al. 2015).
8. First, both coders (a student and the author) independently coded 479 comments from five separate random samples drawn from the total universe of roughly 35,000 comments posted on the news stories but that were not

part of the 3508-comment sample to be analyzed for this book. This was done so we could practice coding and gain proficiency before inter-coder reliability was attempted, as recommended by Lacy et al. "Issues and Best Practices in Content Analysis."
9. Once we were comfortable with the coding procedures, we each independently coded a separate random sample of 303 comments (9% of the total sample) again drawn from the total comments but not part of the study sample, following the recommendation of Daniel Riffe, Stephen Lacy, and Frederick G. Fico, *Analyzing Media Messages: Using Quantitative Content Analysis in Research*, (Mahwah, NJ: Lawrence Erlbaum, 2005). We then assessed inter-coder reliability on this sample using Krippendorf's α, which is the preferable test because it treats coders as independent, controls for agreement by chance and is applicable to variables measured at nominal, ordinal, or interval-ratio levels; see Andrew F. Hayes and Klaus Krippendorf, "Answering the Call for a Standard Reliability Measure for Coding Data," *Communication Methods and Measures* 1, no. 1 (2007): 77–89. The Krippendorf's α for each of the codes is as follows: all capital letters, α = 94; anonymity, α = 95; gender, α = 89; length, α = 95; use of evidence, α = 81; use of legitimate question, α = 0.84; deliberation index, α = 0.85; profanity, α = 0.92; insulting language, α = 0.84; stereotypical/homophobic/racist/sexist/xenophobic speech, α = 0.66; incivility index, α = 0.84. All the Krippendorf's α's were an acceptable 0.80 or higher, indicating at least 81% of agreement between coders exceeded chance, except for stereotypical/homophobic/racist/sexist/xenophobic speech. As a result, both coders were retrained in regard to this code before coding the study sample commenced (Hayes and Krippendorf 2007; Riffe et al. 2005).
10. Once inter-coder reliability was assessed, I coded 2725 (77.7%) of the comments in the sample, and the other coder coded 783 (22.3%).
11. Erika Darics, "Politeness in Computer-Mediated Discourse of a Virtual Team," *Journal of Politeness Research* 6 (2010): 129–150; Zizi Papacharissi, "Democracy Online: Civility, Politeness, and the Democratic Potential of Online Political Discussion Groups," *New Media & Society* 6, no. 2 (2004): 259–283 (Darics 2010; Papacharissi 2004).
12. Kevin Coe, Kate Kenski, and Stephen A. Rains, "Online and Uncivil? Patterns and Determinants of Incivility in Newspaper Website Comments," *Journal of Communication* 64 (2014): 658–679; Papacharissi, "Democracy Online: Civility, Politeness, and the Democratic Potential of Online Political Discussion Groups"; Stroud et al. "Changing Deliberative Norms on News Organizations' Facebook Sites." (Coe et al. 2014).
13. Coe, Kenski, and Rains, "Online and Uncivil? Patterns and Determinants of Incivility in Newspaper Website Comments"; Papacharissi, "Democracy

Online: Civility, Politeness, and the Democratic Potential of Online Political Discussion Groups"; Stroud et al. "Changing Deliberative Norms on News Organizations' Facebook Sites."
14. Jeffrey M. Berry and Sarah Sobieraj, *The Outrage Industry: Political Opinion Media and the New Incivility*, (New York, NY: Oxford University Press, 2014); Papacharissi, "Democracy Online: Civility, Politeness, and the Democratic Potential of Online Political Discussion Groups"; Arthur D. Santana, "Incivility Dominates Online Comments on Immigration," *Newspaper Research Journal* 36, no. 1 (2015): 92–107; Stroud et al. "Changing Deliberative Norms on News Organizations' Facebook Sites"; Sarah Sobieraj and Jeffrey M. Berry, "From Incivility to Outrage: Political Discourse in Blogs, Talk Radio, and Cable News," *Political Communication* 28, no. 1 (2011): 19–41 (Berry and Sobieraj 2014; Papacharissi 2015; Sobieraj and Berry 2011).
15. Santana, "Incivility Dominates Online Comments on Immigration"; Stroud et al. "Changing Deliberative Norms on News Organizations' Facebook Sites"; Sobieraj and Berry, "From Incivility to Outrage: Political Discourse in Blogs, Talk Radio, and Cable News."
16. Stroud et al. "Changing Deliberative Norms on News Organizations' Facebook Sites."
17. Stroud et al. "Changing Deliberative Norms on News Organizations' Facebook Sites."
18. This was tested using a chi square that showed statistically significant relationships for gender and news organization, X^2 (8, $N = 3508$) = 1333.51, $p < 0.001$, and for gender and topic, X^2 (4, $N = 3508$) = 208.24, $p < 0.001$.
19. This was tested using a chi square that showed statistically significant relationships for anonymity and news organization, X^2 (4, $N = 3508$) = 2375.73, $p < 0.001$, and for anonymity and topic, X^2 (2, $N = 3508$) = 241.81, $p < 0.001$.
20. Standard deviation was 44.62 words, and the skewness was 4.05, suggesting the variables was quite positively skewed, and kurtosis was 29.06, indicating the distributed was more peaked than a normal distribution. As a result, I transformed it using logarithmic 10, following the recommendation of Barbara G. Tabachnick and Linda S. Fidell, *Using Multivariate Statistics*, (New York, NY: Pearson, 2007). The logged variable was used in all analyses (Tabachnick and Fidell 2007).
21. This was tested using a multi-factorial analysis of variance (ANOVA) with comment length in words (logged) as the dependent variable, and topic and news organization as independent variable factors. Results showed a statistically significant main effect for topic, F (2, 3505) = 15.49,

$p < 0.001$, $\eta^2 = 0.01$, and for news organization $F\,(4,\,3{,}503) = 87.77$, $p < 0.001$, $\eta^2 = 0.09$.
22. Means reported in the text are not logged for ease of interpretation. The logged values are $M = 1.42$, $SE = 0.02$ for comments posted on the Confederate flag stories, which were significantly different at $p < 0.001$ from those posted on the same-sex marriage stories ($M = 1.31$, $SE = 0.01$) and Super Tuesday stories ($M = 1.33$, $SE = 0.02$).
23. Means reported in the text are not logged for ease of interpretation. The logged values are $M = 1.58$, $SE = 0.02$ for *The New York Times*, which is significantly different at $p < 0.001$ for *NBC News* ($M = 1.38$, $SE = 0.02$), *USA Today* ($M = 1.35$, $SE = 0.04$), the *Huffington Post*, ($M = 1.25$, $SE = 0.01$), and *Fox News* ($M = 1.19$, $SE = 0.02$).
24. Logged means are not significantly different, $p = 0.90$.
25. This was tested using a multi-factorial ANOVA with comment length in words (logged) as the dependent variable and topic and news organization as independent variable factors that also tested an interaction between topic and news organization. Results showed the interaction was statistically significant, $F\,(8,\,3{,}499) = 24.47$, $p = 0.001$, $\eta^2 = 0.05$.
26. This was tested using a chi square, which showed a significant relationship between use of all capital letters in words and topic, $X^2\,(2,\,N = 3508) = 7.94$, $p = 0.02$, but not news organization, $X^2\,(4,\,N = 3508) = 6.16$, $p = 0.19$.
27. Darics, "Politeness in Computer-Mediated Discourse of a Virtual Team"; Papacharissi, "Democracy Online: Civility, Politeness, and the Democratic Potential of Online Political Discussion Groups."
28. Ian Rowe, "Civility 2.0: A Comparative Analysis of Incivility in Online Political Discussion," *Information, Communication & Society* 18, no. 2 (2015): 121–138; Arthur D. Santana, "Virtuous or Vitriolic," *Journalism Practice* 8, no. 1 (2014): 18–33 (Rowe 2015; Santana 2014).
29. This was tested with a multi-factorial ANOVA with anonymity as the independent variable, the incivility index as the dependent variable, and news organization and topic added as additional factors. No significant main effect was found for anonymity, $F\,(1,\,3{,}508) = 1.42$, $p = 0.23$, $\eta^2 = 0.0004$. In addition, the mean for anonymous comments (0.19, $SE = 0.03$) was not significantly different from the mean for comments with what appeared to be real names (0.23, $SE = 0.02$, $p = 0.23$).
30. The multi-factorial ANOVA showed that both topic, $F\,(2,\,3{,}505) = 14.28$, $p < 0.001$, $\eta^2 = 0.008$, and news organization, $F\,(4,\,3{,}503) = 11.47$, $p < 0.001$, $\eta^2 = 0.01$, produced main effects on incivility.

31. Means were significantly different at $p < 0.001$ for comments posted on same-sex marriage stories compared with both Confederate flag and Super Tuesday stories. Means for comments on Confederate flag stories were not significantly different from means for Super Tuesday stories.
32. The multi-factorial ANOVA regarding incivility showed a significant interaction for news organization and topic, $F(8, 3{,}499) = 4.12$, $p < 0.001$, $\eta^2 = 0.009$.
33. This was tested with a multi-factorial ANOVA with anonymity as the independent variable, the deliberation index as the dependent variable, and news organization and topic added as additional factors. No significant main effect was found for anonymity, $F(1, 3{,}506) = 1.27$, $p = 0.26$, $\eta^2 = 0.0004$, but a main effect was found for topic, $F(1, 3{,}506) = 5.50$, $p = 0.004$, $\eta^2 = 0.003$. In addition, the mean for anonymous comments (0.28, $SE = 0.04$) was not significantly different from the mean for comments with what appeared to be real names (0.33, $SE = 0.02$, $p = 0.26$).
34. Means were significantly different at $p < 0.05$.
35. Means were not significantly different at $p = 1.0$.
36. The multi-factorial ANOVA showed a significant main effect for news organization, $F(4, 3{,}503) = 2.88$, $p = 0.02$, $\eta^2 = 0.003$. However, post hoc corrections using Scheffe showed no significant differences between any of the means for deliberation across the five news organizations.
37. The multi-factorial ANOVA showed a significant interaction for topic and news organization for deliberation, $F(8, 3{,}499) = 2.66$, $p = 0.02$, $\eta^2 = 0.006$.
38. Two regressions equations with comment length as the independent variable and the incivility and deliberation indices as the dependent variables were used to test this. Comment length had a significant positive relationship with both incivility ($R^2 = 0.02$, $F = 56.78$, $p < 0.001$) and deliberation ($R^2 = 0.08$, $F = 314.06$, $p < 0.001$). However, the relationship with longer comments was stronger for deliberation ($\beta = 0.30$) than for incivility ($\beta = 0.12$).
39. This was tested using chi squares that showed a significant relationship between use of all capital letters and incivility, $X^2(1, N = 3508) = 12.78$, $p < 0.001$, and deliberation, $X^2(1, N = 3508) = 4.43$, $p = 0.04$.
40. Darics, "Politeness in Computer-Mediated Discourse of a Virtual Team"; Papacharissi, "Democracy Online: Civility, Politeness, and the Democratic Potential of Online Political Discussion Groups."
41. This was tested using two multi-factorial ANOVAs. The first used the incivility index as the dependent variable, and gender, topic, and news organizations as independent variable factors, and no significant differences were found, $F(1, 3{,}506) = 0.19$, $p = 0.82$, $\eta^2 = 0.0$. The second used the

deliberation index as the dependent variable, and no significant differences for gender were found, $F(1, 3,506) = 2.90$, $p = 0.06$, $\eta^2 = 0.0004$.
42. Standard deviation is 0.27.
43. These percentages do not total 21.1% (the total percentage of comment that contains deliberative attributes) because individual comments could contain more than one attribute.
44. Standard deviation is 0.42.
45. This was tested using a t test, $t = -64.56$, $p < 0.001$.
46. These percentages do not total 18.7% (the total percentage of comment that contains incivility attributes) because individual comments could contain more than one attribute.
47. Coe, Kenski, Rains, "Online and Uncivil? Patterns and Determinants of Incivility in Newspaper Website Comments."
48. Gabriel de Tarde, *On Communication and Social* Influence, ed. Terry N. Clark (Chicago, IL: University of Chicago Press, 1889/1969); Elihu Katz, "Back to the Street: When Media and Opinion Leaves Home," *Mass Communication and Society* 17 (2014): 454–463; Papacharissi, "Democracy Online: Civility, Politeness, and the Democratic Potential of Online Political Discussion Groups." (De Tarde 1889; Katz 2014).
49. Jürgen Habermas, "Three Normative Models of Democracy," *Democratic and Constitutional Theory Today* 1, no. 1 (1994): 1–10 (Habermas 1994).
50. Zizi Papacharissi, *Affective Publics*, (New York, NY: Oxford University Press, 2015) (Papacharissi 2015).
51. John G. Geer, *In Defense of Negativity: Attack Ads in Presidential Campaigns*, (Chicago, IL: University of Chicago Press, 2006) (Geer 2006).
52. Gutmann and Thompson, *Democracy and Disagreement*, 1.
53. Gina Masullo Chen, "Online Incivility and Public Deliberation," In *News Scholarship in a Transitional Age: Research in Honor of Pamela J. Shoemaker*, eds. Carol M. Liebler, Brad W. Gorham, and Timothy P. Vos, (New York, NY: Peter Lang; forthcoming in 2017) (Chen 2017).
54. George E. Marcus, W. Russell Neuman, and Michael MacKuen, *Affective Intelligence and Political Judgment*, (Chicago, IL: The University of Chicago Press, 2000) (Marcus et al. 2000).
55. Geer, *In Defense of Negativity: Attack Ads in Presidential Campaigns*.
56. Papacharissi, *Affective Publics*, 10.
57. Papacharissi, *Affective Publics*, 12.
58. Jack Rosenberry, "Users Support Anonymity Despite Increasing Negativity," *Newspaper Research Journal* 32, no. 1 (2011): 6–19; Rowe, "Civility 2.0: A Comparative Analysis of Incivility in Online Political Discussion"; Santana, "Virtuous or Vitriolic." (Rosenberry 2011).

59. Rowe, "Civility 2.0: A Comparative Analysis of Incivility in Online Political Discussion" and Santana, "Virtuous or Vitriolic."
60. Jeff Sonderman, "News Sites Using Facebook Comments See Higher Quality Discussions, More Referrals," *Poynter.org*, August 18, 2011. http://www.poynter.org/2011/news-sites-using-facebook-comments-see-higher-quality-discussion-more-referrals/143192/ (Sonderman 2011).
61. Leonie Rösner and Nicole C. Krämer, "Verbal Venting in the Social Web: Effects of Anonymity and Group Norms on Aggressive Language Use in Online Comments," *Social Media + Society*, July/September (2016): 1–13 (Rösner and Krämer 2016).
62. Abhay Sukumaran, Stephanie Vezich, Melanie McHugh, and Clifford Nass, "Normative Influences on Thoughtful Online Participation," *Proceedings of the CHI 2011: Session: Incentives & User Generated Content*, Vancouver, British Columbia, 3401–3410; Rösner and Krämer, "Verbal Venting in the Social Web: Effects of Anonymity and Group Norms on Aggressive Language Use in Online Comments." (Sukumaran et al. 2011).
63. Arthur D. Santana, "Incivility Dominates Online Comments on Immigration," *Newspaper Research Journal* 36, no. 1 (2015): 92–107 (Santana 2015).

REFERENCES

Berry, Jeffrey M., and Sarah Sobieraj. 2014. *The Outrage Industry: Politics and The New Incivility*. New York: Oxford University Press.
Chen, Gina Masullo. 2017. Online Incivility and Public Deliberation. In *News Scholarship in a Transitional Age: Research in Honor of Pamela J. Shoemaker*, ed. Carol M. Liebler, Brad W. Gorham, and Tim P. Vos. New York: Peter Lang, forthcoming.
Coe, Kevin, Kate Kenski, and Stephen A. Rains. 2014. Online and Uncivil? Patterns and Determinants of Incivility in Newspaper Website Comments. *Journal of Communication* 64: 658–679.
Darics, Erika. 2010. Politeness in Computer-Mediated Discourse of a Virtual Team. *Journal of Politeness Research* 6: 129–150.
De Tarde, Gabriel. 1889/1969. *On Communication and Social Influence*, ed. Terry N. Clark. Chicago: University of Chicago Press.
Geer, John G. 2006. *In Defense of Negativity: Attack Ads in Presidential Campaigns*, 2006. Chicago: University of Chicago Press.
Gutmann, Amy, and Dennis Thompson. 1996. *Democracy and Disagreement*. Cambridge, MA: Harvard University Press.
Habermas, Jürgen. 1994. Three Normative Models of Democracy. *Democratic and Constitutional Theory Today* 1 (1): 1–10.

Hayes, Andrew F., and Klaus Krippendorf. 2007. Answering the Call for a Standard Reliability Measure for Coding Data. *Communication Methods and Measures* 1 (1): 77–89.

Katz, Elihu. 2014. Back to the Street: When Media and Opinion Leaves Home. *Mass Communication and Society* 17: 454–463.

Lacy, Stephen, Brendan R. Watson, Daniel Riffe, and Jennette Lovejoy. 2015. Issues and Best Practices in Content Analysis. *Journalism & Mass Communication Quarterly* 92 (4): 791–811.

Marcus, George E., W. Russell Neuman, and Michael MacKuen. 2000. *Affective Intelligence and Political Judgment*. Chicago: The University of Chicago Press.

Nekmat, Elmie, and William J. Gonzebach. 2013. Multiple Opinion Climates in Online Forums: Role of Website Source Reference and Within-Forum Opinion Congruency. *Journalism & Mass Communication Quarterly* 90 (4): 736–756.

Papacharissi, Zizi. 2004. Democracy Online: Civility, Politeness, and the Democratic Potential of Online Political Discussion. *New Media & Society* 6 (2): 259–283.

Papacharissi, Zizi. 2015. *Affective Publics*. New York: Oxford University Press.

Riffe, Daniel, Stephen Lacy, and Frederick G. Fico. 2005. *Analyzing Media Messages: Using Quantitative Content Analysis in Research*. Mahwah, NJ: Lawrence Erlbaum.

Rosenberry, Jack. 2011. Users Support Anonymity Despite Increasing Negativity. *Newspaper Research Journal* 32 (1): 6–19.

Rösner, Leonie, and Nicole C. Krämer. 2016. Verbal Venting in the Social Web: Effects of Anonymity and Group Norms on Aggressive Language Use in Online Comments. *Social Media + Society*, July/September: 1–13.

Rowe, Ian. 2015. Civility 2.0: A Comparative Analysis of Incivility in Online Political Discussion. *Information, Communication & Society* 18 (2): 121–138.

Santana, Arthur D. 2014. Virtuous or Vitriolic. *Journalism Practice* 8 (1): 18–33.

Santana, Arthur D. 2015. Incivility Dominates Online Comments on Immigration. *Newspaper Research Journal* 36 (1): 92–107.

Sobieraj, Sarah, and Jeffrey M. Berry. 2011. From Incivility to Outrage: Political Discourse in Blogs, Talk Radio, and Cable News. *Political Communication* 28 (1): 19–41.

Sonderman, Jeff. 2011. News Sites Using Facebook Comments See Higher Quality Discussions, More Referrals, *Poynter.org*, August 11. http://www.poynter.org/2011/news-sites-using-facebook-comments-see-higher-quality-discussion-more-referrals/143192/. Accessed 9 Sep 2016.

Stroud, Natalie J., Joshua M. Scacco, Ashley Muddiman, and Alexander L. Curry. 2015. Changing Deliberative Norms on News Organizations' Facebook Sites. *Journal of Computer-Mediated Communication* 20: 188–203.

Sukumaran, Abhay, Stephanie Vezich, Melanie McHugh, and Clifford Nass. 2011. Normative Influences on Thoughtful Online Participation. In *Proceedings of the*

CHI 2011: Session: Incentives & User Generated Content, 3401–3410, Vancouver, BC.

Tabachnick, Barbara A., and Linda S. Fidell. 2007. *Using Multivariate Statistics.* New York: Pearson.

Tenenboim, Ori, and Akiba A. Cohen. 2015. What Prompts Users to Click and Comment? A Longitudinal Study of Online News. *Journalism* 16 (2): 198–217.

PART III

Incivility and Political Participation

CHAPTER 6

Incivility and Speaking Out

During the 2016 presidential campaign, I tried to stay out of the virulent fights that were rampant online. Facebook friends who do not share my political views shared dozens of memes and posts that I viewed as ill-informed or outright lies. I did not comment. I merely hid the posts from my Facebook timeline and sparingly shared my own beliefs on my own wall. Even though I believe strongly in public debate, I also know that sometimes that debate is not possible. When people's views are extremely polarized, they get entrenched, and they cannot see an alternative view, even when they are shown evidence of their flawed beliefs.[1] But one day, I deviated from this routine. I had posted a *New York Times* story about a video that surfaced in which then-presidential candidate Donald Trump bragged about grabbing women by the genitals without consent,[2] and I proclaimed my own disgust with the story in my status update. An acquaintance that I knew as a child but have not seen in 30 years, commented on my post. She accused me of being uneducated and uninformed about the election because I was faulting Trump for this misstep when, in her view, Trump's opponent, Hillary Clinton had done much worse. She recited several popular conspiracy theories about Clinton, and blamed Clinton for her own husband's scandals with women. Even though I knew nothing I would say would sway her, I could not help but respond. I was measured and polite but pointed. I did not insult her as she had insulted me, but I made it clear I disagreed with her comments. I explained in detail why her assertions were incorrect, citing evidence.

So why did I engage this one time and not the others? I propose the reason is something that I call the "defensive effect." The effect posits that when people are confronted with uncivil disagreement—marred by name-calling, insults, or profanity—this ignites an emotional response. Then that emotional response jumpstarts a defense mechanism that makes them more likely to speak out or get politically involved in whatever issue was the focus of the original challenge. In essence, the emotional response triggers a need to re-assert their views by speaking out and mutes a natural drive to remain silent when confronted with views that oppose one's own. As I explain in greater detail in Chap. 2, scholars call this the cross-pressures hypothesis,[3] which argues that disagreement demobilizes people because most of us want to preserve harmony, especially among those we consider friends. When applied to politics, this means that when people are confronted with those who disagree with their views within their *opinion networks* (friends, relatives, neighbors), this introduces ambivalence about their own views, leading them to be less likely to perform political actions, such as voting or even discussing politics.[4] The spiral of silence also plays a role in this effect. The spiral of silence proposes that people make an assessment about whether their views fit those of *most people* based on what their friends and relatives say and what the mass media reports about others' opinions.[5] As a result, they are less apt to speak out if they believe their opinion does not conform to what most other people believe because they fear being socially isolated by expressing an alternative viewpoint.[6] More recent research has found that in today's fragmented media environment, the mass media play a diminished role in this phenomenon,[7] but interpersonal social pressure—especially the type that plays out on social media—may still keep people silent because they want to conform to expectations of their friends and relatives.[8]

Of course, there are exceptions to this trend of staying silent to keep the peace in the face of disagreement. People who feel they hold a majority viewpoint are less likely to feel uncomfortable speaking out when faced with disagreement.[9] Similarly, when people experience a "clash of arguments" between people on both sides of an issue, disagreement may encourage political participation.[10] Specifically, exposure to political disagreement has been found to increase some forms of activism, such as volunteerism.[11] In addition, people who watch highly partisan news become emboldened in their own views,[12] so they may be less ambivalent when confronted with disagreement. This provides background to the defensive effect, which I will explain in greater detail in the rest of this chapter. I also will propose specific underlying mechanisms that are required for the effect to work, and outline hypotheses that I used to test the defensive effect in Chap. 7.

How the "Defensive Effect" Works

Four underlying mechanisms are important for the defensive effect to work. First, the message must be a form a disagreement—it must express a counter opinion[13] to what the person receiving the message believes. Second, the message must by nasty. It must contain markers of incivility, such as profanity, or insults, or name-calling.[14] People do not like when others disagree with them, and even mild disagreement may arouse negative feelings as people try to reconcile what the person is saying with their own beliefs.[15] But it takes uncivil disagreement for the defensive effect to work; civil disagreement is just not arousing enough to ignite the effect.[16]

Third, the topic must be a highly polarizing issue with clear sides, and the person must care deeply enough about the topic for it to elicit an emotional response. People cannot deliberate about a topic about which they care little.[17] In the same way, people will not receive a significant enough jolt of emotion if someone disagrees with them uncivilly about something that matters little to them. A great deal of research shows that uncivil online comments activate negative emotions and make people think or even act more aggressively and retaliate.[18] Emotions are powerful, short-lived states that change from hot to cold, positive to negative in a flash.[19] Negative emotions include feeling angry, anxious, or annoyed, and indicate distress or unrest while positive ones include enthusiasm, alertness or happiness.[20] However, it is important to understand that the defensive effect does not predict how incivility will impact specific emotions,[21] such as anger or happiness. Rather it proposes that incivility will influence negative and positive emotions as a whole that include these specific feelings in what is called the dimensional approach to emotions.[22] The reason is that the defensive effect relies on motivational processes,[23] rather than the "higher-level cognitive processes" required for a discrete emotional approach.[24] In other words, people are responding to incivility at a more primal level, which is discussed in greater detail later in this chapter. Unlike longer-lasting moods, emotions are a momentary spike of feelings that diffuse quickly. As explained in Chap. 2, the evolutionary purpose of emotions was to help guide behavior by providing clues about how people should proceed.[25] Emotions are "potent, volatile, instigators of change"[26] that shape how people vote[27] and lead them to seek answers and learn more about politics or any subject.[28] Affective intelligence theory proposes that when people are confronted with a threat to their worldview, this triggers an affective judgment even before they may be consciously aware of their emotions.[29] For a brief second, the emotion takes over, and reason fades. That moment is the heart of the defensive effect.

The fourth key element of the defensive effect is that the incivility must feel personal in some way. The insult, the criticism, the name-calling, the curse words must challenge the person's constructed sense of self, which is called *face*.[30] Face is how people imagine that others see them. It is the term people use when they say someone has *lost face*, a sense of public scorn or embarrassment. This threat to face challenges people's identity[31] at a very core level, making them feel as if they are less worthy. It causes hurt feelings, which operate like a warning system to people that their value to others is low.[32] It draws on people's earliest roots as humans, when the need to belong to a group was so intense because they might die at the hands of a predator if they were thrust out of the group.[33] Much as a person would withdraw when confronted by a snarling wolf, people recoil when the sense of face is threatened. For a brief second, the sting mimics physical pain.[34] It may even briefly cause the muscles used for smiling to relax[35] or arouse the body's sympathetic nervous system, prompting glands in the hands and feet to fill with sweat that signifies the triggering of a primal fight-or-flight response.[36] When the incivility stimulates negative emotion, it activates what is called the *aversive motivational system*,[37] telling the body to expend cognitive resources—brainpower—on restoring its public identity, or face. In essence, the body responds for a mere second to the social threat much as it would to actual danger, like a tiger giving chase.

For the defensive effect to occur, people must take the affront personally in some way and respond with negative emotion. In essence, if the incivility does not lead to a negative emotional response, it ends there. The person moves on, and no defensive effect occurs. Imagine several people are tweeting about how much they believe Hillary Clinton will destroy the country if elected. If a person reads the tweet, and agrees that Hillary will destroy America, no defensive effect occurs. The person may retweet the comment or merely move on. In that case, there is no disagreement, so there is no reason to defend one's viewpoint. Or consider a case where one reads a news story and is assaulted by a barrage of uncivil comments that argue the U.S.A. should curtail accepting new refugees from Syria for fear they will perpetuate acts of terrorism. The person reading the comments disagrees with this view, and it certainly expresses a polarizing issue. But if the person does not care deeply about this issue or see it as part of his or her core values, it will not generate enough emotion for the defensive effect to take place. Without an intense emotional burst, any concerns the comments raise diffuse too quickly to have any real effect. A final example is a person reading tweets that argue in a vitriolic way rife with name-calling and insults that global warming is a hoax, but the person does not care enough to get involved. The person disagrees with this view, but he or she does not engage, so the tweets do not feel personal. They are merely so much noise on the Internet sounding off. Again, there is no defensive effect.

However, when all four requirements are met, the uncivil disagreement leads to the emotional burst, which serves as the spark. In this case, people's constructed sense of face is threatened, they feel emotional pain as their relational values are challenged. Their primal fight-or-flight response is aroused. They must re-affirm their beliefs by setting the record straight. They may do this in a variety of ways, including experiencing a drive to share their opinions on the issue, to join a Facebook page that supports their view, or even to donate to a political candidate or charity that shares their beliefs on this topic. Scholars in political communication often use intentions to do these types of actions as proxies for civic and political participation[38] because intentions predict what people will actually do.[39] In this instance, the incivility leads directly to a negative emotional experience and indirectly leads to greater intention to participate politically. I have previously tested this effect on three topics—abortion, gun control, and climate change[40]—and the results support this effect. In the next chapter, I test the effect further using three additional heated topics: same-sex marriage, the debate over removing the Confederate flag from government spaces, and the 2016 presidential election.

THE PROPOSED MODEL

The defensive effect is deceptively simple and includes four hypotheses. First, I predicted (H1a) that uncivil disagreement when targeted against a specific person will lead to a burst in negative emotion and a (H1b) deflation of positive emotion. Both positive and negative emotions were considered because earlier research has shown that positive emotion is not just the absence of negative emotion; rather they are two separate emotional experiences.[41] Next, I proposed that both emotional experiences, negative (H2a) and positive (H2b), would lead to greater intention to get politically involved. The rationale for negative emotion leading to political participation has been explained above, but positive emotion may make people feel invigorated, leading them to be more likely to express their political views or act on them. My prior research has shown that people feel positive and negative emotions after any form of disagreement, even if it is not uncivil.[42] So if people are feeling either negative or positive emotion for any reason it may make them more likely to get politically involved. (H3) predicts that if the uncivil disagreement does not create a negative emotional response, the defensive effect will not occur. In fact, incivility in that case is likely to decrease people's intention to get politically involved. Support for this comes from the ample prior research that shows disagreement can have a demobilizing effect.[43] Fig. 6.1 shows this conceptual model. The final piece of the defensive effect is (H4), which proposes that

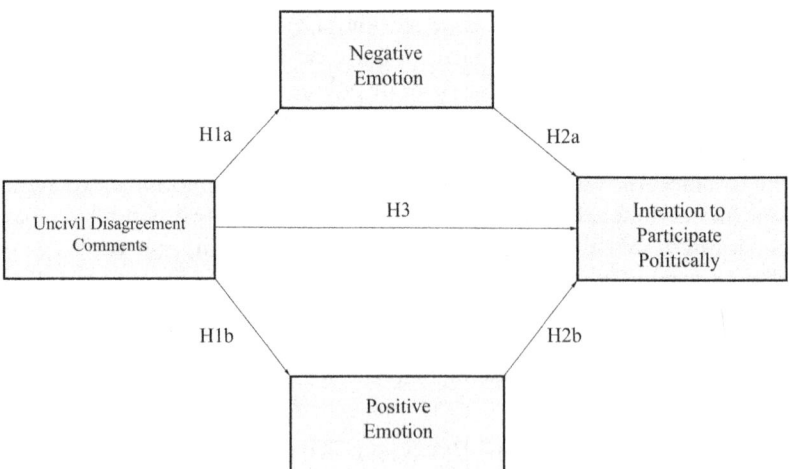

Fig. 6.1 Proposed direct effects of "defensive effect" model

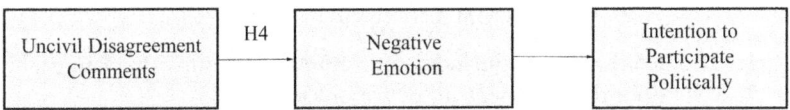

Fig. 6.2 Proposed indirect effect of "defensive effect" model

the incivility will jumpstart a chain reaction that first boosts negative emotion and then leads to increased intention to get politically engaged. This is depicted in Fig. 6.2. In the next chapter, I will test this effect using an experiment.

Conclusion

In summary, if we return to the anecdote that began this chapter, I spoke out that one time on Facebook because my acquaintance's comments, which disagreed with my beliefs and insulted me directly, upset me so much that I felt compelled to respond. Her words were uncivil, they concerned an issue, the election, about which I feel very passionate, and she disagreed vehemently with my cores views about that topic. Her attack felt personal. So, spurred by my own negative emotional response, I defended my beliefs by sharing my own political views in the quasi-public space of my Facebook wall. I was not out of control. I did not lack reason. I even made an attempt to be deliberative, by using rational language and backing up my assertions with evidence. I lived the defensive effect. My goal was not to persuade her. My goal was to set the record straight for others. This example illustrates one of my core beliefs about this effect. While incivility should never be our aim in public discourse, it is an artifact of people talking and debating about topics that move them. Therefore, I do not see the defensive effect as suggesting that we should encourage incivility. In fact, my hope is that we can deliberate about important topics without falling prey to our baser selves. Yet, if the incivility does occur, as it often will, the defensive effect leads to more speech, more discussion, more participation in the political process. As journalism scholar Michael Schudson asserts, the essence of democratic talk is "not equality but publicness."[44] I agree. So if incivility elicits more public discussion, we should embrace the positive result from this decidedly negative experience. In the next chapter, I test the defensive effect model proposed in this chapter.

Classroom Discussion Prompts

1. The defensive effect includes four core mechanisms. Explain each.
2. Why does disagreement influence emotions?
3. Think of your own experiences with reading online comments on social media or news stories. Have you ever experienced the defensive effect? Explain.
4. How comfortable are you with expressing political views that disagree with others? How do you decide whether you should speak or act on them?

Notes

1. Brendan Nyhan and Jason Reifler, "When Corrections Fail: The Persistence of Political Misperceptions," *Political Behavior* 32, no. 2 (2010): 303–330 (Nyhan and Reifler 2010).
2. Susan Dominus, "Donald Trump: King of the Old Boys' Club, and Perhaps Its Destroyer," *The New York Times*, October 7, 2016. http://www.nytimes.com/2016/10/08/magazine/donald-trump-tape.html?smid=fb-nytimes&smtyp=cur&_r=0 (Dominus 2016).
3. Lilach Nir, "Disagreement and Opposition in Social Networks: Does Disagreement Discourage Turnout?" *Political Studies* 59 (2011): 674–692; Lilach Nir, "Ambivalent Social Networks and Their Consequences for Participation," *International Journal of Public Opinion Research* 17, no. 4 (2005): 422–442; Diana C. Mutz, "The Consequences of Cross-Cutting Networks for Political Participation," *American Journal of Political Science* 46, no. 4 (2002): 838–855 (Nir 2005, 2011; Mutz 2002).
4. Nir, "Disagreement and Opposition in Social Networks: Does Disagreement Discourage Turnout?"; Nir, "Ambivalent Social Networks and Their Consequences for Participation"; Scott D. McClurg, "Political Disagreement in Context: The Conditional Effect of Neighborhood Context, Disagreement and Political Talk on Electoral Participation," *Political Behavior* 28 (2006): 349–366 (McClurg 2006).
5. Elisabeth Noelle-Neumann, "The Spiral of Silence: A Theory of Public Opinion," *Journal of Communication* 24 (1974): 43–51; Elisabeth Noelle-Neumann, "The Spiral of Silence," In *A First Look at Communication Theory*, ed. Em Griffin, (New York, NY: McGraw Hill, 2008): 272–286; Yariv Tsfati, Natalie J. Stroud, and Adi Chotiner, "Exposure to Ideological News and Perceived Opinion Climate: Testing the Media Effects Component of Spiral-of-Silence in a Fragmented Media

Landscape," *The International Journal of Press/Politics* 19, no. 1 (2014): 3–23 (Noelle-Neumann 1974, 2008; Tsfati et al. 2014).
6. Elisabeth Noelle-Neumann, "The Spiral of Silence: A Theory of Public Opinion"; Elisabeth Noelle-Neumann, "The Spiral of Silence"; Tsfati, Stroud, and Chotiner, "Exposure to Ideological News and Perceived Opinion Climate: Testing the Media Effects Component of Spiral-of-Silence in a Fragmented Media Landscape," *The International Journal of Press/Politics*, 19, no. 1 (2014): 3–23.
7. Tsfati, Stroud, and Chotiner, "Exposure to Ideological News and Perceived Opinion Climate: Testing the Media Effects Component of Spiral-of-Silence in a Fragmented Media Landscape."
8. Andrew F. Hayes, "Exploring Forms of Self-Censorship: On the Spiral of Silence and the Use of Opinion Expression Avoidance Strategies," *Journal of Communication* 57 (2007): 785–802 (Hayes 2007).
9. McClurg, "Political Disagreement in Context: The Conditional Effect of Neighborhood Context, Disagreement and Political Talk on the Electoral Participation."
10. Nir, "Disagreement and Opposition in Social Networks: Does Disagreement Discourage Turnout?"
11. C.J. Pattie and R.J. Johnson, "Conversation, Disagreement, and Political Participation," *Political Behavior* 31 (2009): 261–285 (Pattie and Johnson 2009).
12. Tsfati, Stroud, and Chotiner, "Exposure to Ideological News and Perceived Opinion Climate: Testing the Media Effects Component of Spiral-of-Silence in a Fragmented Media Landscape."
13. Casey A. Klofstad, Anand Edward Sokhey, and Scott D. McClurg, "Disagreeing About Disagreement: How Conflict in Social Networks Affects Political Behavior," *American Journal of Political Science* 57 (2013): 120–134 (Klofstad et al. 2013).
14. Zizi Papacharissi, "Democracy Online: Civility, Politeness, and the Democratic Potential of Online Political Discussion," *New Media & Society* 6, no. 2 (2004): 259–283; Natalie J. Stroud, Joshua M. Scacco, Ashley Muddiman, and Alexander L. Curry, "Changing Deliberative Norms on News Organizations' Facebook Sites," *Journal of Computer-Mediated Communication* 20 (2015): 188–203 (Papacharissi 2004; Stroud et al. 2015).
15. Leon Festinger, *A Theory of Cognitive Dissonance*, (Palo Alto, CA: Stanford University Press, 1957) (Festinger 1957).
16. Gina Masullo Chen and Pei Zheng. *The "Defensive Effect": Uncivil Comments Indirectly Increase Intention to Participate Politically, Through Negative Affect*, presented to the Mass Communication Division of the

International Communication Association annual conference in Fukuoka, Japan, June 2016; Gina Masullo Chen and Shuning Lu, "Online Political Discourse: Exploring Differences in Effects of Civil and Uncivil Disagreement in News Website Comments," *Journal of Broadcasting & Electronic Media* 61, no. 1 (2017). doi:10.1080/08838151/2016/1273922; Gina Masullo Chen, *Nasty News Story Comments Indirectly Increase Intention to Participate Politically for Women, Mediated Through Negative Affect*, presented to the Mass Communication Division of the Southern States Communication Association at its annual conference in Austin, TX, April 2016 (Chen and Zheng 2016; Chen and Lu 2017; Chen 2016).

17. Amy Gutmann and Dennis Thompson, *Democracy and Disagreement*, (Cambridge, MA: Harvard University Press, 1996) (Gutmann and Thompson 1996).

18. Chen and Lu, "Online Political Discourse: Exploring Differences in Effects of Civil and Uncivil Disagreement in News Website Comments"; Jeanne M. Brett, Mara Olekains, Ray Friedman, Nathan Goates, Cameron Anderson, and Cara Cherry Lisco, "Sticks and Stones: Language, Face, and Online Dispute Resolution," *Academy of Management Journal* 50, no. 1 (2007): 85–99; Bryan T. Gervais, "Incivility Online: Affective and Behavioral Reactions to Uncivil Political Posts in a Web-Based Experiment," *Journal of Information Technology & Politics* 12 (2015): 167–185; Leonie Rösner, Stephan Winter, and Nicole C. Krämer, "Dangerous Minds? Effects of Online Comments on Aggressive Cognitions, Emotions, and Behavior," *Computers in Human Behavior* 58 (2016): 461–470 (Brett et al. 2007; Gervais 2015; Rösner et al. 2016).

19. Paul D. Bolls, "Understanding Emotion from a Superordinate Dimensional Perspective: A Productive Way Forward for Communication Processes and Effects," *Communication Monographs* 77, no. 2 (2010): 146–152 (Bolls 2010).

20. David Watson, Lee A. Clark, and Auke Tellen, "Development and Validation of Briefs Measures of Positive and Negative Affect: The PANAS Scales," *Journal of Personality and Social Psychology* 54, no. 6 (1988): 1063–1070 (Watson et al. 1988).

21. Robin L. Nabi, "The Case for Emphasizing Discrete Emotions in Communication Research," *Communication Monograph* 77, no. 2 (2010): 153–159. http://dx.doi.org/10.1080/03637751003790444 (Nabi 2010).

22. Bolls, "Understanding Emotion from a Superordinate Dimensional Perspective: A Productive Way Forward for Communication Processes and Effects"; Nabi, "The Case for Emphasizing Discrete Emotions in Communication Research."

23. Annie Lang, "The Limited Capacity Model of Mediated Message Processing," *Journal of Communication* 50, no. 1 (2000): 46–70; Annie Lang, "The Limited Capacity Model of Motivated Mediated Message Processing," in *The SAGE Handbook of Mass Media Processes and Effects*, eds. Robin L. Nabi and Mary Beth Oliver, (Thousand Oaks, CA: Sage, 2009): 193–204; Annie Lang, "Using the Limited Capacity Model of Mediated Message Processing to Design Effective Cancer Communication Messages," *Journal of Communication* 53, no. S1 (2006): S57–S80 (Lang 2000, 2006, 2009).
24. Bolls, "Understanding Emotion from a Superordinate Dimensional Perspective: A Productive Way Forward for Communication Processes and Effects," 147.
25. Tori Rodriguez, "Negative Emotions are Key to Well-Being," *Scientific American*, May 1, 2013. http://www.scientificamerican.com/article/negative-emotions-key-well-being/?WT.mc_id=SA_FB_MB_EG (Rodriguez 2013).
26. George E. Marcus, W. Russell Neuman, and Michael MacKuen, *Affective Intelligence and Political Judgment*, (Chicago, IL: The University of Chicago Press, 2000): 26 (Marcus et al. 2000).
27. Renita Coleman and H. Denis Wu, *Image & Emotion in Voter Decisions: The Affect Agenda*, (New York, NY: Lexington Books, 2015) (Coleman and Denis Wu 2015).
28. Bethany Albertson and Shuana Kushner Gadarian, *Anxious Politics: Democratic Citizenship in a Threatening World*, (New York, NY: Cambridge University Press, 2015) (Albertson and Gadarian 2015).
29. Marcus, Neuman, and MacKuen, *Affective Intelligence and Political Judgment*.
30. Penelope Brown and Stephen C. Levinson, *Politeness: Some Universals in Language Usage*, (New York, NY: Cambridge University Press, 1987); Erving Goffman, *Presentation of the Self in Everyday Life*, (Garden City, NJ: Doubleday, 1959) (Brown and Levinson 1987; Goffman 1959).
31. John G. Oetzel and Stella Ting-Toomey, "Face Concerns in Interpersonal Conflict: A Cross-Cultural Empirical Test of Face Negotiation Theory," *Communication Research* 20, no. 6 (2003): 599–624 (Oetzel and Ting-Toomey 2003).
32. Kipling D. Williams, Joseph P. Forgas, and William von Hippel, *The Social Outcast*, (New York, NY: Psychology Press, 2005) (Williams et al. 2005).
33. Roy F. Baumeister and Mark R. Leary, "The Need to Belong: Desire for Interpersonal Attachments as a Fundamental Human Need," *Psychological Bulletin* 117, no. 3 (1995): 497–529 (Baumeister and Leary 1995).

34. Geoff MacDonald and Mark R. Leary, "Why Does Social Exclusion Hurt? The Relationship Between Social Pain and Physical Pain," *Psychological Bulletin* 131, no. 2 (2005): 202–223 (MacDonald and Leary 2005).
35. John T. Cacioppo, Louis G. Tassinary, and Gary G. Berntson, *Handbook of Psychophysiology*, (New York, NY: Cambridge University Press, 2007) (Cacioppo et al. 2007).
36. Michael E. Dawson, Anne M. Schell, and Diane L. Filion, "The Electrodermal System," in *Handbook of Psychophysiology*, eds. John T. Cacioppo, Louis G. Tassinary, and Gary G. Berntson, (New York, NY: Cambridge University Press, 2007): 159–181; Lang, "The Limited Capacity Model of Mediated Message Processing"; Lang, "The Limited Capacity Model of Motivated Mediated Message Processing" (Dawson et al. 2007).
37. Lang, "Using the Limited Capacity Model of Mediated Message Processing to Design Effective Cancer Communication Messages"; Lang, "The Limited Capacity Model of Mediated Message Processing," 2000; Lang, "The Limited Capacity Model of Motivated Mediated Message Processing," 2006.
38. Porismita Borah. "Does it Matter Where You Read the News Story? Interaction of Incivility and News Frames in the Political Blogosphere," *Communication Research*, 41, no. 6 (2014): 809–827; Homero Gil de Zúñiga, Nakwon Jung, and Sebastián Valenzuela, "Social Media Use for News and Individuals' Social Capital, Civic Engagement, and Political Participation," *Journal of Computer-Mediated Communication* 17 (2012), 319–336 (Borah 2014; Gil de Zúñiga et al. 2012).
39. Icek Azjen and Martin E. Fishbein, *Understanding Attitudes and Predicting Social Behavior*, (Englewood Cliff, NJ: Prentice Hall, 1980) (Azjen and Fishbein 1980).
40. Chen and Lu, "Online Political Discourse: Exploring Differences in Effects of Civil and Uncivil Disagreement in News Website Comments"; Chen and Zheng, *Online Public Discourse: Exploring Differences in Responses to Civil and Uncivil Disagreement in News Story Comments*; Chen and Zheng, *The "Defensive Effect": Uncivil Comments Directly Increase Intention to Participate Politically, Through Negative Affect*; Chen, *Nasty News Story Comments Indirectly Increase Intention to Participate Politically for Women, Mediated Through Negative Affect*.
41. Gina Masullo Chen, "Losing *Face* on Social Media: Threats to *Positive Face* Lead to an Indirect Effect on Retaliatory Aggression Through Negative Affect," *Communication Research* 42, no. 6 (2015): 819–838 (Chen 2015).
42. Chen and Lu, "Online Political Discourse: Exploring Differences in Effects of Civil and Uncivil Disagreement in News Website Comments"; Chen and

Zheng, *Online Public Discourse: Exploring Differences in Responses to Civil and Uncivil Disagreement in News Story Comments;* Chen and Zheng, *The "Defensive Effect": Uncivil Comments Indirectly Increase Intention to Participate Politically, Through Negative Affect.*

43. Nir, "Disagreement and Opposition in Social Networks: Does Disagreement Discourage Turnout?" Nir, "Ambivalent Social Networks and Their Consequences for Participation"; Mutz, "The Consequences of Cross-Cutting Networks for Political Participation"; McClurg, "Political Disagreement in Context: The Conditional Effect of Neighborhood Context, Disagreement and Political Talk on Electoral Participation."

44. Michael Schudson, "Why Conversation is Not the Soul of Democracy," *Critical Studies in Mass Communication* 14 (1997): 297–309 (Schudson 1997).

REFERENCES

Albertson, Bethany, and Shauna Kushner Gadarian. 2015. *Anxious Politics: Democratic Citizenship in a Threatening World.* New York: Cambridge University Press.

Azjen, Icek, and Martin E. Fishbein. 1980. *Understanding Attitudes and Predicting Social Behavior.* Englewood Cliff, NJ: Prentice Hall.

Baumeister, Roy F., and Mark R. Leary. 1995. The Need to Belong: Desire for Interpersonal Attachments as a Fundamental Human Need. *Psychological Bulletin* 117 (3): 497–529.

Bolls, Paul D. 2010. Understanding Emotion From a Superordinate Dimensional Perspective: A Productive Way Forward for Communication Processes and Effects. *Communication Monographs* 77 (2): 146–152.

Borah, Porismita. 2014. Does it Matter Where You Read The News Story? Interaction of Incivility and News Frames in the Political Blogosphere. *Communication Research* 41 (6): 809–827.

Brett, Jeanne M., Mara Olekains, Ray Friedman, Nathan Goates, Cameron Anderson, and Cara Cherry Lisco. 2007. Sticks and Stones: Language, Face, and Online Dispute Resolution. *Academy of Management Journal* 50 (1): 85–99.

Brown, Penelope, and Stephen C. Levinson. 1987. *Politeness: Some Universals in Language Usage.* New York: Cambridge University Press.

Cacioppo, John T., Louis G. Tassinary, and Gary G. Berntson. 2007. *Handbook of Psychophysiology.* New York: Cambridge University Press.

Chen, Gina Masullo. 2015. Losing *Face* on Social Media: Threats to *Positive Face* Lead to an Indirect Effect on Retaliatory Aggression Through Negative Affect. *Communication Research* 42 (6): 819–838.

Chen, Gina Masullo. 2016. *Nasty News Story Comments Indirectly Increase Intention to Participate Politically for Women, Mediated Through Negative Affect*. Presented to the Mass Communication Division of the Southern States Communication Association at its Annual Conference in Austin, TX, April.

Chen, Gina Masullo, and Shuning Lu. 2017. Online Political Discourse: Exploring Differences in Effects of Civil and Uncivil Disagreement in News Website Comments. *Journal of Broadcasting and Electronic Media* 61 (1). doi:10.1080/08838151/2016/1273922.

Chen, Gina Masullo, and Pei Zheng. 2016. *The "Defensive Effect": Uncivil Comments Indirectly Increase Intention to Participate Politically, Through Negative Affect*. Presented to the Mass Communication Division of the International Communication Association Annual Conference in Fukuoka, Japan, June 2016.

Coleman, Renita, and H. Denis Wu. 2015. *Image & Emotion in Voter Decisions: The Affect Agenda*. New York: Lexington Books.

Dawson, Michael E., Anne M. Schell, and Diane L. Filion. 2007. The Electrodermal System. In *Handbook of Psychophysiology*, ed. John T. Cacioppo, Louis G. Tassinary, and Gary G. Berntson, 159–191. New York: Cambridge University Press.

Dominus, S. 2016. Donald Trump: King of the Old Boys' Club, and Perhaps Its Destroyer. *The New York Times*, October 7. http://www.nytimes.com/2016/10/08/magazine/donald-trump-tape.html?smid=fb-nytimes&smtyp=cur&_r=0. Accessed 4 Nov 2016.

Festinger, Leon. 1957. *A Theory of Cognitive Dissonance*. Palo Alto, CA: Stanford University Press.

Gervais, Bryan T. 2015. Incivility Online: Affective and Behavioral Reactions to Uncivil Political Posts in a Web-Based Experiment. *Journal of Information Technology and Politics* 12: 167–185.

Gil de Zúñiga, Homero, Nakwon Jung, and Sebastián Valenzuela. 2012. Social Media Use for News and Individuals' Social Capital, Civic Engagement, and Political Participation. *Journal of Computer-Mediated Communication* 17: 319–336.

Goffman, Erving. 1959. *Presentation of the Self in Everyday Life*. Garden City, NY: Doubleday.

Gutmann, Amy, and Dennis Thompson. 1996. *Democracy and Disagreement*. Cambridge, MA: Harvard University Press.

Hayes, Andrew F. 2007. Exploring Forms of Self-Censorship: On the Spiral of Silence and the Use of Opinion Expression Avoidance Strategies. *Journal of Communication* 57: 785–802.

Klofstad, Casey A., Anand Edward Sokhey, and Scott D. McClurg. 2013. Disagreeing About Disagreement: How Conflict in Social Networks Affects Political Behavior. *American Journal of Political Science* 57: 120–134.

Lang, Annie. 2000. The Limited Capacity Model of Mediated Message Processing. *Journal of Communication* 50 (1): 46–70.
Lang, Annie. 2006. Using the Limited Capacity Model of Mediated Message Processing to Design Effective Cancer Communication Messages. *Journal of Communication* 53 (S1): S57–S80.
Lang, Annie. 2009. The Limited Capacity Model of Motivated Mediated Message Processing. In *The SAGE Handbook of Mass Media Processes and Effects*, eds. Robin L. Nabi and Mary Beth Oliver, 193–204. Thousand Oaks, CA: Sage.
MacDonald, Geoff, and Mark R. Leary. 2005. Why Does Social Exclusion Hurt? The Relationship Between Social and Physical Pain. *Psychological Bulletin* 131 (2): 202–223.
Marcus, George E., W. Russell Neuman, and Michael MacKuen. 2000. *Affective Intelligence and Political Judgment*. Chicago, IL: The University of Chicago Press.
McClurg, Scott D. 2006. Political Disagreement in Context: The Conditional Effect of Neighborhood Context, Disagreement and Political Talk on Electoral Participation. *Political Behavior* 28: 349–366.
Mutz, Diana C. 2002. The Consequences of Cross-Cutting Networks for Political Participation. *American Journal of Political Science* 46 (4): 838–855.
Nabi, Robin L. 2010. The Case for Emphasizing Discrete Emotions in Communication Research. *Communication Monograph* 77 (2): 153–159. doi:10.1080/03637751003790444.
Nir, Lilach. 2005. Ambivalent Social Networks and Their Consequences for Participation. *International Journal of Public Opinion Research* 17: 422–442.
Nir, Lilach. 2011. Disagreement and Opposition in Social Networks: Does Disagreement Discourage Turnout? *Political Studies* 59: 674–692.
Noelle-Neumann, Elisabeth. 1974. The Spiral of Silence: A Theory of Public Opinion. *Journal of Communication* 24 (2): 43–51.
Noelle-Neumann, Elisabeth. 2008. Spiral of Silence. In *A First Look at Communication Theory*, ed. Em Griffin, 272–286. New York: McGraw Hill.
Nyhan, Brendan, and Jason Reifler. 2010. When Corrections Fail: The Persistence of Political Misperceptions. *Political Behavior* 30 (2): 303–330.
Oetzel, John G., and Stella Ting-Toomey. 2003. Face Concerns in Interpersonal Conflict: A Cross-Cultural Empirical Test of Face Negotiation Theory. *Communication Research* 30 (6): 599–624.
Papacharissi, Zizi. 2004. Democracy Online: Civility, Politeness, and the Democratic Potential of Online Political Discussion. *New Media and Society* 6 (2): 259–283.
Pattie, C.J., and R.J. Johnson. 2009. Conversation, Disagreement and Political Participation. *Political Behavior* 31: 261–285.

Rodriguez, Tori. 2013. Negative Emotions are Key to Well-Being. *Scientific American*, May 1. http://www.scientificamerican.com/article/negative-emotions-key-well-being/?WT.mc_id=SA_FB_MB_EG. Accessed 21 June 2016.

Rösner, Leonie, Stephan Winter, and Nicole C. Krämer. 2016. Dangerous Minds? Effects of Online Comments on Aggressive Cognitions, Emotions, and Behavior. *Computers in Human Behavior* 58: 461–470.

Schudson, Michael. 1997. Why Conversation is Not the Soul of Democracy. *Critical Studies in Mass Communication* 14: 297–309.

Stroud, Natalie J., Joshua M. Scacco, Ashley Muddiman, and Alexander L. Curry. 2015. Changing Deliberative Norms on News Organizations' Facebook Sites. *Journal of Computer-Mediated Communication* 20: 188–203.

Tsfati, Yariv, Natalie Jomini Stroud, and Adi Chotiner. 2014. Exposure to Ideological News and Perceived Opinion Climate: Testing the Media Effects Component of Spiral-of-Silence in a Fragmented Media Landscape. *The International Journal of Press/Politics* 19 (1): 3–23.

Watson, David, Lee A. Clark, and Auke Tellegen. 1988. Development and Validation of the Brief Measures of Positive and Negative Affect: The PANAS Scales. *Journal of Personality and Social Psychology* 54 (6): 1063–1070.

Williams, Kipling D., Joseph P. Forgas, and William von Hippel. 2005. *The Social Outcast*. New York: Psychology Press.

CHAPTER 7

Testing the "Defensive Effect"

The goal of this chapter is to test in a robust manner what I call the "defensive effect." This effect, explained in greater detail in Chap. 6, proposes that when people are confronted with uncivil disagreement directed at their opinion regarding a topic that is important to them, this incivility may jumpstart a chain reaction. The uncivil disagreement leads to a negative emotional experience, and then this emotional response sparks people to want to speak out politically or get politically involved to reassert their view of the world and combat the disagreeable comment. I proposed a conceptual model in the previous chapter that explains how this effect takes place. In this chapter, I statistically test that model, using three controversial topics in the news. These were the legalization of same-sex marriage in June 2015, the battle that same summer to remove the Confederate battle flag from public spaces, and the 2016 presidential campaign. These are the same topics that I used to analyze real user-generated comments on five news websites. That was deliberate. My goal was to use topics that were highly charged at the time of this writing and that relate to morally loaded issues that connect to people's core values.[1] These are the type of topics that are most likely to draw online comments,[2] especially uncivil ones.[3] These kind of topics are necessary for the "defensive effect" to occur. People cannot have an emotional response to a topic about which they care little. Three topics were used to examine whether the effect occurs in the same way across various news topics, not because I predicted specific differences.

Since I discussed each topic at length in Chap. 4, I will not repeat that in this chapter. Instead, I will first explain how I conducted an experiment to test the "defensive effect," and then I will explore the results of that experiment and how it confirmed my proposed conceptual model of this effect. Finally, I will explain how these effects increase our larger understanding of incivility and public debate.

Recruiting for the Experiment

Before I launched the experiment, I pre-tested the comments and news stories that would be used to make sure they were appropriate for the experiment. The pre-testing process is explained in detail below. All participants for both the pre-test and experiment were recruited through Amazon.com's Mechanical Turk (MTurk), an online tool to find people for small tasks. MTurk uses quota sampling with geographic and demographic variables to create a sample that has been found to be reliable for research targeting a general population and maintains an active self-selected group of respondents.[4] Samples from MTurk have been found to be more representative of the U.S. adult population than student samples, general web samples, or convenience samples.[5] Different people completed the pre-tests and the experiments, and multiple pre-tests were used so that none took more than 10 min to complete. The experiment also took about 10 min, and all participants were compensated 25 cents each. Table 7.1 shows how the participants of the experiment compared to the adult U.S. population.[6] Table 7.2 describes the pre-test participants.

Designing the Experiment

To test the "defensive effect," I created an online experiment. A total of 953 participants[7] were randomly assigned to read one of two stories about each of the three topics: the campaign, the debate over removing the Confederate battle flag from public spaces, or the legalization of same-sex marriage. The six news stories are from real news sites and edited to be roughly consistent in length. All stories were presented as from *The Associated Press*, so the credibility of the news source would not confound results. Three topics were used to assess whether the defensive effect consistently operates across different issues, and not because differences were predicted between issues. Two stories for each topic were used to ensure that any effects I found were not an artifact of a particular story.

Table 7.1 Demographic descriptions of the 953 experiment participants compared to the U.S. population

	Experiment participants (%)	*Adult U.S. population (%)*
Age		
18 to 24 years old	12.4	13.0
25 to 44 years old	39.2	35.0
45 to 64 years old	33.7	35.0
65 or older	14.7	17.0
Race		
White	79.4	63.7
Black/African American	7.5	12.2
Latino/Latina/Hispanic	5.1	16.3
Asian/Pacific Islander	3.1	4.85
Native American	0.9	0.7
Other/Multi-racial	2.7	2.1
No response	1.2	0.0
Gender		
Male	45.3	49.2
Female	54.7	50.8
Political affiliation		
Democrats	38.9	32
Republicans	26	27
Independents	35.1	40

Data for adult U.S. population are based on 2010 U.S. Census and 2016 Gallup Poll
Some percentages do not total exactly 100% because of rounding

Once people read their story, they were prompted to think deeply about the topic and post a comment that expressed their own opinion on the topic. Then they answered questions about their age, gender, race, and personality to provide a delay for hypothetical commenters to respond to their comments. After the delay, the participants returned to the news story to see if anyone had commented. The experiment was designed so that it appeared to the participants that other people were commenting in real time, although the comments were actually created in advance as explained below. A third of the participants received a response to their comments that disagreed with them uncivilly; a third read a comment that disagreed with them civilly; and a third received no comments in response.[8] The no-comment condition was essentially the control condition. After participants read the responses, they answered a series of questions used to test

Table 7.2 Demographic descriptions of the 205 pre-test experiment participants

	N	Age		Gender	Race
		Mean	SD	(Males) (%)	
Pre-test 1: rating comments	74	35.88	11.65	54.1	75.7% White 8.1% Black/African American 8.1% Latino/Latina/Hispanic 6.8% Other/Multi-Racial 1.4% Asian
Pre-test 2: rating comments	20	36.30	12.09	60.0	75.0% White 15.0% Black/African American 10.0% Latino/Latina/Hispanic
Pre-test 3: rating comments	11	34.27	9.57	45.5	54.5% White 18.2% Black/African American 9.1% Asian 9.1% Native American 9.1% Prefer Not to Respond
Pre-test 4: rating news stories	101	41.14	14.41	41.6	83.2% White 8.9% Asian 3.0% Latino/Latina/Hispanic 2.0% Black/African American 2.0% Other/Multi-racial 1.0% Native American

the specific hypotheses explained in Chap. 6. The questions are explored in detail later in this chapter.

Creating the Comments

The comments were the experimental stimuli—the drug of the experiment, if you will. So it was important that the comments be realistic and that they reflected the two experimental conditions—uncivil disagreement and civil disagreement. For example, the uncivil comment had to exhibit the attributes of incivility, specifically: profanity, name-calling, and the use of words in all capital letters to signify yelling online.[9] The ones that depicted civil disagreement had to be free from these attributes of incivility. Both sets of comments had to express disagreement with the experiment participants' view. Because it would be unwieldy to create comments on the fly that exhibited all of these attributes and still made sense, all comments were created in advance and pre-tested. However, the comments exhibited uncivil and civil disagreement in a general enough way that they would seem to be realistic responses, regardless of what the experimental participant actually wrote. It was important that the comments disagreed with the person's view, not the article itself, so the comments did not express a stance on the particular issue. In fact, the same comments were used regardless of the story topic that the experimental participants were assigned to read and comment about. This ensured that no other differences besides tone were exerting effects. It is also worth noting that these same comments were used successfully in four previous experiments I conducted,[10] adding to my confidence that they were accurately depicting the civil and uncivil disagreement being tested in this experiment.

To create the comments, I followed procedures from other studies.[11] I started with dozens of real comments that four undergraduate students had culled from a variety of news websites. Then, I edited the comments so they would be consistent in length and include attributes of incivility. Characters were added into profanity in place of letters (e.g. F&CK) to mimic the way online commenters try to get around profanity filters on websites. All comments used screen names that did not convey gender or race, so these factors would not confuse results. Comments all had the same avatar, designed to mimic the default avatars content-management systems use for people who have not uploaded their own photographs. Then I conducted a series of pre-tests, where people rated the comments on 17 different attributes, such as "rude," "impolite," and "hostile,"[12] used in other studies to see if the comments reflected the two categories: uncivil disagreement and civil disagreement. Based on these ratings, I selected the comments that scored the highest for incivility as the uncivil comments, and those that scored the lowest as the civil comments. This process resulted in three comments for each group. Table 7.3 shows the comments. Pre-test participants rated the news stories for bias,[13] and results showed that they viewed all stories as unbiased. This was important because I did not want perceived bias in the stories to influence how people viewed the comments.

Table 7.3 Comments used in the experiment

	Cronbach's alpha	Mean	Standard deviation
Uncivil disagreement comments			
GOD D&MN are you really so fucking stupid? Obviously can't come up with something better.	0.93	6.35	0.83
Aw look at the little baby crying. How about you SHUT THE F&CK UP.	0.87	6.08	0.91
Do ALL of us a favor and step into traffic. We don't need stupid f&cking people like you around.	0.93	6.40	0.76
Civil disagreement comments			
Thanks for sharing your opinion, but it doesn't persuade me to change my mind.	0.96	3.38	1.23
It's great to hear a different viewpoint—but I don't share your opinion.	0.95	2.47	0.93
I respectfully disagree with you, but I will give your ideas some thought.	0.76	2.00	0.47

Means, standard deviations, and Cronbach's alphas refer to an index of 17 measures that were averaged together for each comment on a 1 to 7 scale, with 7 indicating greater incivility

A series of t tests found that means for the indices for the uncivil disagreement comments were significantly different from the means for the indices for the civil disagreement comments at $p < 0.05$

WHAT QUESTIONS WERE ASKED

Emotional Responses

One of the key issues I was interested in was what type of emotional response incivility produced. So I asked participants to rate how well a series of adjectives described their own feelings immediately after they received the uncivil, civil, or no response to their initial comment on the news stories. This was done to gauge their emotional state. Adjectives that described negative emotions included "angry," "irritable," and "annoyed." Positive adjectives included "excited," "joyful," and "alert."[14]

Intention to Get Politically Engaged

The outcome of the "defensive effect" is that people will express an interest in getting politically engaged. So after I asked participants about their emotional responses to the comments they received (or no comments in the control), I identified 17 possible actions of political engagement drawn from earlier studies[15] to see how likely they were to want to do them. Activities included "forwarding an email," "sharing content on social media," or "trying to persuade others to one's view."[16] Each statement was phrased as if it related specifically to the topic of the news story the person read. For example, people who read a story about the campaign were asked how likely they were to perform these actions regarding their opinion on the campaign. Similarly, people who read one of the same-sex marriage stories were asked about their likelihood to perform these actions regarding their viewpoints on this issue.

Control Variables

All three topics in the news that were the focus of this study—same-sex marriage, the debate over removing the Confederate battle flag from public spaces, and the campaign—have clear partisan sides. In addition, people's pre-existing attitudes toward the topics of the story might influence results. As a result, I controlled for each of these factors in statistical analyses. Participants were asked to rate their support or opposition to same-sex marriage and to removing the Confederate flag from public spaces,[17] and also to indicate their political beliefs on a 7-item scale where 1 was *most conservative* and 7 was *most liberal*.[18] These ratings were used in all analyses as controls.

Manipulation Check

After participants answered all the study questions, I asked them to rate whether the comments posted in response to their comments were civil or uncivil.[19] This was done to make sure that they had noticed the differences in comments that form the stimuli for the experiment. Results showed that the manipulation was effective.[20] People who received the uncivil comments were significantly more likely to rate them as uncivil than those who received the civil comments.

TESTING THE "DEFENSIVE EFFECT"

Before conducting specific hypothesis tests, I examined whether any of the variables were inter-related with each other. Results showed that people exposed to uncivil comments were more likely to exhibit negative

Table 7.4 Correlations between all variables

	Negative emotion	Positive emotion	Intention to get politically engaged	Gender	Age	Political beliefs
Exposure to uncivil comments	0.12**	−0.03	−0.07*	0.00	0.00	−0.02
Exposure to civil comments	−0.03	0.00	0.03	−0.02	−0.01	0.04
Negative emotion		−0.03	0.25**	0.08*	−0.25**	0.25**
Positive emotion			0.30**	−0.05	0.13**	−0.08*
Intention to get politically engaged				0.03	−0.14**	0.12**
Gender					0.08*	0.07*
Age						−0.07*
Political beliefs						

Pearson's r correlation coefficients are shown. Statistically significant correlations are indicated with asterisks
*** $p < 0.001$; ** $p < 0.01$; * $p < 0.05$

emotion, and were less likely to express an intention to engage politically. In contrast, civil comments showed no significant relationships with any of the variables. Compared to older people, younger people were less likely to feel negative emotion or want to be politically engaged. Women were more likely than men to be liberals, but men were more likely to feel positive emotions. People who exhibited both positive and negative emotions were more likely to report an intention to be engaged politically. Democrats or liberals were more likely to exhibit negative feelings, but conservatives and Republican were less likely to report positive emotions. Table 7.4 shows these correlations.

Effects of Incivility

My first hypothesis predicted that when people were exposed to uncivil comments, they would feel an increase in negative emotion and a decrease in positive emotion. This is the first part of the "defensive effect." Results[21] showed that incivility caused people to feel more negative emotion, but it had no effect on positive emotion. Therefore, H1 was partially supported. Those exposed to incivility scored on average 2.14[22] on the 1 to 7 negative emotion scale, where 7 indicates greater negative emotion. This was significantly more negative emotion than recorded by those exposed to civil responses (average of 1.83) or those exposed to no responses (average of 1.94). The emotional response is small, which is unsurprising. Since the incivility is a brief affront from strangers, it would be unlikely to spike emotions wildly. People's feelings toward same-sex marriage and their political beliefs also played a role. Those who oppose same-sex marriage exhibited more negative emotion than those who support it, and Democrats and liberals felt greater negative feelings than conservatives and Republicans.[23] Similarly, those who oppose same-sex marriage exhibited greater positive emotion.[24] My second hypothesis[25] proposed that emotional experiences—either positive of negative—would make people more likely to express an intention to get politically involved. That's exactly what happened. If people had an emotional response, regardless of whether it was positive or negative, they were likely to report wanting to express themselves politically. Results suggested that the experience of heightened emotions in general produced this effect, regardless of whether they received responses that uncivilly or civilly disagreed with them. Table 7.5 shows the results.

My third and fourth hypotheses predicted that uncivil disagreement had a different effect on intention to participate politically, depending on whether the incivility increased the person's negative emotion. If people were challenged uncivilly, but that incivility did not spike their negative emotion, then incivility produced a chilling effect on any intention to participate politically. In other words, people who were confronted with disagreement in a nasty way but who did not get upset by it, were less likely to want to speak or act politically. In fact, in that case, incivility had a silencing effect. But if the incivility boosted their negative emotional response, this triggered a chain reaction called the "defensive effect" that made them more likely to express an intention to engage politically. In essence, the negative emotional response was needed for incivility to increase intention to get politically engaged in a process called mediation.[26] In all cases, this occurred only for uncivil disagreement. Being disagreed with civilly did not upset people or cause them to be more or less likely to want to get politically engaged. In essence, these findings showed that the incivility—not the disagreement by itself—is what sparks negative emotion

Table 7.5 Unstandardized OLS path analysis coefficients for direct effects of uncivil and civil disagreement

	Mediators				Outcome variable	
	Negative emotion		Positive emotion		Political participation	
	Coeff.	SE	Coeff.	SE	Coeff.	SE
Uncivil condition[a]						
Uncivil disagreement comments	0.34**	0.10	−0.10	0.11	−0.31**	0.11
Negative emotion					0.32***	0.04
Positive emotion					0.33***	0.03
Controls						
Civil disagreement comments	0.11	0.10	−0.02	0.11	−0.04	0.11
Political beliefs	0.08**	0.03	−0.04	0.04	0.15***	0.03
Attitude toward same-sex marriage	0.05*	0.02	0.07**	0.02	0.01	0.02
Attitude toward removing Confederate flag	0.04	0.02	−0.01	0.02	0.01	0.02
	$R^2 = 0.03$		$R^2 = 0.02$		$R^2 = 0.19$	
	$F(5, 934)$ = 4.83***		$F(5, 934)$ = 3.13**		$F(7, 932)$ = 30.43***	
Civil condition[a]						
Civil disagreement comments	0.11	0.11	−0.02	0.11	−0.04	0.11
Negative emotion					0.32***	0.04
Positive emotion					0.33***	0.03
Controls						
Uncivil disagreement comments	0.34***	0.10	−0.10	0.11	−0.31**	0.11
Political beliefs	0.08**	0.03	−0.04	0.04	0.15***	0.03
Attitude toward same-sex marriage	0.05	0.02	0.07**	0.02	0.01	0.02
Attitude toward removing Confederate flag	0.03	0.02	−0.02	0.02	0.01	0.02
	$R^2 = 0.03$		$R^2 = 0.02$		$R^2 = 0.19$	
	$F(5, 934)$ = 4.83***		$F(5, 934)$ = 3.13		$F(7, 932)$ = 30.43***	

[a]Experimental conditions were dichotomously coded, so coefficients can be interpreted compared to the control group
Coeff = Unstandardized regression coefficient derived from PROCESS model 4. *SE* = standard error
*$p < 0.05$ **$p < 0.01$ ***$p < 0.001$

and jumpstarts the defensive effect. Figures 7.1 and 7.2 show this. It is important to note, as well, that in all these results, no significant differences were found based on the topic of the news story or the version of the news story. This suggests the "defensive effect" is issues, not the artifact of a particular topic or news story.

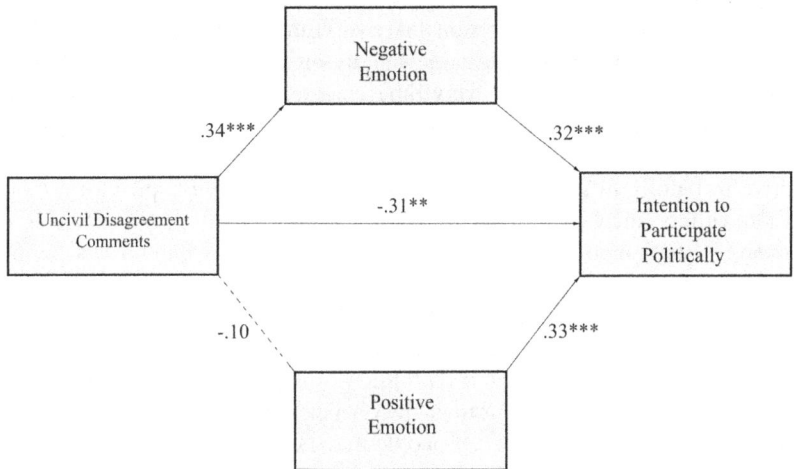

Fig. 7.1 Direct effects of "defensive effect" model
Unstandardized ordinary least squares path analysis coefficients are shown. Asterisks indicate statistically significant paths (***$p < 0.001$; **$p < 0.01$). The dashed line represents a non-significant path. The statistical model included attitude toward same-sex marriage, attitude toward removing the Confederate flag from public spaces, and political beliefs as controls. They are not pictured in the interest of parsimony.

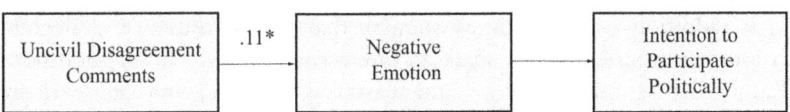

Fig. 7.2 Indirect effect of "defensive effect" model
An unstandardized ordinary least square path analysis coefficient is shown. Mediation was tested using 5,000 bias-corrected bootstrap samples, which indicated a significant mediation effect at $p < 0.05$. The statistical model included attitude toward same-sex marriage, attitude toward removing the Confederate flag from public spaces, and political beliefs as controls. They are not pictured in the interest of parsimony.

What This All Means

These findings offer two additions to our understanding of how incivility influences political participation. First, uncivil and civil disagreement have markedly different effects on people. People do not like it when others disagree with them. Disagreement may lead to cognitive dissonance[27] or even anger or aggression.[28] Disagreement may annoy us, but most of us can handle it, as long as it remains civil. But when disagreement turns uncivil, marked by profanity, name-calling, insults, and words in all capital letters to indicate yelling,[29] everything changes. Uncivil disagreement has the power to diminish interest in getting politically involved, perhaps for fear that others will attack. Like early human ancestors who felt a strong drive to belong in groups,[30] people may feel they cannot speak or act out when others uncivilly disagree with them. The fear of being isolated is so strong[31] that people stay quiet. However, if the incivility upsets people enough, they lose that fear. The emotional responses are momentarily strong enough, that they disinhibit people. The result is people want to speak or act on their political beliefs. Part of the explanation for this may be that people—when confronted with uncivil disagreement—want to set the record straight by reasserting their own beliefs, and, in so doing, neutralize the threat to those beliefs.[32] Or people may be acting impulsively, without thinking, driven by emotions. Another explanation is that expressing intention to get politically involved is a coping mechanism to deal with the uncertainty and discomfort of negative feelings.[33] It is vital to understand that this does not suggest that incivility is an asset because it may foment interest in political participation. These findings certainly should not be interpreted as support for incivility. Instead, I suggest that these findings help us understand how incivility influences people, so, perhaps, we can take steps to quell the nasty talk. It is hard to stop something unless we understand the cause.

In addition, these findings suggest that both positive and negative emotional experiences can spark an interest in politics. This is good news. Rather than seeing emotions and reason as separate, mutually exclusive aspects of the human experiences, these results suggest overlap. An emotional response may drive us or move us to become involved politically, when, hopefully, our more rational side takes over. These findings point to a balance between emotional and rational states and suggest that good (discussion and debate) can come from bad (incivility). Finally, these findings suggest strongly that the defensive effect is robust. I had previously tested it regarding abortion, gun control, and climate change.[34] These results showed it applies equally well to same-sex marriage, the debate over the Confederate flag, or the campaign. This is important because it shows this effect is not a quirk that happens only with one topic. Instead, this offered evidence of a broader understanding of how communication processes relate to how people behave.

In summary, these findings strongly showed that emotions are intrinsic to our political experience. Either positive or negative, emotions move us. They may help us examine key issues in a more nuanced way than reason alone can do. When emotions are negative, they stir people to act to remove the unpleasantness and regain their "affective balance."[35] As people read and respond to online comments, this process likely happens over and over. They feel an emotional response, good or bad, and it shapes how they respond, and, in some case, sparks them to act. This offers hope for the potential of online comments to be deliberative, open to various voices, rational, and to be supported by evidence.[36] Even amid the incivility of these comments, people were invigorated to get politically involved.

Classroom Discussion Prompts

1. Considering the way the defensive effect operates, can incivility ever be considered a good thing? Defend your answer.
2. This chapter tests the defensive effect on three topics. Name them and explain why these topics were used.
3. Think of some other topics in the news and propose whether the defensive effect may work with them. Explain your answer.
4. Is it better to have less political participation and more peaceful exchanges or more political participation but less peaceful exchanges? Defend your answer.

Notes

1. Elmie Nekmat and William J. Gonzebach, "Multiple Opinion Climates in Online Forums: Role of Website Source References and Within-Forum Opinion Congruency," *Journalism & Mass Communication Quarterly* 90, no. 4 (2013), 736–656; Amy Gutmann and Dennis Thompson, *Democracy*

and Disagreement, (Cambridge, MA: Harvard University Press, 1996) (Nekmat and Gonzebach 2013; Gutmann and Thompson 1996).
2. Ori Tenenboim and Akiba A. Cohen, "What Prompts Users to Click and Comment: A Longitudinal Study of Online News," *Journalism* 16, no. 2 (2015): 198–217; Patrick Weber, "Discussions in the Comment Sections: Factors Influencing Participation and Interactivity in Online Newspapers' Reader Comments," *New Media & Society* 10, no. 6 (2013): 941–957; Natalie J. Stroud, Joshua M. Scacco, Ashley Muddiman, and Alexander L. Curry, "Changing Deliberative Norms on News Organizations' Facebook Sites," *Journal of Computer-Mediated Communication* 20 (2015): 188–203 (Tenenboim and Cohen 2015; Weber 2013; Stroud et al. 2015).
3. Mustafa Oz, Pei Zheng, and Gina Masullo Chen, *Social Media, Politeness and Discussion Quality*, presented to the World Association for Public Opinion Research Annual Conference in Austin, TX, April 2016 (Oz et al. 2016).
4. Gabriele Paolacci, Jesse Chandler, Panagiotis G. Ipeirotis, "Running Experiments on Amazon Mechanical Turk," *Judgment and Decision Making* 5, no. 5 (2010): 411–419 (Paolacci et al. 2010).
5. D. Jasun Carr, Matthew Barnidge, Byung Gu Lee, and Stephanie Jean Tsang, "Cynics and Skeptics: Evaluating the Credibility of Mainstream and Citizen Journalism," *Journalism & Mass Communication Quarterly* 9, no. 3 (2014): 452–470; Adam J. Berinsky, Gregory A. Huber, and Gabriel S. Lenz, "Evaluating Online Labor Markets for Experimental Research: Amazon.com's Mechanical Turk," *Political Analysis* 20, no. 3 (2012): 351–368 (Carr et al. 2014; Berinsky et al. 2012).
6. Age, gender, and race percentages on Table 7.1 for the adult U.S. population are taken from the 2010 U.S. Census. Political affiliation percentages for the U.S. population are from the September 2016 Gallup Poll, accessed on October 2, 2016 at: http://www.gallup.com/poll/15370/party-affiliation.aspx. Racial breakdowns for the adult U.S. population came from the U.S. Census and National Population Estimates, as disseminated by InfoPlease, accessed on October 2, 2016 at: http://www.infoplease.com/ipa/A0762156.html.
7. The Institutional Review Board at The University of Texas at Austin approved the project on January 19, 2016.
8. This resulted in a 3 (news topic: same-sex marriage, confederate flag, campaign) by 3 (tone: uncivil, civil, control) by 2 (story version: story 1, story 2) multi-factorial design with all between-subjects variables. Of the total sample, 325 read and commented about the Confederate flag, 299 read and commented about the campaign, and 329 read and comments about same-sex marriage. In regard to tone, 318 participants were exposed

to uncivil disagreement, 316 to civil disagreement, and 319 to the no-comment control. For each topic, 471 participants got the first version of the story, and 482 received the second version of the story.
9. Kevin Coe, Kate Kenski, and Stephen A. Rains, "Online and Uncivil? Patterns and Determinants of Incivility in Newspaper Website Comments," *Journal of Communication* 64 (2014): 658–679; Erika Darics, "Politeness in Computer-Mediated Discourse of a Virtual Team," *Journal of Politeness Research* 6, no. 1 (2010): 129–150; Zizi Papacharissi, "Democracy Online: Civility, Politeness, and Democratic Potential of Online Political Discussion," *New Media & Society* 6, no. 2 (2004): 259–283 (Coe et al. 2014; Darics 2010; Papacharissi 2004).
10. Gina Masullo Chen and Shuning Lu, "Online Political Discourse: Exploring Differences in Effects of Civil and Uncivil Disagreement in News Website Comments," *Journal of Broadcasting & Electronic Media* 61, no. 1 (2017). doi:10.1080/08838151/2016/1273922; Gina Masullo Chen, *Nasty News Story Comments Indirectly Increase Intention to Participate Politically for Women, Mediated Through Negative Affect*, presented to the Mass Communication Division of the Southern States Communication Association at its annual conference in Austin, TX, in April 2016; Gina Masullo Chen and Pei Zheng, *Online Public Discourse: Exploring Differences in Responses to Civil and Uncivil Disagreement in News Story Comments*, presented to the Mass Communication and Society Division of the Association for Education in Journalism and Mass Communication at its annual conference in Minneapolis, MN, in August, 2016; Gina Masullo Chen and Pei Zheng, *The "Defensive Effect": Uncivil Comments Directly Increase Intention to Participate Politically, Through Negative Affect*, presented to the Mass Communication Division of the International Communication Association at its annual conference in Fukuoka, Japan, in June 2016 (Chen 2016; Chen and Lu 2017; Chen and Zheng 2016a, b).
11. Gina Masullo Chen, "Losing *Face* on Social Media: Threats to *Positive Face* lead to an Indirect Effect on Retaliatory Aggression Through Negative Affect," *Communication Research* 42, no. 6 (2015): 819–838; Arthur C. Graesser, *Prose Comprehension Beyond the Word*, (New York, NY: Springer-Verlag, 1981); Michael A. Shapiro and T. Makana Chock, "Media Dependency and Perceived Reality of Fiction and News," *Journal of Broadcasting & Electronic Media* 8, no. 1 (2004): 675–695 (Chen 2015; Graesser 1981; Shapiro and Chock 2004).
12. Pre-test participants rated the comments on 17 adjectives drawn from the *Positive Face* Threat Scale from William R. Cupach and Christine L. Carson, "Characteristics and Consequences of Interpersonal Complaints Associated with Perceived Face Threat," *Journal of Social and Personal Relationships* 19, no. 4 (2002): 443–462. Using a 1 (*does not describe this*

comment at all) to 7 (*describes this comment extremely well*) scale, pre-test participants rated each comment for the following attributes: *uncivil, negative, not supportive, disagreement, impolite, rude, insensitive, hostile, would show contempt for a person receiving it, would damage a relationship between two people,* and *would make a person look badly to others.* They also rated whether each comment was *civil, positive, supportive, tactful, justified, not disagreement, polite,* and *would not bother someone at all.* These items were reverse coded so that a higher number indicated a greater incivility. Ratings were averaged into indices, and those with the highest means were used as uncivil comments, and those with the lowest means were civil comments. Cronbach's α's for the indices for all comments ranged from 0.76 to 0.96, showing high or acceptable reliability. Uncivil comments had means that ranged from 6.08 to 6.40, showing they were perceived as threats to *face*. Civil comments' means ranged from 2.00 to 3.38, showing they were not perceived as threats to *face*. A series of t tests found that means for the indices for the uncivil disagreement comments were significantly different from the means for the indices for the civil disagreement comments at $p < 0.05$. No significant differences between means were found within conditions, suggesting comments in each condition were perceived equally (Cupach and Carson 2002).

13. To do this, pre-test participants rated each story on a 1 (*biased toward one side on the top*) to 7 (*biased toward the other side on the topic*) scale. Means for the stories ranged from 3.88 to 4.37, indicating respondents viewed the stories as unbiased. Paired t tests showed the scores for each story were not significantly different at $p < 0.05$, suggesting they were suitable for use in the experiment.

14. Adjectives were drawn from the Positive Affect Negative Affect Scale (PANAS) by David Watson, Lee A. Clark, and Auke Tellegen, "Development and Validation of the Brief Measures of Positive and Negative Affect: The PANAS Scales," *Journal of Personality and Social Psychology* 54, no. 6 (1988): 1063–1070. Experiment subjects rated on 1 (*not at all*) to 7 (*extremely*) scale how much the following emotions described how they felt at the very moment. The positive adjectives were: *excited, strong, interested, enthusiastic, elated, alert, inspired, determined, joyful,* and *active.* The negative emotions were: *upset, guilty, jittery, ashamed, depressed, angry, irritable, annoyed, distressed,* and *hostile.* Items were each averaged into two indices with high reliability (negative affect: $M = 1.98$, $SD = 1.21$, Cronbach's $\alpha = 0.94$; positive affect: $M = 4.09$, $SD = 1.42$, Cronbach's $\alpha = 0.93$) (Watson et al. 1988).

15. Porismita Borah, "Does it Matter Where Your Read the News Story?" *Communication Research* 41, no: 6(2014): 809–827; Homero Gil de Zúñiga, Nakwon Jung, Sebastián Valenzuela, "Social Media Use for News

and Individuals' Social Capital, Civic Engagement, and Political Participation," *Journal of Computer-Mediated Communication* 17 (2012): 319–336 (Borach 2014; Gil de Zúñiga et al. 2012).
16. Subjects rated on a 1 (*not at all likely*) to 7 (*extremely likely*) scale how likely they were to perform 17 actions of political participation in support of their views on the issue they commented on during the experiment. The items were: contacting a news organization; forwarding an email; circulating an online petition; joining or liking a Facebook group; sharing one's opinion in a letter to an editor; attending a public meeting; participating in a rally; posting a bumper sticker or yard sign; posting a message on social media; sharing, favoriting, or liking a message on social media; following a social media account; engaging in community problem-solving; donating money; persuading others to one's viewpoint; reading or watching a news report; sharing or liking a video; or changing one's profile to support the issue. I then conducted an exploratory principal component analysis (PCA) to determine how the statements loaded into factors with my data. Before conducting the PCA, I checked that data were suitable for performing this analysis, using Bartlett's test of sphericity, as recommended by M.S. Bartlett, "A Note on Multiplying Factors for Various Chi-Square Approximations," *Journal of the Royal Statistical Society, Series B (Methodological)* 16, no. 2 (1954): 296–289. The result of the test was significant, so the data were appropriate for PCA, $X^2 = 5972.92$, df = 55, $p < 0.001$. I also performed a Kaiser-Meyer-Olkin (KMO) test, which evaluates sampling adequacy, as recommended by Henry F. Kaiser, "A Second Generation Little Jiffy," *Psychometrika* 35, no. 4 (1970): 401–415. The test achieved an excellent value of 0.94, so it was valid to perform the PCA on these data. To determine factors, I used the traditional method for figuring out the number of factors, relying on components with eigenvalues greater than 1. I also generated a scree plot test, as recommended in Raymond B. Cattell, "The Scree Test for the Number of Factors," *Multivariate Behavioral Research* 1, no. 2 (1966): 245–276. Both methods suggested one factor that explained 59.98% of variance. Items were then averaged into an index with high reliability, ($M = 3.29$, $SD = 1.48$, Cronbach's $\alpha = 0.92$) (Bartlett 1954; Kaiser 1970 and Cattell 1966).
17. Participants rated on a 1 (*strongly disagree*) to 7 (*strongly agree*) scale whether they opposed same-sex marriage ($M = 2.92$, $SD = 2.32$) or were opposed to removing the Confederate flag from public spaces ($M = 3.34$, $SD = 2.23$). Both questions were used as statistical controls in analyses.
18. Participants rated their beliefs on a 1 (*strongly conservative*) to 7 (*strongly liberal*) scale and on a 1 (*strongly Republican*) to 7 (*strongly Democrat*) scale. Responses were strongly correlated, $r = 0.73$, $p < 0.001$. They were averaged together into an index with acceptable reliability, ($M = 4.26$,

SD = 1.52, Cronbach's α = 0.84). This measure was used as a control in all analyses.
19. This manipulation question came after the dependent variable questions and was embedded in unrelated questions, so it would not effect changes in the dependent variables.
20. This was tested by asking participants to rate how civil the comments were on a 1 to 7 scale, where a 7 would mean the comment was most civil. Results were analyzed using a one-way ANOVA with condition (civil versus uncivil) as the independent variable. Those in the control condition did not answer this question because they did not receive any comments. The manipulation was effective, $F(1, 527) = 1441.09$, $p < 0.001$, $\eta^2 = 0.73$. Subjects in the civil condition ($M = 5.80$, $SE = 0.08$) rated the comments posted in response to their comments as significantly more civil than those in the uncivil condition ($M = 1.40$, $SE = 0.08$).
21. These were tested using two multi-factorial between-subjects ANOVAs with a 3 (tone of comments: civil, uncivil, no comments) by 3 (topic: campaign, same-sex marriage, Confederate flag) by 2 (story version: one or two) design. Negative emotion was the dependent variable for one model, and positive emotion was for the other. Both models included political beliefs, attitude toward same-sex marriage, and attitude toward removing the Confederate flag as covariates. In addition, I tested interactions between tone of comments and the topic and between version of the story and topic, but neither produced significant results, so they were removed from the model. For negative emotion, condition showed a significant main effect, $F(2, 950) = 6.80$, $p = 0.01$, $\eta^2 = 0.01$. For positive emotion, no main effect was found, $F(2, 950) = 0.40$, $p = 0.16$, $\eta^2 = 0.001$.
22. Those exposed to uncivil responses reported significantly more negative emotion ($M = 2.18$, $SE = 0.07$) than those exposed to civil responses ($M = 1.94$, $SE = 0.07$, $p = 0.04$) and to those in the no-response control ($M = 1.83$, $SE = 0.07$, $p = 0.001$).
23. For negative emotion, opposition toward same-sex marriage produced a significant main effect, $F(2, 950) = 4.75$, $p = 0.03$, $\eta^2 = 0.005$, as did political beliefs, $F(2, 950) = 6.39$, $p = 0.01$, $\eta^2 = 0.01$.
24. For positive emotion, opposition toward same-sex marriage produced a significant main effect, $F(2, 950) = 7.41$, $p = 0.01$, $\eta^2 = 0.01$.
25. Hypotheses 2, 3, and 4 were tested using PROCESS, a mediation and moderation modeling tool that estimates direct and indirect effects using ordinary least squares (OLS) path analysis and a bootstrapping technique. PROCESS was developed by Andrew F. Hayes, *Introduction to Mediation, Moderation, and Conditional Process Analysis*, (New York, NY: Guilford, 2013). This analysis technique required that each experimental condition be analyzed as a separate variable that compares it to the control, following

the recommendation of Andrew F. Hayes and Kristopher J. Preacher, "Statistical Mediation Analysis with a Multi-categorical Independent Variable," *British Journal of Mathematical and Statistical Psychology* 67, no. 3 (2014): 451–470. Therefore, separate PROCESS 4 models were run with incivility and civility as predictors, and negative and positive emotion as a mediators, and intention to participate politically as an outcome variable. Attitude toward same-sex marriage, attitude toward removing the Confederate flag from public space, and political beliefs were used as covariates. In each model, civility or incivility were included as covariates when that condition was not the predictor (Hayes 2013; Hayes and Preacher 2014).

26. Mediation was tested using 5,000 bias-corrected bootstrapping confidence intervals, which provides a reliable test of whether mediation occurred, according to Hayes, *Introduction to Mediation, Moderation, and Conditional Process Analysis*. Bootstrapping involves resampling the original data thousands of times and calculating the indirect effect of each sample to create a sampling distribution. The distribution is used to create a confidence interval for each effect, and a confidence interval that does not include zero indicates the presence of a statistically significant effect.

27. Leon Festinger, *A Theory of Cognitive Dissonance*, (Palo Alto, CA: Stanford University Press, 1957) (Festinger 1957).

28. Chen and Lu, "Online Political Discourse: Exploring Differences in Effects of Civil and Uncivil Disagreement in News Website Comments"; George E. Marcus, W. Russell Neuman, and Michael MacKuen, *Affective Intelligence and Political Judgment*, (Chicago, IL: University of Chicago Press, 2000); Bryan M. Parsons, "Social Networks and the Affective Impact of Political Disagreement," *Political Behavior* 32, no. 2 (2010): 181–204; Jeanne M. Brett, Mara Olekains, Ray Friedman, Nathan Goates, Cameron Anderson, and Cara Cherry Lisco, "Sticks and Stones: Language, Face, and Online Dispute Resolution," *Academy of Management Journal* 50, no. 1 (2007): 85–99 (Marcus et al. 2000; Parsons 2010; Brett et al. 2007).

29. Coe et al., "Online and Uncivil? Patterns and Determinants of Incivility in Newspaper Website Comments"; Darics, "Politeness in Computer-Mediated Discourse of a Virtual Team"; Papacharissi, "Democracy Online: Civility, Politeness, and Democratic Potential of Online Political Discussion."

30. Roy F. Baumeister and Mark F. Leary, "The Need to Belong: Desire for Interpersonal Attachments as a Fundamental Human Need," *Psychological Bulletin* 117, no. 3 (1995): 497–529 (Baumeister and Leary 1995).

31. Andrew F. Hayes, "Exploring Forms of Self-Censorship: On the Spiral of Silence and the Use of Opinion Expression Avoidance Strategies," *Journal*

of Communication 57 (2007): 785–802; Elisabeth Noelle-Neumann, "Spiral of Silence." In *A First Look at Communication Theory*, eds. Em Griffin, (New York, NY: McGraw Hill, 2008): 272–286; Bryan M. Parsons, "Social Networks and the Affective Impact of Political Agreement," *Political Behavior* 32, no. 2 (2010): 181–204 (Hayes 2007; Noelle-Neumann 2008).
32. Brett et al., "Sticks and Stones: Language, Face, and Online Dispute Resolution."
33. Bethany Albertson and Shauna Kushner Gadarian, *Anxious Politics: Democratic Citizenship in a Threatening World*, (New York, NY: Cambridge University Press, 2015) (Albertson and Gadarian 2015).
34. Chen and Lu, "Online Political Discourse: Exploring Differences in Effects of Civil and Uncivil Disagreement in News Website Comments"; Chen, *Nasty News Story Comments Indirectly Increase Intention to Participate Politically for Women, Mediated Through Negative Affect*; Chen and Zheng, "*Online Public Discourse: Exploring Differences in Responses to Civil and Uncivil Disagreement in News Story Comments*"; Chen and Zheng, *The "Defensive Effect": Uncivil Comments Directly Increase Intention to Participate Politically, Through Negative Affect*.
35. Albertson and Gadarian, *Anxious Politics: Democratic Citizenship in a Threatening World*, p. xxi.
36. Amy Gutmann and Dennis Thompson, *Democracy and Disagreement*, (Cambridge, MA: Harvard University Press, 1996); James S. Fishkin, *Democracy and Deliberation*, (New Haven, CT: Yale University Press, 1991); Lawrence R. Jacobs, Fay Lomax Cook, and Michael X. Delli Carpini, *Talking Together: Public Deliberation and Political Participation in America*, (Chicago, IL: University of Chicago Press, 2009) (Fishkin 1991; Jacobs et al. 2009).

REFERENCES

Albertson, Bethany, and Shauna Kushner Gadarian. 2015. *Anxious Politics: Democratic Citizenship in a Threatening World*. New York: Cambridge University Press.

Bartlett, M.S. 1954. A Note on Multiplying Factors for Various Chi-Square Approximations. *Journal of the Royal Statistical Society, Series B (Methodological)* 16 (2): 296–289.

Baumeister, Roy F., and Mark R. Leary. 1995. The Need to Belong: Desire for Interpersonal Attachments as a Fundamental Human Need. *Psychological Bulletin* 117 (3): 497–529.

Berinsky, A.J., Gregory A. Huber, and Gabriel S. Lenz. 2012. Evaluating Online Labor Markets for Experimental Research: Amazon.com's Mechanical Turk. *Political Analysis* 20 (3): 351–368.

Borah, Porismita. 2014. Does it Matter Where You Read the News Story? Interaction of Incivility and News Frames in the Political Blogosphere. *Communication Research* 41 (6): 809–827.

Brett, Jeanne M., Mara Olekains, Ray Friedman, Nathan Goates, Cameron Anderson, and Cara Cherry Lisco. 2007. Sticks and Stones: Language, Face, and Online Dispute Resolution. *Academy of Management Journal* 50 (1): 85–99.

Carr, D.Jasun, Matthew Barnidge, Byung Gu Lee, and Stephanie Jean Tsang. 2014. Cynics and Skeptics: Evaluating the Credibility of Mainstream and Citizen Journalism. *Journalism & Mass Communication Quarterly* 9 (3): 452–470.

Cattell, Raymond B. 1966. The Scree Test of the Number of Factors. *Multivariate Behavioral Research* 1 (2): 245–276.

Chen, Gina Masullo. 2015. Losing *Face* on Social Media: Threats to *Positive Face* Lead to an Indirect Effect on Retaliatory Aggression Through Negative Affect. *Communication Research* 42 (6): 819–838.

Chen, Gina Masullo. 2016. *Nasty News Story Comments Indirectly Increase Intention to Participate Politically for Women, Mediated Through Negative Affect*. Presented to the Mass Communication Division of the Southern States Communication Association at its Annual Conference in Austin, TX.

Chen, Gina Masullo, and Pei Zheng. 2016a. *Online Public Discourse: Exploring Differences in Responses to Civil and Uncivil Disagreement in News Story Comments*. Presented to the Mass Communication and Society Division of the Association for Education in Journalism and Mass Communication Annual Conference in Minneapolis, MN.

Chen, Gina Masullo, and Pei Zheng. 2016b. *The 'Defensive Effect': Uncivil Comments Indirectly Increase Intention to Participate Politically, Through Negative Affect*. Presented to the Mass Communication Division of the International Communication Association Annual Conference in Fukuoka, Japan.

Chen, Gina Masullo, and Shuning Lu. 2017. Online Political Discourse: Exploring Differences in Effects of Civil and Uncivil Disagreement in News Website Comments. *Journal of Broadcasting & Electronic Media* 61 (1). doi:10.1080/08838151/2016/1273922.

Coe, Kevin, Kate Kenski, and Stephen A. Rains. 2014. Online and Uncivil? Patterns and Determinants of Incivility in Newspaper Website Comments. *Journal of Communication* 64: 658–679.

Cupach, William R., and Christine L. Carson. 2002. Characteristics and Consequences of Interpersonal Complaints Associated with Perceived Face Threat. *Journal of Social and Personal Relationships* 19 (4): 443–462.

Darics, Erika. 2010. Politeness in Computer-Mediated Discourse of a Virtual Team. *Journal of Politeness Research* 6: 129–150.
Festinger, Leon. 1957. *A Theory of Cognitive Dissonance*. Palo Alto, CA: Stanford University Press.
Fishkin, James S. 1991. *Democracy and Deliberation*. New Haven, CT: Yale University Press.
Gil de Zúñiga, Homero, Nakwon Jung, and Sebastián Valenzuela. 2012. Social Media Use for News and Individuals' Social Capital, Civic Engagement, and Political Participation. *Journal of Computer-Mediated Communication* 17: 319–336.
Graesser, Arthur C. 1981. *Prose Comprehension Beyond the Word*. New York: Springer.
Gutmann, Amy, and Dennis Thompson. 1996. *Democracy and Disagreement*. Cambridge, MA: Harvard University Press.
Hayes, Andrew F. 2007. Exploring Forms of Self-Censorship: On the Spiral of Silence and the Use of Opinion Expression Avoidance Strategies. *Journal of Communication* 57: 785–802.
Hayes, Andrew F. 2013. *Introduction to Mediation, Moderation, and Conditional Process Analysis*. New York: Guilford.
Hayes, Andrew F., and Kristopher J. Preacher. 2014. Statistical Mediation Analysis with a Multi-Categorical Independent Variable. *British Journal of Mathematical and Statistical Psychology* 67 (3): 451–470.
Jacobs, Lawrence R., Fay Lomax Cook, and Michael X. Delli Carpini. 2009. *Talking Together: Public Deliberation and Political Participation in America*, Chicago: University of Chicago Press.
Kaiser, Henry F. 1970. A Second Generation Little Jiffy. *Psychometrika* 35 (4): 401–415.
Marcus, George E., W. Russell Neuman, and Michael MacKuen. 2000. *Affective Intelligence and Political Judgment*. Chicago: The University of Chicago Press.
Nekmat, Elmie, and William J. Gonzebach. 2013. Multiple Opinion Climates in Online Forums: Role of Website Source Reference and Within-Forum Opinion Congruency. *Journalism & Mass Communication Quarterly* 90 (4): 736–756.
Noelle-Neumann, Elisabeth. 2008. Spiral of Silence. In *A First Look at Communication Theory*, ed. Em Griffin, 272–286. New York: McGraw Hill.
Oz, Mustafa, Pei Zheng, and Gina Masullo Chen. 2016. *Social Media, Politeness and Discussion Quality*. Presented at the World Association for Public Opinion Research Annual Conference in Austin, TX.
Paolacci, Gabriele, Jessie Chander, and Panagiotis G. Ipeirotis. 2010. Running Experiments on Amazon Mechanical Turk. *Judgment and Decision Making* 5 (5): 411–419.

Papacharissi, Zizi. 2004. Democracy Online: Civility, Politeness, and the Democratic Potential of Online Political Discussion. *New Media & Society* 6 (2): 259–283.

Parsons, Bryan M. 2010. Social Networks and the Affective Impact of Political Agreement. *Political Behavior* 32 (2): 181–204.

Shapiro, Michael A., and T. Makana Chock. 2004. Media Dependency and Perceived Reality of Fiction and News. *Journal of Broadcasting & Electronic Media* 8 (1): 675–695.

Stroud, Natalie J., Joshua M. Scacco, Ashley Muddiman, and Alexander L. Curry. 2015. Changing Deliberative Norms on News Organizations' Facebook Sites. *Journal of Computer-Mediated Communication* 20: 188–203.

Tenenboim, Ori, and Akiba A. Cohen. 2015. What Prompts Users to Click and Comment? A Longitudinal Study of Online News. *Journalism* 16 (2): 198–217.

Watson, David, Lee A. Clark, and Auke Tellegen. 1988. Development and Validation of the Brief Measures of Positive and Negative Affect: The PANAS Scales. *Journal of Personality and Social Psychology* 54 (6): 1063–1070.

Weber, Patrick. 2013. Discussions in the Comments Sections: Factors Influencing Participation and Interactivity in Online Newspapers' Reader Comments. *New Media & Society* 10 (6): 941–957.

PART IV

What This Means for Public Debate

CHAPTER 8

Conclusion: Where Do We Go from Here?

While incivility has long been part of the human condition and U.S. politics, we live in a particular moment where vitriol has been normalized into nearly every aspect of life. Tweens and teens regularly confront cyber bullying through Snapchat or other online platforms.[1] Racist rants, harassment of journalists, and even targeted death threats have become the norm online.[2] President Donald Trump has come under fire for using Twitter to orally pounce on people, including an 18-year-old college student,[3] and actor Meryl Streep,[4] who criticized him at the Golden Globe Awards in January 2017. Incivility has even been weaponized, as when Russia hired social media trolls to spread disparaging information in an effort to undermine faith in U.S. democracy during the 2016 presidential election, according to U.S. intelligence agencies.[5] People feel uninhibited on social media or in news site comment streams,[6] whether they use a real name or not, and this online culture has fomented a "new digital space for malfeasance and indiscretion."[7] Rancor can spread across the web in a flash, generating a virtual mêlée in minutes. While the nastiness is not new, the speed and publicness of online communication makes incivility particularly potent in this context. At the same time, politics has become increasingly acerbic,[8] fueled by partisan media outlets that reinforce people's existing beliefs[9] and "blunt the persuasive power of antagonistic views."[10] The result is the online space—the "broader sociopolitical deliberative arena to which journalism contributes"[11]—becomes inhospitable to engagement, sounding the death knell of the Internet's potential to be a unfettered platform[12] for discussion and debate that mimics the salons and cafés of days gone by.[13]

Wow, that sounds depressing. But wait. There is a glimmer of hope. In this chapter, I will detail my findings from earlier chapters, offering strong evidence that online discussions, while often mired in incivility, provide the potential for what I call "deliberative moments" even if the truly reciprocal public deliberation[14] of the sanitized public sphere that sociologist Jürgen Habermas[15] imagined eludes us online. These deliberative moments are brief forms of public deliberation, small bites, if you will, that offer some support for the ideals of free debate, inclusiveness of viewpoints, and discussions across difference encompassed by democratic deliberation.[16] I explain the key findings from this book by answering the two main questions I posed in Chap. 1: Can online comment streams on news websites ever foster the robust and important public debate that democracy requires? What influence does incivility in these streams have on political participation and the larger public discussion about issues of the day? Next I synthesize the larger themes that we can draw from these findings to provide a greater understanding about public debate. Finally, I offer some suggestions for where we go from here, based on what I found in this research.

ONLINE COMMENTS AND PUBLIC DEBATE

In Chap. 2, I explored the concept of deliberative democracy, specifically in the context of online discussions. I argued that this type of discussion is vital to our society and that it takes on greater urgency in the computer-mediated space of commenting streams. We may not cluster at the post office or lean over the backyard fence to chat as frequently as people did in days gone by. However, in many ways, online discussions have replaced or at least augmented these types of face-to-face conversations. Thus, these online conversations become vitally important. They offer the room for more voices but also the danger that the most informed of those voices may be drowned out. Evidence is mixed on whether the digital space offers room for deliberation.[17] Deliberation is marked by openness to others' ideas, a forum for everyone, a focus on rationality and well-reasoned solutions, and respectful consideration of others' views.[18] It is within this context that I propose the idea of "deliberative moments." I define these moments as short episodes of public deliberation. These moments should foster openness to others' views, discussion across disagreement, varied viewpoints, and such attributes as asking a question to understand another's view better or using evidence, such as documents or facts and figures, to support one's own opinion. I concede these moments are often all too brief, as ephemeral as a Snapchat picture that disappears in 10 s. The value of these moments is that they open the door at least a crack to true discussion, even if that door shuts rather quickly if things escalate. Is opening the door a crack to true discussion worth it? I say, yes. A partially open door is better than one that is perpetually shut. Speech, even if imperfect, is better than silence. Political scientists Amy Gutmann and Dennis Thompson urge that deliberation should not be confined to formal settings but "embrace virtually any setting in which citizens come together on a regular basis to reach collective decisions about public issues."[19] I agree. While face-to-face discussions may offer the "gold standard"[20] of deliberation, we cannot afford to give up the digital space as hopeless.

However, as I outlined in Chap. 3, the online space is particularly vulnerable to misuse. Online communication lacks the cues of face-to-face speech, like tone of voice and facial expressions, and, as a result, people may feel deindividuated online,[21] as if they are hidden in plain sight. They may see the other disembodied voices online as fair game for their malice or vitriol. That's why the incivility—marked by profanity; name-calling; insults; and homophobic, racist, sexist, xenophobic, and bigoted speech[22]—flourishes. That is why I propose we live with a little incivility, even if it sprinkled amid what could be deliberative discourse. Certainly, civil speech is the goal, but I would rather an emotionally impassioned debate that dips into incivility, than no debate at all. That is why I ask the question in Chap. 4: Can incivility and deliberation co-exist? I propose a model of the "zone of deliberative moments" to show how they can. I argue that non-normative speech ranges from mere impoliteness to virulent hate speech, but incivility within the zone of deliberative moments falls somewhere in between. Agreement and silence are innocuous but also do little to move a debate, so they fall outside the deliberative zone. Hate speech, marked by vicious attacks based on one's race, gender, sexuality, ethnicity, national origin, or religion, along with trolling—intentional efforts to get a rise out of people and harm them[23]—are beyond hope. They also fall outside the deliberative zone. One cannot deliberate while hate filled. Yet, between these poles, I argue, there is a sweet spot that is not so polite that it prohibits disagreement or discord but not so nasty that it makes rational speech impossible. This deliberative zone may include occasional profanity, name-calling, or even insults mixed in with asking legitimate questions and using evidence to support one's viewpoints. It is imperfect speech, but important speech.

In Chap. 5, I tested this conceptual model, analyzing 3508 user-generated comments posted on news stories about same-sex marriage, the debate over removing the Confederate flag from government spaces, and the 2016 presidential campaign. The comments were drawn from five news organizations: *Fox News*, the *Huffington Post*, *NBC News*, *The New York Times*, and *USA Today*. Overall, my findings showed that deliberation was more frequent that incivility. More than 25% of comments contained deliberative attributes, while nearly 18% were uncivil. More importantly, my findings showed that deliberation and incivility could co-exist, particularly when the incivility is relatively tame. Nearly 19% of the deliberative comments also contained some incivility, while uncivil attributes were present in 14.5% of deliberative comments. This is important because it suggests that a curse, an insult, or playing with letters to make a normal word aversive (e.g. "Demoncrats") does not necessarily preclude deliberation from taking place. While certainly, incivility may not help the discourse, this finding suggests that people can still make important points even if their speech is rough around the edges. Commenting streams may just be a place where emotions escalate, as people try to assert deeply held moral convictions. This is telling because profanity is an easy item to spot and flag in comment streams. But the more nuanced—and harder to flag items—such as sweeping xenophobic statements may do more harm. Some topics, such as the Super Tuesday primaries and the Confederate flag debate, elicited more incivility than the Supreme Court decision legalizing same-sex marriage across all five news sites studies, except *Fox News*. This suggest some topics are so polarizing that deliberation may be less possible. At *Fox*, the most civil comments were about the Confederate flag. At the same time, my findings showed that deliberation was highest for the Confederate flag issue and Super Tuesday for all the news organizations, except *The New York Times*, where same-sex marriage provoked more deliberation than the flag issue. This creates a quandary for our society. Disagreements about issues that are important and deeply held, such as those concerning race and politics, are among the most valuable to discuss. Yet, my findings showed that these topics were more challenging to discuss because they often generate incivility.

Looking to the future, this suggests more help is needed to enable a quality conversation about these types of topics. Some evidence suggests that comments streams can be improved if a positive tone is set in them early[24] or if recognizable journalists engage with commenters.[25] Commenting policies that warn users about the rules of the site, pre-moderate comments, or remove offending comments have been found to play a role in encouraging civility,[26] and some news sites require that commenters link to their Facebook profiles in an effort to curb incivility by connecting to the person's real identity.[27] With only five news sites in my content analysis, I do not have enough sites to make predictions about whether these commenting policies influence incivility. However, it is notable that *NBC News* was the only site of the five I studied that did not offer an explicit commenting policy, and its comments were most uncivil. At the same time, comments that went through a person's Facebook profile at *USA Today* and *Huffington Post* were not the most civil of my sample. The *Huffington Post* was mainly on a par with *Fox News* and *The New York Times* in terms of incivility, but *USA Today* was more uncivil. This suggests that that if we want to improve comments, commenting policies may play an important role. Yet, merely shifting commenting streams to Facebook will not solve the problem of nasty talk. My findings clearly showed that blaming incivility on anonymity of commenters alone is misplaced. Though some studies[28] have found a link between anonymity of commenters and incivility, I did not. My analysis showed that incivility differed by the news organization and the topic of the comments, but not by anonymity of the commenters. This supports an experimental study that showed that anonymity did not lead to aggressive language.[29] Certainly, it would be foolish to suggest anonymity plays no role in incivility, but I would urge news organizations and scholars to be cautious before blaming anonymity alone for online rancor. Like most complex problems, curbing incivility will require several strategies, not just one.

Other notable findings deserve mention. As others have found, my data suggest quite strongly that men are more frequent commenters than women,[30] although neither gender was more likely to be uncivil or deliberative. This suggests that women either feel less comfortable commenting or fear attacks, supporting much other evidence that the gender equanimity that the Internet was supposed to provide[31] has not occurred. This is unsurprising given the attacks on female gamers,[32] journalists,[33] and feminists[34] that happen all the time online. Yet, it suggests great urgency to the problem of curbing this particular type of abuse. We cannot have a robust debate if half the population feels unsafe trying to engage. Certainly, increased comment moderation may help this problem, as well as rapid blocking and banning commenters who wage such attacks. Speed is necessary to keep one misogynistic comment from escalating into a diatribe. It is also clear that words in all capital letters in online speech do not indicate only yelling, as earlier scholars, suggest.[35] My findings showed that using all capitals is clearly linked to incivility. Perhaps, one way to quell incivility, at least in part, would be to create commenting systems that do not allow people to type in all capital letters. If one person cannot "scream" at another, the other person is less likely to yell back.[36]

So to return to my first question: Can online comment streams on news websites ever foster the robust and important public debate that democracy requires? The answer is a guarded yes. Some of this debate is clearly happening, but not enough. It is hidden, mixed in with the messiness and vitriol. Shopping provides a telling analogy. If you shop at a large department store (think Macy's), all the clothing is organized by brand, size, and style. It is easy to find what one wants. But head to a discount store like TJ Maxx or Marshalls, and the clothing is pooled on the floor. Shirts are mixed in with dresses and shorts. A man's trousers may be hung on a rack next to a baby's pajamas. It takes some digging to uncover what you want, but, when you do, it's a real find. I think comment streams are a bit like this. The deliberation does not scream out at you, but when you search, you can find it. And when you do, these deliberative moments are worth protecting. The online space offers such potential for engagement that I am unready to give up on it. I do not believe that abandoning commenting streams, as National Public Radio, Reuters, the *Chicago Sun-Times*, and others have done, is the overall solution. Instead, we need to recognize what works about commenting—the engagement, the airing of views, the back-and-forth debate —and curb what does not. This is no easy fix. Surely, part of the answer is strongly moderating comments, highlighting thoughtful commenters to encourage more like them, and warning commenters of the rules of the road. Efforts like the Coral Project, a collaboration of *The New York Times, The Washington Post*, and Mozilla, is working to change how commenting occurs using open-source tools to calm the incivility.[37] One project, for example, identifies trustworthy commenters and highlights them.[38] Another tries to curate parts of online conservations, particularly around very polarizing topics,[39] rather than revealing a free-for-all. The Knight Foundation, which funds the Coral Project, solicited ideas from journalists on how to improve comments, and their suggestions included organizing content better and increasing participation among readers, while encouraging diverse voices.[40] More ideas like this are needed. Of course, there is also a time when comments should just be shut off on a particular stories if efforts to control the conversation fail.

INCIVILITY AND POLITICAL PARTICIPATION

In Chap. 6, I shifted to the second major focus of this book—how does online incivility influence political participation? Earlier in the book, I examined how disagreement in general influences people. Exposure to differing views is unlikely to change people's minds, but it may help them see another viewpoint, increase tolerance for alternative opinions, or even create a more informed public.[41] Yet, exposure to disagreement also can reinforce people's existing opinions[42] or make them ambivalent about what they believe.[43] The influence of exposure to disagreement in one's social group may demobilize people from participating politically[44] or silence them for fear of social rejection,[45] although these effects are greatest if people feel as if they are in the political minority in their community.[46] At an interpersonal level, exposure to disagreement may upset people briefly, but when the disagreement is nasty, everything changes. Uncivil disagreement boosts negative emotions and makes people aggressive.[47] This background provides the basis for what I call the "defensive effect." The defensive effect predicts that when people are confronted with uncivil disagreement—rife with name-calling, insults, or profanity—this begins a chain reaction. First, it stirs negative emotions, and then this emotional response triggers a defense mechanism, making them more likely to speak out or get politically involved in the issue. In essence, if the incivility boosts their negative emotions enough, it discounts a natural urge to stay quiet in the face of disagreement. In contrast, civil disagreement has no effect on people's intention to get politically involved. If uncivil disagreement does not trigger a negative emotional response, it makes people less likely—not more likely—to speak out politically. Basically, the emotional response changes the experience.

In Chap. 7, I tested the defensive effect in an experiment with 953 participants. My findings suggested quite strongly that the effect occurs, and that it operates in the same way across a variety of topics. So what does this mean for our understanding of how incivility influences political participation? I submit that it offers some good news. Clearly, comment streams and social media will never be completely free from acrimony. Incivility, whether we like it or not, is part of what makes us human; it is here to stay. Yet, the defensive effect offers hope for deliberation. Disagreement has long been seen as offering a chilling effect on political speech and participation,[48] although not in every case. Incivility, however, can open the door to more speech and, perhaps, more action. Now some may suggest there is little value in defensiveness or inciting people to act out. I disagree. I think this effect is not merely defensiveness. It suggests that incivility can help people tap into their deeply held beliefs and feel less constrained by the fact that some see things differently than others. Political participation is vital in a democracy, so if incivility jumpstarts action, that serves a greater good. Instead of ambivalence or silence in the face of cross-cutting viewpoints, people confronted with uncivil disagreement are spurred to do something—write a letter to the editor, post a yard sign, or donate money. Overall, these findings suggest that emotions and reason can work together: An emotional response from incivility leads to a rational act, getting politically engaged. Without the incivility, people still may get involved, but many will remain apathetic. An engaged electorate is too important to be left to a minority, so putting up with some incivility may be the cost of greater engagement. As President Barack Obama said in his final speech as president in January 2017: "Change only happens when ordinary people get involved, and they get engaged, and they come together to demand it."[49]

Where Do We Go from Here?

That brings me to the most important question of this chapter: Where do we go from here? As I explained earlier in this chapter, technological changes in commenting systems,[50] encouraging participation from diverse voices,[51] and intense moderation all will help improve the potential for public debate in these platforms. Having journalists or experts answer questions in comment streams or set a positive tone also offer great promise.[52] However, what is even more vital is that attitudes about commenting streams should change. I hear so often from both journalists and friends that comment streams are cesspools. "Don't read the comments," they warn. But in analyzing thousands of comments, that is not what I found. Certainly, there was incivility. Comments made me cringe or wonder about the humanity of my fellow Americans. Some made me embarrassed for my country. Many made me angry. Yet, so many comments offered thoughtful points or showed a populace that cares deeply about its country, its laws, and its people. Not every commenter was eloquent. Many could use a lesson in spelling and grammar. But there was often heart in what was being said, so that, more than anything else, I found writing this book gives me hope for the future of online discourse. Of course, most of these comments had been subjected to moderation. But that does not negate the potential of comments to provide a public debate. News organizations must moderate. That is clear.

What we also must do is dive in. Join the conversation. The more positive, thoughtful, intelligent voices we have in comment streams, the more likely it is that a conversation will not digress. Chose your news site wisely. As this study shows, different sites foster widely varying online communities. Put on your armor before you go in: Take no affront personally, count to 10 or even step away from the computer before responding, be judicious about which comments warrant your reply. Trying to reason with someone in the throes of an uncivil episode is likely fruitless. Yet, offering a supportive comment to someone who has been challenged may calm others down, or at least let that person know she is not alone. When you do comment, model deliberation, regardless of whether the topic is presidential politics or a discussion of the latest movie. Be rational, reasonable, ask questions, and support your own views with evidence. And if you do get incensed by what you find, channel that passion into political action, as the defensive effect predicts. Online speech does not have to be perfect to have value. We cannot afford to leave the online space to the trolls and miscreants.

Notes

1. Alyson Shontell, "13-Year-Old Describes How Kids are Bullied on Snapchat," *Business Insider*, June 26, 2014. http://www.businessinsider.com/how-kids-are-bullied-on-snapchat-2014-6; Gianluca Gini and Dorothy L. Espelage, "Peer Victimization, Cyberbullying, and Suicide Risk in Children and Adolescents," *Journal of the American Media Association* 312, no. 5 (2014): 545–546 (Shontell 2014; Gini and Espelage 2014).
2. Abby Ohlheiser, "Just How Offensive Did Milo Yiannopoulos Have to be to Get Banned from Twitter?" *The Washington Post*, July 21, 2016. https://www.washingtonpost.com/news/the-intersect/wp/2016/07/21/what-it-takes-to-get-banned-from-twitter/?utm_term=.55bc937413a4; Abby Ohlheiser, "Martin Shkreli Was Suspended From Twitter for 'Targeted Harassment' of Journalist," *The Washington Post*, January 8, 2017. https://www.washingtonpost.com/news/the-intersect/wp/2017/01/08/martin-shkreli-was-suspended-from-twitter-for-targeted-harassment-

of-a-journalist/?utm_term=.3688b7892648; Sarah Ashley O'Brien, "The Year in Harassment: 2016 Sunk Lower Than Rock Bottom," December 20, 2016. http://money.cnn.com/2016/12/20/technology/2016-internet-harassment/ (Ohlheiser 2016, 2017; O'Brien 2016).
3. Jenna Johnson, "What Happens When Donald Trump Attacks a Private Citizen on Twitter," *The Washington Post*, December 8, 2016. https://www.washingtonpost.com/politics/this-is-what-happens-when-donald-trump-attacks-a-private-citizen-on-twitter/2016/12/08/a1380ece-bd62-11e6-91ee-1adddfe36cbe_story.html?utm_term=.595a42aa5063 (Johnson 2016).
4. Elahe Izadi and Amy B. Wang, "Meryl Streep Called Out Donald Trump at Golden Globes. He Responds By Calling Her 'Over-Rated,'" *The Washington Post*, January 9, 2017. https://www.washingtonpost.com/news/arts-and-entertainment/wp/2017/01/08/meryl-streep-called-out-donald-trump-at-the-golden-globes-read-her-speech-here/?utm_term=.7b28d8698d59 (Izadi and Wang 2017).
5. An unclassified version of the intelligence report was released to the public through the media on January 6, 2017. http://www.nytimes.com/interactive/2017/01/06/us/politics/document-russia-hacking-report-intelligence-agencies.html?_r=0.
6. Russell Spears, Tom Postmes, Martin Le, and Anka Wolbert, "When Are Net Effects Gross Products? The Power of Influence and Influence of Power in Computer-Mediated Communication," *Journal of Social Issues* 58, no. 1 (2012): 91–107 (Spears et al. 2012).
7. Gina Masullo Chen and Hinda Mandell, "Conclusion: Predicting a New Scandal Environment in the Twenty-First Century," in *Scandal in a Digital Age*, eds. Hinda Mandell and Gina Masullo Chen, (New York, NY: Palgrave Macmillan, 2016): 210 (Chen and Mandell 2016).
8. Diana C. Mutz, *In-Your-Face Politics: The Consequences of Uncivil Media*, (Princeton, NJ: Princeton University Press, 2015) (Mutz 2015).
9. Matthew Levendusky, *How Partisan Media Polarize America*, (Chicago, IL: The University of Chicago Press, 2013); Michael D. Slater, "Reinforcing Spirals: The Mutual Influence of Media Selectivity and Media Effects and Their Impact on Individual Behavior and Society Identity," *Communication Theory* 17 (2007): 281–303; Natalie J. Stroud, "Media Use and Political Dispositions: Revisiting the Concept of Selective Exposure," *Political Behavior* 30 (2008): 241–266; Natalie J. Stroud, "Polarization and Partisan Selective Exposure," *Journal of Communication* 60 (2010): 556–576 (Levendusky 2013; Slater 2007; Stroud 2008, 2010).

10. Kathleen Hall Jamieson and Joseph N. Cappella, *Echo Chamber: Rush Limbaugh and the Conservative Media Establishment*, (New York, NY: Oxford University Press, 2008): preface (Jamieson and Cappella 2008).
11. Stephen D. Reese and Pamela J. Shoemaker, "A Media Sociology for the Networked Public Sphere: The Hierarchy of Influences Model," *Mass Communication and Society*, 19 (2016): 389–410 (Reese and Shoemaker 2016).
12. Steffen Albrecht, "Whose Voice is Heard in Online Deliberation? A Study of Participation and Representation in Political Debates on the Internet," *Information, Communication & Society* 8, no. 1 (2006): 62–82; Zizi Papacharissi, "Democracy Online: Civility, Politeness, and Democratic Potential of Online Political Discussion Groups," *New Media & Society* 6, no. 2 (2004): 259–283 (Albrecht 2006; Papacharissi 2004).
13. Gabriel de Tarde, *On Communication and Society Influence*, ed. Terry N. Clark, (Chicago, IL: University of Chicago Press, 1889/1969); Jürgen Habermas, "Three Normative Models of Democracy," *Democratic and Constitutional Theory Today* 1, no. 1 (1994): 1–10 (De Tarde 1889/1969; Habermas 1994).
14. James S. Fishkin, *Democracy and Deliberation*, (New Haven, CT: Yale University Press, 1991) (Fishkin 1991).
15. Habermas, "Three Normative Models of Democracy."
16. Fishkin, *Democracy and Deliberation*; Amy Gutmann and Dennis Thompson, *Democracy and Disagreement*, (Cambridge, MA: Harvard University Press, 1996); Lawrence R. Jacobs, Fay Lomax Cook, and Michael X. Delli Carpini, *Talking Together: Public Deliberation and Political Participation in America*, (Chicago, IL: University of Chicago Press, 2009); Hélène Landemore, "Democratic Reason: The Mechanism of Collective Intelligence in Politics." In *Collective Wisdom: Principles and Mechanisms*, eds. Hélène Landemore and John Elster, (New York, NY: Cambridge University Press, 2012) (Gutmann and Thompson 1996; Jacobs et al. 2009; Landemore 2012).
17. Lindita Camaj and Arthur D. Santana, "Political Deliberation on Facebook During Electoral Campaigns: Exploring the Relevance of Moderator's Technical Role and Political Ideology," *Journal of Information, Technology & Politics* 12, no. 4 (2015): 325–341; Edith Manosevitch and Dana Walker, "Reader Comments to Online Opinion Journalism: A Space of Public Deliberation," *International Symposium of Online Journalism* 10 (2009): 10–30; Carolos Ruiz, David Domingo, Josep Lluís Micó, Javier Díaz-Noci, Koldo Meso, and Pere Maship, "Public Sphere 2.0? The Democratic Qualities of Citizen Debates in Online Newspapers," *The International Journal of Press/Politics* 16, no. 4 (2011): 463–487; Jennifer Stromer-Galley, "Diversity of Political Conversation on the Internet: Users'

Perspectives," *Journal of Computer-Mediated Communication* 8, no. 3 (2003): n.p. (Camaj and Santana 2015; Manosevitch and Walker 2009; Ruiz et al. 2011; Stromer-Galley 2003).
18. Fishkin, *Democracy and Deliberation*; John Gastil, *Political Communication and Deliberation*, (Cambridge, MA: Harvard University Press, 1996); John Gastil and Laura W. Black, "Public Deliberation as the Organizing Principles of Political Communication Research," *Journal of Public* Deliberation 4, no. 1 (2008): Article 3, 7; Gutmann and Thompson, *Democracy and Disagreement*; Jacobs, Cook, and Delli Carpini, *Talking Together: Public Deliberation and Political Participation in America* (Gastil 1996; Gastil and Black 2008).
19. Gutmann and Thompson, *Democracy and Disagreement*, 12.
20. Jacobs, Cook, and Delli Carpini, *Talking Together: Public Deliberation and Political Participation in America*, 35.
21. Spears et al., "When Are Net Effects Gross Products? The Power of Influence and Influence of Power in Computer-Mediated Communication."
22. Jeffrey M. Berry and Sarah Sobieraj, *The Outrage Industry: Politics and the New Incivility*, (New York, NY: Oxford University Press, 2014); Papacharissi, "Democracy Online: Civility, Politeness, and Democratic Potential of Online Political Discussion Groups"; Natalie J. Stroud, Joshua M. Scacco, Ashley Muddiman, and Alexander L. Curry, "Changing Deliberative Norms on News Organizations' Facebook Sites," *Journal of Computer-Mediated Communication* 20 (2015): 188–203 (Berry and Sobieraj 2014; Stroud et al. 2015).
23. Kristi K. Cole, "It's Like She's Eager to be Verbally Abused: Twitter, Trolls, and (En) Gendering Disciplinary Rhetoric," *Feminist Media Studies* 15, no. 2 (2015): 356–358; Erin E. Buckels, Paul D. Trapnell, Delroy L. Paulhus, "Trolls Just Want to Have Fun," *Personality and Individual Difference* 67 (2014): 97–102; Karem Erjavec and Melita Poler Kovačič, "'You Don't Understand, This is a New War!' Analysis of Hate Speech in News Web Sites' Comments," *Mass Communication and Society* 15 (2012): 899–920; Patrick B. O'Sullivan and Andrew J. Flanagin, "Reconceptualizing 'Flaming' and Other Problematic Messages," *New Media & Society* 5, no. 1 (2003): 69–94 (Cole 2015; Buckels et al. 2014; Erjavec and Kovačič 2012; O'Sullivan and Flanagin 2003).
24. Abhay Sukumaran, Stephanie Vezich, Melanie McHugh, and Clifford Nass. "Normative Influences on Thoughtful Online Participation," *Proceedings of the CHI 2011: Session: Incentives & User Generated Content*, (Vancouver, British Columbia, 2011): 3401–3410 (Sukumaran et al. 2011).
25. Stroud et al., "Changing Deliberative Norms on News Organizations' Facebook Sites."

26. Thomas B. Ksiazek, "Civil Interactivity: How News Organizations' Commenting Policies Explain Civility and Hostility in User Comments," *Journal of Broadcasting & Electronic Media* 59, no. 4 (2015): 556–573 (Ksiazek 2015).
27. Jeff Sonderman, "News Sites Using Facebook Comments See Higher Quality Discussions, More Referrals," Poynter.org, August 18, 2011. http://www.poynter.org/2011/news-sites-using-facebook-comments-see-higher-quality-discussion-more-referrals/143192/ (Sonderman 2011).
28. Jack Rosenberry, "Users Support Anonymity Despite Increasing Negativity," *Newspaper Research Journal* 32, no. 1 (2011): 6–19; Ian Rowe, "Civility 2.0: A Comparative Analysis of Incivility in Online Political Discussion," *Information, Communication & Society* 18, no. 2 (2015): 121–138; Arthur D. Santana, "Virtuous or Vitriolic," *Journalism Practice* 8, no. 1 (2014): 18–33 (Rosenberry 2011; Rowe 2015; Santana 2014).
29. Leonie Rösner and Nicole C. Krämer, "Verbal Venting in the Social Web: Effect of Anonymity and Group Norms on Aggressive Language Use in Online Comments," *Social Media + Society*, July/September (2016): 1–13 (Rösner and Krämer 2016).
30. Hans K. Meyer and Michael Clary Carey, "Men More Likely to Post Online Newspaper Comments," *Newspaper Research Journal* 36, no. 4 (2015): 469–481 (Meyer and Carey 2015).
31. Ebo Bosah, *Cyberghetto or Cybertopia? Race, Class and Gender on the Internet*, (Westport, CT: Praeger, 1998); Gina Masullo Chen, "Don't Call Me That: A Techno-Feminist Critique of the Term *Mommy Blogger*," *Mass Communication and Society* 16, no. 4 (2013): 510–532; Dustin Harp and Mark Tremayne, "The Gendered Blogosphere: Examining Inequality Using Network and Feminist Theory," *Journalism & Mass Communication Quarterly* 32, no. 2 (2006): 247–264; Susan C. Herring, Inna Kouper, Lois Ann Scheidt, and Elijah Wright, "Women and Children Last: The Discursive Construction of Weblogs," *Into the Blogsphere: Rhetoric, Community and Culture Weblogs*, eds. Laura Gurak, Smilijana Antonijevic, Laurie Johnson, Clancy Ratcliff, and Jennifer Reyman, (Minneapolis, MN: University of Minnesota, 2004) (Ebo 1998; Chen 2013; Harp and Tremayne 2006; Herring et al. 2004).
32. Andrea Braithwaite, "It's About Ethics in Games Journalism? Gamergaters and Geek Masculinity," *Social Media + Society*, October/December, no. 4 (2016): 1–10; Shira Chess and Adrienne Shaw, "A Conspiracy of Fishes, or, How We Learned to Stop Worrying About GamerGate and Embrace Hegemonic Masculinity," *Journal of Broadcasting & Electronic Media* 59, no. 1 (2015): 208–220 (Braithwaite 2016; Chess and Shaw 2015).

33. Maeve Duggan, "Online Harassment," *Pew Research Center*, October 22, 2014. http://www.pewinternet.org/2014/10/22/online-harassment/; Lindsey Wotanis and Laurie McMillan, "Performing Gender on YouTube: How Jenna Marbles Negotiates a Hostile Online Environment," *Feminist Media Studies* 14, no. 6 (2014): 912–928 (Duggan 2014; Wotanis and McMillan 2014).
34. Cole, "'It's Like She's Eager to Be Verbally Abused': Twitter, Trolls and (En)Gendering Disciplinary Rhetoric."
35. Erika Darics, "Politeness in Computer-Mediated Discourse of a Virtual Team," *Journal of Politeness Research* 13, no. 6 (2010): 129–150; Papacharissi, "Democracy Online: Civility, Politeness, and the Democratic Potential of Online Political Discussion." (Darics 2010).
36. Chen and Lu, "Online Political Discourse: Exploring Differences in Effects of Civil and Uncivil Disagreement in News Website Comments," *Journal of Broadcasting and Electronic Media* 61, no. 1 (2017). doi:10.1080/08838151/2016/1273922 (Chen and Lu 2017).
37. Nausicaa Renner, "As Sites Abandon Comments, The Coral Project Aims to Turn the Tide," *Columbia Journalism Review*, August 23, 2016. http://www.cjr.org/tow_center/improving_audience_engagement_coral_project.php (Renner 2016).
38. Renner, "As Sites Abandon Comments, The Coral Project Aims to Turn the Tide."
39. Renner, "As Sites Abandon Comments, The Coral Project Aims to Turn the Tide."
40. Rodrigo Zamith and Seth C. Lewis, "From Public Spaces to Public Sphere: Rethinking Systems for Reader Comments on Online News Sites," *Digital Journalism* 2, no. 4 (2014): 558–574 (Zamith and Lewis 2014).
41. Diana C. Mutz, "Cross-Cutting Social Networks: Testing Democratic Theory in Practice," *American Political Science Review* 96, no. 1 (2002): 11–126; Vincent Price, Joseph N. Cappella, and Lilach Nir, Does Disagreement Contribute to More Deliberative Opinion? *Political Communication* 19 (2002): 95–112 (Mutz 2002a; Price et al. 2002).
42. Mutz, "Cross-Cutting Social Networks: Testing Democratic Theory in Practice."
43. Mutz, "Cross-Cutting Social Networks: Testing Democratic Theory in Practice"; Lilach Nir, "Ambivalent Social Networks and Their Consequences for Participation," *International Journal of Public Opinion Research* 17 (2005): 422–442 (Nir 2005).
44. Scott D. McClurg, "Political Disagreement in Context: The Condition Effect of Neighborhood Context, Disagreement and Political Talk in Electoral Participation," *Political Behavior* 28 (2006): 349–366; Mutz, "Cross-Cutting Social Networks: Testing Democratic Theory in Practice";

Diana C. Mutz, "The Consequences of Cross-Cutting Networks for Political Participation," *American Journal of Political Science* 46, no. 1 (2002): 838–855; Nir, "Ambivalent Social Networks and Their Consequences for Participation"; Lilach Nir, "Disagreement and Opposition in Social Networks: Does Disagreement Discourage Turnout," *Political Studies* 59 (2011): 674–692 (McClurg 2006; Mutz 2002b; Nir 2011).
45. Magdalena E. Wojcieszak and Vincent Price, "Perceived Versus Actual Disagreement: Which Influences Deliberative Experiences?" *Journal of Communication* 62 (2012): 418–436 (Wojcieszak and Price 2012).
46. McClurg, "Political Disagreement in Context: The Conditional Effect of Neighborhood Context, Disagreement and Political Talk on the Electoral Participation."
47. Chen and Lu, "Online Political Discourse: Exploring Differences in Effects of Civil and Uncivil Disagreement in News Website Comments."
48. McClurg, "Political Disagreement in Context: The Condition Effect of Neighborhood Context, Disagreement and Political Talk in Electoral Participation"; Mutz, "Cross-Cutting Social Networks: Testing Democratic Theory in Practice"; Mutz, "The Consequences of Cross-Cutting Networks for Political Participation"; Nir, "Ambivalent Social Networks and Their Consequences for Participation"; Nir, "Disagreement and Opposition in Social Networks: Does Disagreement Discourage Turnout."
49. The transcript and video of President Barack Obama's speech is available at: https://www.nytimes.com/2017/01/10/us/politics/obama-farewell-address-speech.html.
50. Renner, "As Sites Abandon Comments, The Coral Project Aims to Turn the Tide."
51. Zamith and Lewis, "From Public Spaces to Public Sphere: Rethinking Systems for Reader Comments on Online News Sites."
52. Stroud et al., "Changing Deliberative Norms on News Organizations' Facebook Sites"; Sukumaran et al., "Normative Influences on Thoughtful Online Participation."

References

Albrecht, Steffen. 2006. Whose Voice Is Heard in Online Deliberation? A Study of Participation and Representation in Political Debates on the Internet. *Information, Communication and Society* 8 (1): 62–82.
Berry, Jeffrey M., and Sarah Sobieraj. 2014. *The Outrage Industry: Politics and the New Incivility*. New York: Oxford University Press.
Braithwaite, Andrea. 2016. It's About Ethics in Games Journalism? Gamergaters and Geek Masculinity. *Social Media + Society* 4: 1–10.

Buckels, Erin E., Paul D. Trapnell, and Delroy L. Paulhus. 2014. Trolls Just Want to Have Fun. *Personality and Individual Differences* 62: 97–102.

Camaj, Lindita, and Arthur D. Santana. 2015. Political Deliberation on Facebook During Electoral Campaigns: Exploring the Relevance of Moderator's Technical Role and Political Ideology. *Journal of Information, Technology and Politics* 12 (4): 325–341.

Chen, Gina Masullo. 2013. Don't Call Me That: A Techno-Feminist Critique of the Term *Mommy Blogger*. *Mass Communication and Society* 16 (4): 510–532.

Chen, Gina Masullo, and Hinda Mandell. 2016. Conclusion: Predicting a New Scandal Environment in the Twenty-First Century. In *Scandal in a Digital Age*, ed. Hinda Mandell and Gina Masullo Chen. New York: Palgrave Macmillan.

Chen, Gina Masullo, and Shuning Lu. 2017. Online Political Discourse: Exploring Differences in Effects of Civil and Uncivil Disagreement in News Website Comments. *Journal of Broadcasting and Electronic Media* 61 (1). doi:10.1080/08838151/2016/1273922.

Chess, Shira, and Adrienne Shaw. 2015. A Conspiracy of Fishes, or, How We Learned to Stop Worrying About #GamerGate and Embrace Hegemonic Masculinity. *Journal of Broadcasting and Electronic Media* 59 (1): 208–220.

Cole, Kristi K. 2015. 'It's Like She's Eager to Be Verbally Abused': Twitter, Trolls, and (En)Gendering Disciplinary Rhetoric. *Feminist Media Studies* 15 (2): 356–358.

Darics, Erika. 2010. Politeness in Computer-Mediated Discourse of a Virtual Team. *Journal of Politeness Research* 6: 129–150.

De Tarde, Gabriel. 1889/1969. *On Communication and Social Influence*, ed. Terry N. Clark. Chicago: University of Chicago Press.

Duggan, Maeve. 2014. Online Harassment. *Pew Research Center*, October 22. http://www.pewinternet.org/2014/10/22/online-harassment/. Accessed 11 Jan 2017.

Ebo, Bosah. 1998. *Cyberghetto or Cybertopia? Race, Class and Gender on the Internet*, ed. Wesport, CT: Praeger.

Erjavec, Karmen, and Melita Poler Kovačič. 2012. 'You Don't Understand, This is a New War!' Analysis of Hate Speech in News Web Sites' Comments. *Mass Communication and Society* 15: 899–920.

Fishkin, James S. 1991. *Democracy and Deliberation*. New Haven, CT: Yale University Press.

Gastil, John. 1996. *Political Communication and Deliberation*. Cambridge, MA: Harvard University Press.

Gastil, John, and Laura W. Black. 2008. Public Deliberation as the Organizing Principle of Political Communication Research. *Journal of Public Deliberation* 4 (1): Article 3.

Gini, Gianluca, and Dorothy L. Espelage. 2014. Peer Victimization, Cyberbullying, and Suicide Risk in Children and Adolescents. *Journal of the American Medical Association* 312 (5): 545–546.

Gutmann, Amy, and Dennis Thompson. 1996. *Democracy and Disagreement*. Cambridge, MA: Harvard University Press.

Habermas, Jürgen. 1994. Three Normative Models of Democracy. *Democratic and Constitutional Theory Today* 1 (1): 1–10.

Herring, Susan C., Inna Kouper, Lois Ann Scheidt, and Elijah Wright. 2004. Women and Children Last: The Discursive Construction of Weblogs. In *Into the Blogsphere: Rhetoric, Community and Culture Weblogs*, ed. Laura Gurak, Smilijana Antonijevic, Laurie Johnson, Clancy Ratcliff, and Jennifer Reyman. Minneapolis, MN: University of Minnesota.

Harp, Dustin, and Mark Tremayne. 2006. The Gendered Blogosphere: Examining Inequality Using Network and Feminist Theory. *Journalism and Mass Communication Quarterly* 32 (2): 247–264.

Izadi, Elahe, and Amy B. Wang. 2017. Meryl Streep Called Out Donald Trump at Golden Globes. He Responds By Calling her 'Over-Rated.' *The Washington Post*, January 9. https://www.washingtonpost.com/news/arts-and-entertainment/wp/2017/01/08/meryl-streep-called-out-donald-trump-at-the-golden-globes-read-her-speech-here/?utm_term=.7b28d8698d59. Accessed 10 Jan 2017.

Jacobs, Lawrence R., Fay Lomax Cook, and Michael X. Delli Carpini. 2009. *Talking Together: Public Deliberation and Political Participation in America*. Chicago: University of Chicago Press.

Jamieson, Kathleen Hall, and Joseph N. Cappella. 2008. *Echo Chamber: Rush Limbaugh and the Conservative Media Establishment*. New York: Oxford University Press.

Johnson, Jenna, 2016. What Happens When Donald Trump Attacks a Private Citizen on Twitter. *The Washington Post*, December 8. https://www.washingtonpost.com/politics/this-is-what-happens-when-donald-trump-attacks-a-private-citizen-on-twitter/2016/12/08/a1380ece-bd62-11e6-91ee-1adddfe36cbe_story.html?utm_term=.595a42aa5063. Accessed 10 Jan 2017.

Ksiazek, Thomas B. 2015. Civil Interactivity: How News Organizations' Commenting Policies Explain Civility and Hostility in User Comments. *Journal of Broadcasting and Electronic Media* 59 (4): 556–573.

Landemore, Hélène. 2012. Democratic Reason: The Mechanism of Collective Intelligence in Politics. In *Collective Wisdom: Principles and Mechanisms*, ed. Hélène Landemore, and John Elster, 251–289. New York: Cambridge University Press.

Levendusky, Matthew. 2013. *How Partisan Media Polarize America*. Chicago: University of Chicago Press.

Manosevitch, Edith, and Dana Walker. 2009. Reader Comments to Online Opinion Journalism: A Space of Public Deliberation. *International Symposium of Online Journalism* 10: 10–30.

McClurg, Scott D. 2006. Political Disagreement in Context: The Conditional Effect of Neighborhood Context, Disagreement and Political Talk on Electoral Participation. *Political Behavior* 28: 349–366.

Meyer, Hans K., and Michael C. Carey. 2015. Men More Likely to Post Online Newspaper Comments. *Newspaper Research Journal* 36 (4): 469–481.

Mutz, Diana C. 2002a. Cross-Cutting Social Networks: Testing Democratic Theory in Practice. *American Political Science Review* 96 (1): 111–126.

Mutz, Diana C. 2002b. The Consequences of Cross-Cutting Networks for Political Participation. *American Journal of Political Science* 46 (4): 838–855.

Mutz, Diana C. 2015. *In-Your-Face Politics: The Consequences of Uncivil Media*. Princeton, NJ: Princeton University Press.

Nir, Lilach. 2011. Disagreement and Opposition in Social Networks: Does Disagreement Discourage Turnout? *Political Studies* 59: 674–692.

Nir, Lilach. 2005. Ambivalent Social Networks and Their Consequences for Participation. *International Journal of Public Opinion Research* 17: 422–442.

O'Brien, Sarah Ashley. 2016. The Year in Harassment: 2016 Sunk Lower Than Rock Bottom. December 20. http://money.cnn.com/2016/12/20/technology/2016-internet-harassment/. Accessed 10 Jan 2017.

Ohlheiser, Abby. 2016. Just How Offensive Did Milo Yiannopoulos Have to Be to Get Banned from Twitter? *The Washington Post*, July 21. https://www.washingtonpost.com/news/the-intersect/wp/2016/07/21/what-it-takes-to-get-banned-from-twitter/?utm_term=.27ca27d651fa. Accessed 9 Dec 2016.

Ohlheiser, Abby. 2017. Martin Shkreli Was Suspended From Twitter for 'Targeted Harassment' of Journalist, *The Washington Post*, January 8. https://www.washingtonpost.com/news/the-intersect/wp/2017/01/08/martin-shkreli-was-suspended-from-twitter-for-targeted-harassment-of-a-journalist/?utm_term=.3688b7892648. Accessed 10 Jan 2017.

O'Sullivan, Patrick B., and Andrew J. Flanagin. 2003. Reconceptualizing 'Flaming' and Other Problematic Messages. *New Media & Society* 5 (1): 69–94.

Papacharissi, Zizi. 2004. Democracy Online: Civility, Politeness, and the Democratic Potential of Online Political Discussion. *New Media & Society* 6 (2): 259–283.

Price, Vincent, Joseph N. Cappella, and Lilach Nir. 2002. Does Disagreement Contribution to More Deliberative Opinion? *Political Communication* 19: 95–112.

Reese, Stephen D., and Pamela J. Shoemaker. 2016. A Media Sociology for the Network Public Sphere: The Hierarchy of Influence Model. *Mass Communication and Society* 19: 389–410.

Renner, Nausicaa. 2016. As Sites Abandon Comments, The Coral Project Aims to Turn the Tide. *Columbia Journalism Review*, August 23. http://www.cjr.org/tow_center/improving_audience_engagement_coral_project.php. Accessed 10 Jan 2017.

Rosenberry, Jack. 2011. Users Support Anonymity Despite Increasing Negativity. *Newspaper Research Journal* 32 (1): 6–19.

Rösner, Leonie, and Nicole C. Krämer. 2016. Verbal Venting in the Social Web: Effects of Anonymity and Group Norms on Aggressive Language Use in Online Comments. *Social Media + Society*, July/September: 1–13.

Rowe, Ian. 2015. Civility 2.0: A Comparative Analysis of Incivility in Online Political Discussion. *Information, Communication and Society* 18 (2): 121–138.

Ruiz, Carlos, David Domingo, Josep Lluís Micó, Javier Díaz-Noci, Koldo Meso, and Pere Masip. 2011. Public Sphere 2.0? The Democratic Qualities of Citizen Debates in Online Newspapers. *The International Journal of Press/Politics* 16 (4): 463–487.

Santana, Arthur D. 2014. Virtuous or Vitriolic. *Journalism Practice* 8 (1): 18–33.

Shontell, Alyson. 2014. 13-Year-Old Describes How Kids are Bullied on SnapChat. *Business Insider*, June 26. http://www.businessinsider.com/how-kids-are-bullied-on-snapchat-2014-6. Accessed 10 Jan 2017.

Slater, Michael D. 2007. Reinforcing Spirals: The Mutual Influence of Media Selectivity and Media Effects and Their Impact on Individual Behavior and Society Identity. *Communication Theory* 17: 281–303.

Sonderman, Jeff. 2011. News Sites Using Facebook Comments See Higher Quality Discussions, More Referrals. *Poynter.org*, August 11. http://www.poynter.org/2011/news-sites-using-facebook-comments-see-higher-quality-discussion-more-referrals/143192/. Accessed 9 Sept 2016.

Spears, Russell, Tom Postmes, Martin Le, and Anka Wolbert. 2012. When Are Net Effects Gross Products? The Power of Influence and Influence of Power in Computer-Mediated Communication. *Journal of Social Issues* 58 (1): 91–107.

Stromer-Galley, Jennifer. 2003. Diversity of Political Conversation on the Internet: Users' Perspectives. *Journal of Computer-Mediated Communication* 8 (3): n.p.

Stroud, Natalie J. 2008. Media Use and Political Dispositions: Revisiting the Concept of Selective Exposure. *Political Behavior* 30: 341–366.

Stroud, Natalie J. 2010. Polarization and Partisan Selective Exposure. *Journal of Communication* 60: 556–576.

Stroud, Natalie J., Joshua M. Scacco, Ashley Muddiman, and Alexander L. Curry. 2015. Changing Deliberative Norms on News Organizations' Facebook Sites. *Journal of Computer-Mediated Communication* 20: 188–203.

Sukumaran, Abhay, Stephanie Vezich, Melanie McHugh, and Clifford Nass. 2011. Normative Influences on Thoughtful Online Participation. In *Proceedings of the CHI 2011: Session: Incentives and User Generated Content*, 3401–3410. Vancouver, BC.

Wojcieszak, Magdalena E., and Vincent Price. 2012. Perceived Versus Actual Disagreement: Which Influences Deliberative Experiences? *Journal of Communication* 62: 418–436.

Wotanis, Lindsey, and Laurie McMillan. 2014. Performing Gender on YouTube: How Jenna Marbles Negotiates a Hostile Online Environment. *Feminist Media Studies* 14 (6): 912–928.

Zamith, Rodrigo, and Seth C. Lewis. 2014. From Public Spaces to Public Sphere: Rethinking Systems for Reader Comments on Online News Sites. *Digital Journalism* 2 (4): 558–574.

Bibliography

Akpan, Nsikan. 2016. The Very Real Consequences of Fake News Stories and Why Our Brain Can't Ignore Them. *PBS News Hour*, December 5. http://www.pbs.org/newshour/updates/real-consequences-fake-news-stories-brain-cant-ignore/. Accessed 6 Dec 2016.

Albertson, Bethany, and Shauna Kushner Gadarian. 2015. *Anxious Politics: Democratic Citizenship in a Threatening World*. New York: Cambridge University Press.

Albrecht, Steffen. 2006. Whose Voice is Heard in Online Deliberation? A Study of Participation and Representation in Political Debates on the Internet. *Information, Communication & Society* 8 (1): 62–82.

Andersson, Lynne M., and Christine M. Pearson. 1999. Tit for Tat? The Spiraling Effect of Incivility in the Workplace. *Academy of Management Review* 24 (3): 452–471.

Arendt, Hannah. 1958. *The Human Condition*. Chicago: The University of Chicago Press.

Baek, Young Min, Magdalena Wojcieszak, and Michael X. Delli Carpini. 2011. Online Versus Face-to-Face Deliberation? Who? Why? What? With What Effects? *New Media & Society* 14 (3): 363–383.

Bai, Qiyu, Weipeng Lin, and Lei Wang. 2016. Family Incivility and Counterproductive Work Behavior: A Moderated Mediation Model of Self-Esteem and Emotional Regulation. *Journal of Vocational Behavior* 94: 11–19.

Barker-Plummer, Bernadette, and Dave Barker-Plummer. 2017. Hashtag Feminism, Digital Media, and New Dynamics of Social Change: A Case Study of #YesAllWomen. In *Social Media and Politics: A New Way to Participate in the Political Process*, ed. Glenn W. Richardson Jr., 79–96. Santa Barbara, CA: Praeger.

Bartlett, M.S. 1954. A Note on Multiplying Factors for Various Chi-Square Approximations. *Journal of the Royal Statistical Society, Series B (Methodological)* 16 (2): 296–289.

Baumeister, Roy F., and Mark R. Leary. 1995. The Need to Belong: Desire for Interpersonal Attachments as a Fundamental Human Need. *Psychological Bulletin* 117 (3): 497–529.

Baym, Nancy K., and danah boyd. 2012. Socially Mediated Publicness: An Introduction. *Journal of Broadcasting & Electronic Media* 56 (3): 320–329.

Becker, Ron. 2006. *Gay TV and Straight America*. New Brunswick, NJ: Rutgers University Press.

Berinsky, A.J., Gregory A. Huber, and Gabriel S. Lenz. 2012. Evaluating Online Labor Markets for Experimental Research: Amazon.com's Mechanical Turk. *Political Analysis* 20 (3): 351–368.

Berry, Jeffrey M., and Sarah Sobieraj. 2014. *The Outrage Industry: Politics and the New Incivility*. New York, NY: Oxford University Press.

Blinder, Alan, and Richard Pérez-Peña. 2015. Kentucky Clerk Denies Same-Sex Marriage Licenses, Defying Court. *NYTimes.com*, September 1. http://www.nytimes.com/2015/09/02/us/same-sex-marriage-kentucky-kim-davis.html. Accessed 25 Aug 2016.

Bolls, Paul D. 2010. Understanding Emotion from a Superordinate Dimensional Perspective: A Productive Way Forward for Communication Processes and Effects. *Communication Monographs* 77 (2): 146–152.

Borah, Porismita. 2014. Does it Matter Where You Read the News Story? Interaction of Incivility and News Frames in the Political Blogosphere. *Communication Research* 41 (6): 809–827.

Braithwaite, Andrea. 2016. It's About Ethics in Games Journalism? Gamergaters and Geek Masculinity. *Social Media + Society* 4: 1–10.

Brett, Jeanne M., Mara Olekains, Ray Friedman, Nathan Goates, Cameron Anderson, and Cara Cherry Lisco. 2007. Sticks and Stones: Language, Face, and Online Dispute Resolution. *Academy of Management Journal* 50 (1): 85–99.

Brost, Lori. 2013. Editors Have Mixed Feelings on User-Generated Comments. *Newspaper Research Journal* 34 (3): 101–115.

Brown, Penelope, and Stephen C. Levinson. 1987. *Politeness: Some Universals in Language Usage*. New York: Cambridge University Press.

Buckels, Erin E., Paul D. Trapnell, and Delroy L. Paulhus. 2014. Trolls Just Want to Have Fun. *Personality and Individual Differences* 62: 97–102.

Burns, Alexander, Maggie Haberman, and Jonathan Martin. 2016. Donald Trump Apology Caps Day of Outrage Over Lewd Tape. *The New York Times*, October 7. http://www.nytimes.com/2016/10/08/us/politics/donald-trump-women.html. Accessed 12 Dec 2016.

Cacioppo, John T., Louis G. Tassinary, and Gary G. Berntson. 2007. *Handbook of Psychophysiology*. New York: Cambridge University Press.

Camaj, Lindita, and Arthur D. Santana. 2015. Political Deliberation on Facebook During Electoral Campaigns: Exploring the Relevance of Moderator's Technical Role and Political Ideology. *Journal of Information, Technology & Politics* 12 (4): 325–341.

Carr, D.Jasun, Matthew Barnidge, Byung Gu Lee, and Stephanie Jean Tsang. 2014. Cynics and Skeptics: Evaluating the Credibility of Mainstream and Citizen Journalism. *Journalism & Mass Communication Quarterly* 9 (3): 452–470.

Cattell, Raymond B. 1966. The Scree Test of the Number of Factors. *Multivariate Behavioral Research* 1 (2): 245–276.

Cavna, Michael. 2013. 'Nobody Knows You're a Dog': As Iconic Internet Cartoon Turns 20, Creator Peter Steiner Knows the Idea is as Relevant as Ever. *The Washington Post*, July 13. https://www.washingtonpost.com/blogs/comic-riffs/post/nobody-knows-youre-a-dog-as-iconic-internet-cartoon-turns-20-creator-peter-steiner-knows-the-joke-rings-as-relevant-as-ever/2013/07/31/73372600-f98d-11e2-8e84-c56731a202fb_blog.html. Accessed 23 May 2016.

Chen, Gina Masullo. 2011. Tweet This: A Uses and Gratifications Perspective on How Active Twitter Use Gratifies a Need to Connect with Others. *Computers in Human Behavior* 27: 755–762.

Chen, Gina Masullo. 2012. Why Do Women Write Personal Blogs? Satisfying Needs for Self-Disclosure and Affiliation Tell Part of the Story. *Computers in Human Behavior* 28: 171–180.

Chen, Gina Masullo. 2013. Don't Call Me That: A Techno-Feminist Critique of the Term *Mommy Blogger*. *Mass Communication and Society* 16 (4): 510–532.

Chen, Gina Masullo. 2015. Losing *Face* on Social Media: Threats to *Positive Face* Lead to an Indirect Effect on Retaliatory Aggression Through Negative Affect. *Communication Research* 42 (6): 819–838.

Chen, Gina Masullo, and Zainul Abedin. 2014. Exploring Differences in How Men and Women Respond to Threats to *Positive Face* on Social Media. *Computers in Human Behavior* 38: 118–126.

Chen, Gina Masullo. 2016. Social Media: From Digital Divide to Empowerment. In *The Routledge Companion to Media and Race*, ed. Christopher P. Campbell. New York: Routledge.

Chen, Gina Masullo, T. Makana Chock, Hillary Gozigian, Ryan Rogers, Arushi Sen, Valarier N. Schweisberger, Joseph Steinhardt, and Yi Wang. 2011. Personalizing News Websites Attracts Young Readers. *Newspaper Research Journal* 32 (4): 22–38.

Chen, Gina Masullo, and Paromita Pain. 2016. Normalizing Online Comments. *Journalism Practice, Online First.*. doi:10.1080/17512786.2016.1205954.

Chen, Gina Masullo. 2016, April. Nasty News Story Comments Indirectly Increase Intention to Participate Politically for Women, Mediated Through Negative Affect. In *Presented to the Mass Communication Division of the Southern States Communication Association at its Annual Conference*, Austin, TX.

Chen, Gina Masullo. 2017. Online Incivility and Public Deliberation. In *News Scholarship in a Transitional Age: Research in Honor of Pamela J. Shoemaker*, ed. Carol M. Liebler, Brad W. Gorham, and Tim P. Vos. New York: Peter Lang.

Chen, Gina Masullo, and Hinda Mandell. 2016. Conclusion: Predicting a New Scandal Environment in the Twenty-First Century. In *Scandal in a Digital Age*, ed. Hinda Mandell and Gina Masullo Chen. New York: Palgrave Macmillan.

Chen, Gina Masullo, and Pei Zheng. 2016 August. Online Public Discourse: Exploring Differences in Responses to Civil and Uncivil Disagreement in News Story Comments. In *Presented to the Mass Communication and Society Division of the Association for Education in Journalism and Mass Communication Annual Conference*, Minneapolis, MN.

Chen, Gina Masullo, and Pei Zheng. 2016 June. The 'Defensive Effect': Uncivil Comments Indirectly Increase Intention to Participate Politically, Through Negative Affect. In *Presented to the Mass Communication Division of the International Communication Association Annual Conference*, Fukuoka, Japan.

Chen, Gina Masullo, and Shuning Lu. 2017. Online Political Discourse: Exploring Differences in Effects of Civil and Uncivil Disagreement in News Website Comments. *Journal of Broadcasting & Electronic Media* 61 (1). doi:10.1080/08838151/2016/1273922.

Chess, Shira, and Adrienne Shaw. 2015. A Conspiracy of Fishes, or, How We Learned to Stop Worrying About #GamerGate and Embrace Hegemonic Masculinity. *Journal of Broadcasting & Electronic Media* 59 (1): 208–220.

Chokshi, Niraj. 2016. How #BlackLivesMatter Came to Define a Movement. *The New York Times*, August 22. http://www.nytimes.com/2016/08/23/us/how-blacklivesmatter-came-to-define-a-movement.html. Accessed 24 Aug 2016.

Chozik, Amy. 2016. Hillary Clinton Calls Many Trump Backers 'Deplorables,' and GOP Pounces. *The New York Times*, September 10. http://www.nytimes.com/2016/09/11/us/politics/hillary-clinton-basket-of-deplorables.html. Accessed 12 Dec 2016.

Chung, Myojung, Greg J. Munno, and Brian Moritz. 2015. Triggering Participation: Exploring the Effects of Third-Person and Hostile Media Perceptions on Online Participation. *Computers in Human Behavior* 53: 452–461.

Clarke, Allan. 2016. Facebook Memes Compare Aboriginal Athlete to Gorilla That Was Fatally Shot. *BuzzFeed*, June 1. https://www.buzzfeed.com/allanclarke/facebook-memes-compare-adam-goodes-to-the-gorilla-that-was-f?utm_term=.vcqRN7Mqa#.lb6zDXZAV. Accessed 23 June 2016.

Clayton, Cornell W. 2012. Historical Perspectives on the Role of Civility in American Democracy. In *Civility and Democracy in America: A Reasoned Understanding*, ed. Cornell W. Clayton and Richard Elgar, 1–4. Pullman, WA: Washington University Press.

Clayton, Cornell W., and Richard Elgar. 2012. Civility and American Democracy. In *Civility and democracy in America: A reasoned understanding*, ed. Cornell W. Clayton and Richard Elgar, ix–xxii. Pullman, WA: Washington University Press.

Coe, Kevin, Kate Kenski, and Stephen A. Rains. 2014. Online and Uncivil? Patterns and Determinants of Incivility in Newspaper Website Comments. *Journal of Communication* 64: 658–679.

Cole, Kristi K. 2015. It's Like She's Eager to Be Verbally Abused: Twitter, Trolls, and (En)Gendering Disciplinary Rhetoric. *Feminist Media Studies* 15 (2): 356–358.

Coleman, Renita, and H. Denis Wu. 2015. *Image & Emotion in Voter Decisions: The Affect Agenda*. New York, NY: Lexington Books.

Colleoni, Elanor, Alessandro Rozza, and Adam Arvidsson. 2014. Echo Chamber or Public Sphere? Predicting Political Orientation and Measuring Political Homophily in Twitter Using Big Data. *Journal of Communication* 64 (2): 317–332.

Cooks, Leda, Mari Castañeda Paredes, and Erica Scharrer. 2002. There's 'O Place' Like Home: Searching for Community on Oprah.com. In *Women & Everyday Uses of the Internet: Agency & Identity*, ed. Mia Consalvo and Susanna Paasonen, 133–167. New York: Peter Lang.

Cupach, William R., and Christine L. Carson. 2002. Characteristics and Consequences of Interpersonal Complaints Associated with Perceived Face Threat. *Journal of Social and Personal Relationships* 19 (4): 443–462.

Daft, Richard L., and Robert H. Lengel. 1986. Information Richness: A New Approach to Managerial Behavior and Organizational Design. In *Research in Organizational Behavior*, ed. Barry M. Staw and Larry L. Cummings, 554–571. Greenwich, CT: Jai.

Dahlberg, Lincoln. Re-Constructing Digital Democracy: An Outline of Four Positions. *New Media & Society* 13 (6): 855–872.

Daniels, Jessie. 2009. *Cyber Racism: White Supremacy Online and the New Attack on Civil Rights*. Lanham, MD: Rowman and Littlefield.

Darics, Erika. 2010. Politeness in Computer-Mediated Discourse of a Virtual Team. *Journal of Politeness Research* 6: 129–150.

Dawson, Michael E., Anne M. Schell, and Diane L. Filion. 2007. The Electrodermal System. In *Handbook of Psychophysiology*, ed. John T. Cacioppo, Louis G. Tassinary, and Gary G. Berntson, 159–191. New York: Cambridge University Press.

De Tarde, Gabriel. 1889/1969. *On Communication and Social Influence*, ed. Terry N. Clark. Chicago, IL: University of Chicago Press.

Dehue, Francine, Catherine Bolman, and Trinjntje Völlink. 2008. Cyberbullying: Youngsters' Experiences and Parental Perception. *Cyberpsychology & Behavior* 11 (2): 217–223.

Diakopoulos Nicholas, and Mor Naaman. 2011. Towards Quality Discourse in Online News Comments. In *Proceedings of the CSCW*, March 19–23, Hangzhou, China.

Dominus, Susan. 2016. Donald Trump: King of the Old Boys' Club, and Perhaps Its Destroyer. *The New York Times*, October 7. http://www.nytimes.com/2016/10/08/magazine/donald-trump-tape.html?smid=fb-nytimes&smtyp=cur&_r=0. Accessed 4 Nov 2016.

Duggan, Maeve. 2014. Online Harassment. *Pew Research Center*, October 22. http://www.pewinternet.org/2014/10/22/online-harassment/. Accessed 11 Jan 2017.

Ebo, Bosah. 1998. ed.*Cyberghetto or Cybertopia? Race, Class and Gender on the Internet*. Wesport, CT: Praeger.

Eisenberger, Naomi I., Matthew D. Lieberman, and Kipling D. Williams. 2003. Does Rejection Hurt? An fMRI Study of Social Exclusion. *Science* 203: 290–292.

Eisenstadt, Marnie. 2016. Syracuse's Public Housing Creates Prisons of Poverty; What If They Could Move to Suburbs? *Syracuse.com*, April 14. http://www.syracuse.com/poverty/2016/04/syracuses_public_housing_creat.html. Accessed 13 May 2016.

Ellis, Justin. 2015. What Happened When 7 News Sites Got Rid of Reader Comments. *Nieman Journalism Lab*, September 15. http://www.niemanlab.org/2015/09/what-happened-after-7-news-sites-got-rid-of-reader-comments/. Accessed 23 Aug 2016.

Entous, Adam, Ellen Nakashima, and Greg Miller. 2016. Secret CIA assessment says Russia was Trying to Help Trump Win White House. *The Washington Post*, December 9. https://www.washingtonpost.com/world/national-security/obama-orders-review-of-russian-hacking-during-presidential-campaign/2016/12/09/31d6b300-be2a-11e6-94ac-3d324840106c_story.html?utm_term=.e589066144fe. Accessed 12 Dec 2016.

Erjavec, Karmen, and Melita Poler Kovačič. 2012. 'You Don't Understand, This is a New War!' Analysis of Hate Speech in News Web Sites' Comments. *Mass Communication and Society* 15: 899–920.

Festinger, Leon. 1957. *A Theory of Cognitive Dissonance*. Palo Alto, CA: Stanford University Press.

Fishkin, James S. 1991. *Democracy and Deliberation.* New Haven, CT: Yale University Press.
Forni, P.M. 2008. *The Civility Solution: What to Do When People are Rude.* New York, NY: St. Martin's Press.
Frijda, Nico H. 1984. *The Emotions.* New York: Cambridge University Press.
Gastil, John. 2008. *Political Communication and Deliberation.* Thousand Oaks, CA: SAGE.
Gastil, John, and Laura W. Black. 2008. Public Deliberation as the Organizing Principle of Political Communication Research. *Journal of Public Deliberation* 4 (1): Article 3.
Geer, John G. 2006. *In Defense of Negativity: Attack Ads in Presidential Campaigns,* 2006. Chicago, IL: University of Chicago Press.
Gershman, Jacob, and Tamara Audi. 2015. Court Rules Baker Can't Refuse to Make Wedding Cake for Gay Couple. *Wall Street Journal,* August 13. http://www.wsj.com/articles/court-rules-baker-cant-refuse-to-make-wedding-cake-for-gay-couple-1439506296. Accessed 25 Aug 2016.
Gervais, Bryan T. 2015. Incivility Online: Affective and Behavioral Reactions to Uncivil Political Posts in a Web-Based Experiment. *Journal of Information Technology & Politics* 12: 167–185.
Gil de Zúñiga, Homero, Nakwon Jung, and Sebastián Valenzuela. 2012. Social Media Use for News and Individuals' Social Capital, Civic Engagement, and Political Participation. *Journal of Computer—Mediated Communication* 17: 319–336.
Gillmor, Dan. 2004. *We the Media.* Santa Rosa, CA: O'Reilly Media.
Gini, Gianluca, and Dorothy L. Espelage. 2014. Peer Victimization, Cyberbullying, and Suicide Risk in Children and Adolescents. *Journal of the American Medical Association* 312 (5): 545–546.
Goffman, Erving. 1959. *Presentation of the Self in Everyday Life.* Garden City, NY: Doubleday.
Graesser, Arthur C. 1981. *Prose Comprehension Beyond the Word.* New York: Springer-Verlag.
Graham, Todd, and Tamara Witschge. 2003. In Search of Online Deliberation: Towards a New Method of Examining the Quality of Online Discussions. *Communications* 28: 173–204.
Granovetter, Mark. 1973. The Strength of Weak Ties. *American Journal of Sociology* 78 (6): 1360–1380.
Grice, H.P. 1969. Utterer's Meaning and Intention. *The Philosophical Review* 78 (2): 147–177.
Grinberg, Emanuella. 2016. Battle Over Symbols Continues with Mississippi State Flag. *CNN.com,* June 19. http://www.cnn.com/2016/06/19/us/mississippi-state-flag/. Accessed 25 Aug 2016.

Gutmann, Amy, and Dennis Thompson. 1996. *Democracy and Disagreement*. Cambridge, MA: Harvard University Press.

Habermas, Jürgen. 1994. Three Normative Models of Democracy. *Democratic and Constitutional Theory Today* 1 (1): 1–10.

Han, Soo-Hye, and LeAnn M. Brazeal. 2015. Playing Nice: Modeling Civility in Online Political Discussions. *Communication Research Reports* 32 (1): 20–28.

Harp, Dustin, and Mark Tremayne. 2006. The Gendered Blogosphere: Examining Inequality Using Network and Feminist Theory. *Journalism & Mass Communication Quarterly* 32 (2): 247–264.

Hatcher, John A., and Mary Currin-Percival. 2016. Does the Structural Pluralism Model Predict Differences in Journalists' Perceptions of Online Comments? *Digital Journalism* 4 (3): 302–320.

Hayes, Andrew F. 2007. Exploring Forms of Self-Censorship: On the Spiral of Silence and the Use of Opinion Expression Avoidance Strategies. *Journal of Communication* 57: 785–802.

Hayes, Andrew F. 2013. *Introduction to Mediation, Moderation, and Conditional Process Analysis*. New York: Guilford.

Hayes, Andrew F., and Klaus Krippendorf. 2007. Answering the Call for a Standard Reliability Measure for Coding Data. *Communication Methods and Measures* 1 (1): 77–89.

Hayes, Andrew F., and Kristopher J. Preacher. 2014. Statistical Mediation Analysis with a Multi-Categorical Independent Variable. *British Journal of Mathematical and Statistical Psychology* 67 (3): 451–470.

Herring, Susan C., Inna Kouper, Lois Ann Scheidt, and Elijah Wright. 2004. Women and Children Last: The Discursive Construction of Weblogs. In *Into the Blogsphere: Rhetoric, Community and Culture Weblogs*, ed. Laura Gurak, Smilijana Antonijevic, Laurie Johnson, Clancy Ratcliff, and Jennifer Reyman. Minneapolis, MN: University of Minnesota.

Herschcovis, M.Sandy. 2011. 'Incivility, Social Undermining, Bullying … Oh My!': A Call to Reconcile Constructs within Workplace Aggression Research. *Journal of Organizational Communication* 32 (3): 499–519.

Himelboim, Itai, Stephen McCreery, and Marc Smith. 2013. Birds of a Feather Tweet Together: Integrating Network and Content Analyses to Examine Cross-Ideology Exposure on Twitter. *Journal of Computer-Mediated Communication* 18 (2): 40–60.

Huckfeldt, Robert, Jeannette Morehouse Mendez, and Tracy Osborn. 2004. Disagreement, Ambivalence, and Engagement: The Political Consequences of Heterogeneous Networks. *Political Psychology* 25 (1): 65–95.

Huckfeldt, Robert, Ken'Ichi Ikeda, and Franz Urban Pappi. 2005. Patterns of Disagreement in Democratic Politics: Comparing Germany, Japan, and the United States. *American Journal of Political Science* 49 (3): 497–514.

Huffadine, Leith. 2016. 'Utterly Appalling': Racist Memes Comparing Retired Star Adam Goodes to Shot Gorilla Harambe Pulled From Facebook. *Daily Mail.com*, June 1. http://www.dailymail.co.uk/news/article-3621232/Shocking-racist-memes-compared-retired-indigenous-AFL-star-Adam-Goodes-gorilla.html. Accessed 23 June 2016.

Hughey, Matthew W. 2012. Show Me Your Papers! Obama's Birth and the Whiteness of Belonging. *Qualitative Sociology* 35: 163–181.

Hughey, Matthew W., and Jessie Daniels. 2013. Racist Comments at Online News Sites: A Methodological Dilemma for Discourse Analysis. *Media, Culture & Society* 35 (3): 332–337.

Hunzinger, Erica. 2016, July 19. Two Weeks of Shock, Tragedy. *Austin American-Statesman*, B4.

Hwang, Hyunseo, Zhondang Pan, and Ye Sun. 2008. Influence of Hostile Media Perceptions on Willingness to Engage in Discursive Activities: An Examination of Mediating Role of Media Indignation. *Media Psychology* 11 (1): 76–97.

Izadi, Elahe, and Amy B. Wang. 2017. Meryl Streep Called Out Donald Trump at Golden Globes. He Responds By Calling her 'Over-Rated.' *The Washington Post*, January 9. https://www.washingtonpost.com/news/arts-and-entertainment/wp/2017/01/08/meryl-streep-called-out-donald-trump-at-the-golden-globes-read-her-speech-here/?utm_term=.7b28d8698d59. Accessed 10 Jan 2017.

Jacobs, Lawrence R., Fay Lomax Cook, and Michael X. Delli Carpini. 2009. *Talking Together: Public Deliberation and Political Participation in America*. Chicago, IL: University of Chicago Press.

Jamieson, Kathleen Hall, and Joseph N. Cappella. 2008. *Echo Chamber: Rush Limbaugh and the Conservative Media Establishment*. New York, NY: Oxford University Press.

Jarvie, Jenny. 2016. Mississippi Law Opens a New Front on the Battle Over Gay Rights. *Los Angeles Times*, April 5. http://www.latimes.com/nation/nationnow/la-na-mississippi-law-service-denial-gays-20160405-story.html. Accessed 25 Aug 2016.

Jensen, Elizabeth. 2016. NPR Website to Get Rid of Comments. *NPR.org*, August 17. http://www.npr.org/sections/ombudsman/2016/08/17/489516952/npr-website-to-get-rid-of-comments. Accessed 23 Aug 2016.

Jensen, Elizabeth. 2016. Mailbag: Saying Goodbye to Comments, *NPR.org*, August 24. http://www.npr.org/sections/ombudsman/2016/08/24/491099942/mailbag-saying-goodbye-to-comments?utm_campaign=storyshare&utm_source=twitter.com&utm_medium=social. Accessed 24 Aug 2016.

Johnson, Jenna, 2016. What Happens When Donald Trump Attacks a Private Citizen on Twitter. *The Washington Post*, December 8. https://www.washingtonpost.com/politics/this-is-what-happens-when-donald-trump-attacks-a-private-citizen-on-twitter/2016/12/08/a1380ece-bd62-11e6-91ee-1adddfe36cbe_story.html?utm_term=.595a42aa5063. Accessed 10 Jan 2017.

Kaiser, Henry F. 1970. A Second Generation Little Jiffy. *Psychometrika* 35 (4): 401–415.
Katz, Elihu. 2014. Back to the Street: When Media and Opinion Leaves Home. *Mass Communication and Society* 17: 454–463.
Kennedy, Kathleen A., and Emily Pronin. 2008. When Disagreement Gets Ugly: Perceptions of Bias and the Escalation of Conflict. *Personality and Social Psychology Bulletin* 34 (6): 833–848.
Khaldarova, Irina, and Mervi Pantti. 2016. Fake News. *Journalism Practice* 10 (7): 891–901.
Kim, Younghwan. 2015. Does Disagreement Mitigate Polarization? How Selective Exposure and Disagreement Affect Political Polarization. *Journalism & Mass Communication Quarterly* 92 (4): 915–937.
Klinger, Ulrike, and Uta Russmann. 2015. The Sociodemographics of Political Public Deliberation: Measuring Deliberative Quality in Different User Groups. *Communications* 40 (4): 471–484.
Klofstad, Casey A., Anand Edward Sokhey, and Scott D. McClurg. 2013. Disagreeing About Disagreement: How Conflict in Social Networks Affects Political Behavior. *American Journal of Political Science* 57: 120–134.
Knight, Cameron, and Mallorie Sullivan. 2016. *Gorilla Killed after 3-Year-Old Falls into Zoo Enclosure*. Cincinnati (Ohio) Enquirer, June 18. http://www.cincinnati.com/story/news/2016/05/28/police-child-taken-hospital-after-falling-into-gorilla-pen/85095094/. Accessed 23 June 2016.
Ksiazek, Thomas B. 2015. Civil Interactivity: How News Organizations' Commenting Policies Explain Civility and Hostility in User Comments. *Journal of Broadcasting & Electronic Media* 59 (4): 556–573.
Lacy, Stephen, Brendan R. Watson, Daniel Riffe, and Jennette Lovejoy. 2015. Issues and Best Practices in Content Analysis. *Journalism & Mass Communication Quarterly* 92 (4): 791–811.
Landemore, Hélène. 2012. Democratic Reason: The Mechanism of Collective Intelligence in Politics. In *Collective Wisdom: Principles and Mechanisms*, ed. Hélène Landemore, and John Elster, 251–289. New York, NY: Cambridge University Press.
Lang, Annie. 2000. The Limited Capacity Model of Mediated Message Processing. *Journal of Communication* 50 (1): 46–70.
Lang, Annie. 2006. Using the Limited Capacity Model of Mediated Message Processing to Design Effective Cancer Communication Messages. *Journal of Communication* 53 (S1): S57–S80.
Lang, Annie. 2009. The Limited Capacity Model of Motivated Mediated Message Processing. In *The SAGE Handbook of Mass Media Processes and Effects*, ed. Robin L. Nabi and Mary Beth Oliver, 193–204. Thousand Oaks, CA: Sage.

Lang, Hai. 2014. The Organizational Principles of Online Political Discussion: A Relational Event Stream Model for Analysis of Web Forum Deliberation. *Human Communication Research* 40: 483–507.

Lasswell, Harold D. 1941. *Democracy Through Public Opinion*. Menasha, WI: George Banta Publishing Co.

Lazarus, Richard S. 1984. On the Primacy of Cognition. *American Psychologist* 39 (2): 124–129.

Leary, Mark R., and Roy F. Baumeister. 2000. The Nature and Function of Self-esteem: Sociometer Theory. *Advances in Experimental Social Psychology* 32: 1–62.

Leary, Mark R. 2010. Affiliation, Belonging, and Acceptance: The Pursuit of Interpersonal Connection. *Handbook of Social Psychology*, ed. Susan T. Fiske, Daniel T. Gilbert, and Gardner Lindzey, 864–897. Hoboken, NJ: Wiley.

Lee, Francis L.F. 2009. The Impact of Political Discussion in a Democratizing Society: The Moderating Role of Disagreement and Support for Democracy. *Communication Research* 36 (3): 379–399.

Lee, Francis, L.F. 2012. Does Discussion With Disagreement Discourage All Types of Political Participation? Survey Evidence from Hong Kong. *Communication Research* 39 (4): 543–562.

Lee, Michelle Ye Hee. 2015. Donald Trump's False Comments Connecting Mexican Immigrants and Crime. *The Washington Post*, July 18. https://www.washingtonpost.com/news/fact-checker/wp/2015/07/08/donald-trumps-false-comments-connecting-mexican-immigrants-and-crime/?utm term=.ccfc 38734c56. Accessed 7 Dec 2016.

Leonard, Tom. 2016. They Should Have Seen Him Coming. *British Journalism Review* 27 (2): 16–21.

Levendusky, Matthew. 2013. *How Partisan Media Polarize America*. Chicago, IL: University of Chicago Press.

Logevall, Fredrik. 2012. The Paradox of Civility. *Civility and Democracy in America: A Reasoned Understanding*, ed. Cornell W. Clayton and Richard Elgar, 5–12. Pullman, WA: Washington University Press.

Loke, Jaime. 2012. Old Turf, New Neighbors. *Journalism Practice* 6 (2): 233–249.

Lopez, Lori Kido. 2009. The Radical Act of 'Mommy Blogging': Refining Motherhood Through the Blogosphere. *New Media & Society* 11 (5): 729–747.

Mabweazara, Hayes, A. 2014. Reader Comments on Zimbabwean Newspaper Websites. *Digital Journalism* 2 (1): 44–61.

MacDonald, Geoff, and Mark R. Leary. 2005. Why Does Social Exclusion Hurt? The Relationship Between Social and Physical Pain. *Psychological Bulletin* 131 (2): 202–223.

Maheshwari, Sapna. 2016. How Fake News Goes Viral: A Case Study. *The New York Times*, November 20. http://www.nytimes.com/2016/11/20/business/media/how-fake-news-spreads.html. Accessed 12 Dec 2016.

Manosevitch, Edith, and Dana Walker. 2009. Reader Comments to Online Opinion Journalism: A Space of Public Deliberation. *International Symposium of Online Journalism* 10: 10–30.

Marchi, Regina. 2012. With Facebook, Blogs, and Fake News, Teens Reject Journalistic "Objectivity." *Journal of Communication Inquiry* 36 (3): 246–262.

Marcus, George E., W. Russell Neuman, and Michael MacKuen. 2000. *Affective Intelligence and Political Judgment*. Chicago: The University of Chicago Press.

Masci, David, and Mike Lipka. 2015. Where Christian Churches, Other Religions Stand on Gay Marriage. *Pew Research Center*, December 15. http://www.pewresearch.org/fact-tank/2015/12/21/where-christian-churches-stand-on-gay-marriage/. Accessed 25 Aug 2016.

Matsunaga, Masaki. 2011. Underlying Circuits of Social Support for Bullied Victims: An Appraisal-Based Perspective on Supportive Communication and Postbullying Adjustment. *Human Communication Research* 37: 174–206.

Matz, David C., and Wendy Wood. 2005. Cognitive Dissonance in Groups: The Consequences of Disagreement. *Journal of Personality and Social Psychology* 88: 22–37.

McClurg, Scott D. 2006. The Electoral Relevance of Political Talk: Examining Disagreement and Expertise in Social Networks on Political Participation. *American Journal of Political Science* 50 (3): 737–754.

McClurg, Scott D. 2006. Political Disagreement in Context: The Conditional Effect of Neighborhood Context, Disagreement and Political Talk on Electoral Participation. *Political Behavior* 28: 349–366.

Meet the Press. 2016. Are You Excited About Super Tuesday? *NBCNews.com*, March 1. http://www.nbcnews.com/meet-the-press/are-you-excited-about-super-tuesday-we-are-n529226. Accessed 25 Aug 2016.

Mehra, Bharat, Cecelia Merkel, and Ann Peterson Bishop. 2004. The Internet for Empowerment of Minority and Marginalized Groups. *New Media & Society* 6 (6): 781–802.

Meltzer, Kimberly. 2015. Journalistic Concern About Uncivil Political Talk in Digital Media: Responsibility, Credibility, and Academic Influence. *The International Journal of Press/Politics* 20 (1): 85–107.

Metts, Sandra, and William R. Cupach. 2015. Face Theory: Goffman's Dramatist Approach to Interpersonal Interaction. In *Engaging Theories in Interpersonal Communication*, ed. Leslie A. Baxter and Dawn O. Braithwaite, 203–214. Thousand Oaks, CA: Sage.

Meyer, Hans K., and Michael C. Carey. 2014. In Moderation: Examining How Journalists' Attitudes Toward Online Comments Affect the Creation of Community. *Journalism Practice* 8 (2): 213–228.

Meyer, Hans K., and Michael C. Carey. 2015. Men More Likely to Post Online Newspaper Comments. *Newspaper Research Journal* 36 (4): 469–481.

Min, Seong-Jae. 2007. Online Vs. Face-To-Face Deliberation: Effects on Civic Engagement. *Journal of Computer-Mediated Communication* 12: 1369–1387.

Mitchell, Amy, Jeffrey Gottfried, Jocelyn Kiley, and Katerina Eva Matsa. 2014. Political Polarization & Media Habits. Pew Research Center, October 21. http://www.journalism.org/2014/10/21/political-polarization-media-habits/. Accessed 1 Feb 2016.

Mitra, Ananda. 2001. Marginal Voices in Cyberspace. *New Media & Society* 3 (1): 29–48.

Mohan, Geoffrey. 2016. Facebook's Zuckerberg Offers Plan to Counter Fake News Sites. *Los Angeles Times*, November 19. http://www.latimes.com/business/la-fi-fakenews-facebook-20161119-story.html. Accessed 21 Dec 2016.

Molina, Maribel. 2016. Twitter Users React to Austin ISD Not Cancelling, Delaying Classes. *Austin American-Statesman*, May 19. http://austin.blog.statesman.com/2016/05/19/twitter-users-react-to-austin-isd-not-cancelling-delaying-classes/. Accessed 19 May 2016.

Montgomery, Scott. 2016. Beyond Comments: Finding Better Ways to Connect with You. *NPR.org*, August 23. http://www.npr.org/sections/thisisnpr/2016/08/17/490208179/beyond-comments-finding-better-ways-to-connect-with-you. Accessed 23 Aug 2016.

Moscowitz, Leigh. 2013. *The Battle Over Marriage: Gay Rights Activism Through the Media*. Chicago, IL: University of Illinois Press.

Mother Jones. 2015. Here's What Appears to be Dylann Roof's Racist Manifesto. *MotherJones.com*, June 20. http://www.motherjones.com/politics/2015/06/alleged-charleston-shooter-dylann roof-manifesto-racist. Accessed 25 Aug 2016.

Mutz, Diana C. 2002. Cross-Cutting Social Networks: Testing Democratic Theory in Practice. *American Political Science Review* 96 (1): 111–126.

Mutz, Diana C. 2002. The Consequences of Cross-Cutting Networks for Political Participation. *American Journal of Political Science* 46 (4): 838–855.

Mutz, Diana C. 2015. *In-Your-Face Politics: The Consequences of Uncivil Media*. Princeton, NJ: Princeton University Press.

Nabi, Robin L. 2010. The Case for Emphasizing Discrete Emotions in Communication Research. *Communication Monograph* 77 (2): 153–159. doi:10.1080/03637751003790444.

Nardi, Bonnie A., Diane J. Schiano, Michelle Gumbrecht, and Luke Swartz. 2004. Why We Blog. *Communications of the ACM* 47 (2): 41–46.

Nekmat, Elmie, and William J. Gonzebach. 2013. Multiple Opinion Climates in Online Forums: Role of Website Source Reference and Within-Forum Opinion Congruency. *Journalism & Mass Communication Quarterly* 90 (4): 736–756.

Nielsen, Carolyn. 2012. Newspaper Journalists Support Online Comments. *Newspaper Research Journal* 33 (1): 86–100.

Nir, Lilach. 2005. Ambivalent Social Networks and Their Consequences for Participation. *International Journal of Public Opinion Research* 17: 422–442.

Nir, Lilach. 2011. Disagreement and Opposition in Social Networks: Does Disagreement Discourage Turnout? *Political Studies* 59: 674–692.

Noelle-Neumann, Elisabeth. 1974. The Spiral of Silence: A Theory of Public Opinion. *Journal of Communication* 24 (2): 43–51.

Noelle-Neumann, Elisabeth. 2008. Spiral of Silence. In *A First Look at Communication Theory*, ed. Em Griffin, 272–286. New York: McGraw Hill.

Nyhan, Brendan, and Jason Reifler. 2010. When Corrections Fail: The Persistence of Political Misperceptions. *Political Behavior* 30 (2): 303–303.

Oetzel, John G., and Stella Ting-Toomey. 2003. Face Concerns in Interpersonal Conflict: A Cross-Cultural Empirical Test of Face Negotiation Theory. *Communication Research* 30 (6): 599–624.

Ohlheiser, Abby. 2016. Just How Offensive Did Milo Yiannopoulos Have to Be to Get Banned from Twitter? *The Washington Post*, July 21. https://www.washingtonpost.com/news/the-intersect/wp/2016/07/21/what-it-takes-to-get-banned-from-twitter/?utm_term=.27ca27d651fa. Accessed 9 Dec 2016.

Ohlheiser, Abby. 2017. Martin Shkreli Was Suspended From Twitter for 'Targeted Harassment; of Journalist, *The Washington Post*, January 8. https://www.washingtonpost.com/news/the-intersect/wp/2017/01/08/martin-shkreli-was-suspended-from-twitter-for-targeted-harassment-of-a-journalist/?utm_term=.3688b7892648. Accessed 10 Jan 2017.

Olweus, Dan. 1993. *Bullying at School: What We Know and What We can Do*. Oxford, UK: Blackwell.

Oz, Mustafa, Pei Zheng, and Gina Masullo Chen. 2016 April. Social Media, Politeness and Discussion Quality. In *Presented at the World Association for Public Opinion Research Annual Conference*, Austin, TX.

O'Brien, Sarah Ashley. 2016. The Year in Harassment: 2016 Sunk Lower Than Rock Bottom. December 20. http://money.cnn.com/2016/12/20/technology/2016-internet-harassment/. Accessed 10 Jan 2017.

O'Keefe, Ed, and Paul Kane. 2016. McConnell Announces Senate Probe of Suspected Russian Election Interference: 'The Russians Are Not Our Friends.' *The Washington Post*, December 12. https://www.washingtonpost.com/news/powerpost/wp/2016/12/12/schumer-on-congressional-probe-of-russia-i-dont-want-this-to-turn-into-a-benghazi-investigation/?utm_term=.880d5944b09b . Accessed 12 Dec 2016.

O'Sullivan, Patrick B., and Andrew J. Flanagin. 2003. Reconceptualizing 'Flaming' and Other Problematic Messages. *New Media & Society* 5 (1): 69–94.

Paolacci, Gabriele, Jessie Chander, and Panagiotis G. Ipeirotis. 2010. Running Experiments on Amazon Mechanical Turk. *Judgment and Decision Making* 5 (5): 411–419.

Papacharissi, Zizi. 2004. Democracy Online: Civility, Politeness, and the Democratic Potential of Online Political Discussion. *New Media & Society* 6 (2): 259–283.

Papacharissi, Zizi. 2015. *Affective Publics*. New York: Oxford University Press.
Papacharissi, Zizi. 2013. *A Private Sphere: Democracy in a Digital Age*. Malden, MA: Polity.
Parsons, Bryan M. 2010. Social Networks and the Affective Impact of Political Agreement. *Political Behavior* 32 (2): 181–204.
Pattie, C.J., and R.J. Johnson. 2009. Conversation, Disagreement and Political Participation. *Political Behavior* 31: 261–285.
Pedersen, Sarah, and Caroline Macafee. 2007. Gender Differences in British Blogging. *Journal of Computer-Mediated Communication* 12: 1471–1492.
Pitts, Leonard. 2010. Anonymity Brings Out the Worst in Expression. *The Gazette.com*, April 1. http://gazette.com/anonymity-brings-out-the-worst-in-expression/article/96545. Accessed 20 June 2016.
Podsiadly, Adrzej, and Malgorzata Gamain-Wilk. 2016. Personality Traits as Predictors or Outcomes of Being Exposed to Bullying in the Workplace. *Personality and Individual Differences*, Advance Online Publication. doi:10.1016/j.paid.2016.08.001. Accessed 7 Dec 2016.
Price, Vincent, Joseph N. Cappella, and Lilach Nir. 2002. Does Disagreement Contribute to More Deliberative Opinion? *Political Communication* 19: 95–112.
Putnam, Linda L., and Dennis K. Mumby. 2014. *The Sage Handbook of Organizational Communication*. Thousand Oaks, CA: Sage.
Pérez-Peña, Richard. 2010. News Sites Rethink Anonymous Online Comments. *The New York Times*, April 1. http://www.nytimes.com/2010/04/12/technology/12comments.html?_r=0. Accessed 24 June 2016.
Rappeport, Alan. 2016. Who Won the Debate? Hillary Clinton, the 'Nasty Woman.' *The New York Times*, October 20. http://www.nytimes.com/2016/10/21/us/politics/who-won-the-third-debate.html. Accessed 12 Dec 2016.
Reader, Bill. 2012. "Free Press Vs. Free Speech? The Rhetoric of 'Civility' in Regard to Anonymous Online Comments." *Journalism & Mass Communication Quarterly* 89, no. 3: 495–512.
Reese, Stephen D. 2016. The New Geography of Journalism Research. *Digital Journalism* 4 (7): 818–826.
Reese, Stephen D., and Pamela J. Shoemaker. 2016. A Media Sociology for the Network Public Sphere: The Hierarchy of Influence Model. *Mass Communication and Society* 19: 389–410.
Reeves, Byron, and Clifford Nass. 1996. *The Media Equation*. Cambridge, MA: Cambridge University Press.
Renner, Nausicaa. 2016. As Sites Abandon Comments, The Coral Project Aims to Turn the Tide. *Columbia Journalism Review*, August 23. http://www.cjr.org/tow_center/improving_audience_engagement_coral_project.php. Accessed 10 Jan 2017.

Rheingold, Howard. 2000. *The Virtual Community: Homesteading on the Electronic Frontier.* Cambridge, MA: MIT Press.

Riffe, Daniel, Stephen Lacy, and Frederick G. Fico. 2005. *Analyzing Media Messages: Using Quantitative Content Analysis in Research.* Mahwah, NJ: Lawrence Erlbaum.

Robles, Frances, Jason Horowitz, and Shaila Dewan. 2015. Dylann Roof, Suspect in Charleston Shooting Flew the Flag of White Power. *The New York Times*, June 18. http://www.nytimes.com/2015/06/19/us/on-facebook-dylann-roof-charleston-suspect-wears-symbols-of-white-supremacy.html?_r=0. Accessed 25 Aug 2016.

Robles, Frances, Richard Fausset, and Michael Barbaro. 2015. Nikki Haley, South Carolina Governor, Calls for Removal of Confederate Battle Flag. *The New York Times*, June 22. http://www.nytimes.com/2015/06/23/us/south-carolina-confederate-flag-dylann-roof.html. Accessed 25 Aug 2016.

Rodriguez, Tori. 2013. Negative Emotions are Key to Well-Being. *Scientific American*, May 1. http://www.scientificamerican.com/article/negative-emotions-key-well-being/?WT.mc_id=SA_FB_MB_EG. Accessed 21 June 2016.

Rosenberry, Jack. 2011. Users Support Anonymity Despite Increasing Negativity. *Newspaper Research Journal* 32 (1): 6–19.

Rowe, Ian. 2015. Civility 2.0: A Comparative Analysis of Incivility in Online Political Discussion. *Information, Communication & Society* 18 (2): 121–138.

Ruiz, Carlos, David Domingo, Josep Lluís Micó, Javier Díaz-Noci, Koldo Meso, and Pere Maship. 2011. Public Sphere 2.0? The Democratic Qualities of Citizen Debates in Online Newspapers. *The International Journal of Press/Politics* 16 (4): 463–487.

Rösner, Leonie, and Nicole C. Krämer. 2016. Verbal Venting in the Social Web: Effects of Anonymity and Group Norms on Aggressive Language Use in Online Comments. *Social Media + Society* 1–13. July/September.

Rösner, Leonie, Stephan Winter, and Nicole C. Krämer. 2016. Dangerous Minds? Effects of Online Comments on Aggressive Cognitions, Emotions, and Behavior. *Computers in Human Behavior* 58: 461–470.

Santana, Arthur D. 2011. Online Readers' Comments Represent New Opinion Pipeline. *Newspaper Research Journal* 32 (3): 66–88.

Santana, Arthur D. 2014. Virtuous or Vitriolic. *Journalism Practice* 8 (1): 18–33.

Santana, Arthur D. 2015. Incivility Dominates Online Comments on Immigration. *Newspaper Research Journal* 36 (1): 92–107.

Schneider, Bill. 2015. What Makes Donald Trump a New Kind of Candidate? *Reuters.com*, August 12. http://blogs.reuters.com/great-debate/2015/08/12/what-makes-donald-trump-a-new-kind-of-candidate/. Accessed 25 Aug 2016.

Schradie, Jen. 2012. The Trend of Class, Race, and Ethnicity in Social Media Inequality: Who Still Cannot Afford to Blog. *Information, Communication & Society* 15 (4): 555–571.

Schudson, Michael. 1997. Why Conversation Is Not the Soul of Democracy. *Critical Studies in Mass Communication* 14: 297–309.

Shapiro, Michael A., and T. Makana Chock. 2004. Media Dependency and Perceived Reality of Fiction and News. *Journal of Broadcasting & Electronic Media* 8 (1): 675–695.

Shifman, Limor. 2014. *Memes in Digital Culture*. Cambridge, MA: MIT Press.

Shoemaker, Pamela J. 1982. The Perceived Legitimacy of Deviant Political Groups: Two Experiments on Media Effects. *Communication Research* 9 (2): 249–286.

Shoemaker, Pamela J. 1984. Media Treatment of Deviant Groups. *Journalism Quarterly* 61 (1): 66–82.

Shontell, Alyson. 2014. 13-Year-Old Describes How Kids are Bullied on SnapChat. *Business Insider*, June 26. http://www.businessinsider.com/how-kids-are-bullied-on-snapchat-2014-6. Accessed 10 Jan 2017.

Slater, Michael D. 2007. Reinforcing Spirals: The Mutual Influence of Media Selectivity and Media Effects and Their Impact on Individual Behavior and Society Identity. *Communication Theory* 17: 281–303.

Sobieraj, Sarah, and Jeffrey M. Berry. 2011. From Incivility to Outrage: Political Discourse in Blogs, Talk Radio, and Cable News. *Political Communication* 28 (1): 19–41.

Sonderman, Jeff. 2011. News Sites Using Facebook Comments See Higher Quality Discussions, More Referrals, *Poynter.org*, August 11. http://www.poynter.org/2011/news-sites-using-facebook-comments-see-higher-quality-discussion-more-referrals/143192/. Accessed 9 Sep 2016.

Spears, Russell, Tom Postmes, Martin Le, and Anka Wolbert. 2002. When Are Net Effects Gross Products? The Power of Influence and Influence of Power in Computer-Mediated Communication. *Journal of Social Issues* 58 (1): 91–107.

Stromer-Galley, Jennifer. 2003. Diversity of Political Conversation on the Internet: Users' Perspectives. *Journal of Computer-Mediated Communication* 8 (3): n.p.

Stroud, Natalie J. 2008. Media Use and Political Dispositions: Revisiting the Concept of Selective Exposure. *Political Behavior* 30: 341–366.

Stroud, Natalie J. 2010. Polarization and Partisan Selective Exposure. *Journal of Communication* 60: 556–576.

Stroud, Natalie J., Joshua M. Scacco, Ashley Muddiman, and Alexander L. Curry. 2015. Changing Deliberative Norms on News Organizations' Facebook Sites. *Journal of Computer-Mediated Communication* 20: 188–203.

Stroud, Natalie J., Joshua M. Scacco, Ashley Muddiman, and Alexander L. Curry. 2015. Changing Deliberative Norms on News Organizations' Facebook Sites. *Journal of Computer-Mediated Communication* 20: 188–203.

Sukumaran, Abhay, Stephanie Vezich, Melanie McHugh, and Clifford Nass. 2011. Normative Influences on Thoughtful Online Participation. *Proceedings of the CHI 2011: Session: Incentives & User Generated Content*, 3401–3410. Vancouver, BC.

Suler, John. 2004. The Online Disinhibition Effect. *CyberPsychology & Behavior* 7 (3): 321–326.

Tabachnick, Barbara A., and Linda S. Fidell. 2007. *Using Multivariate Statistics*. New York: Pearson.

Tenenboim, Ori, and Akiba A. Cohen. 2015. What Prompts Users to Click and Comment? A Longitudinal Study of Online News. *Journalism* 16 (2): 198–217.

The Guardian. 2016. 'It feels like censorship': Guardian Readers on NPR's Decision to Close Comments. *The Guardian*, August 19. https://www.theguardian.com/media/2016/aug/19/npr-comments-decision-guardian-readers?CMP=twt_gu. Accessed 23 Aug 2016.

The New York Times. 2016. Who is Running for President. *The New York Times*, July 26. http://www.nytimes.com/interactive/2016/us/elections/2016-presidential-candidates.html. Accessed 25 Aug 2016.

Thrift, Samantha C. 2014. #YesAllWomen as Feminist Meme Event. *Feminist Media Studies* 14 (6): 1090–1092.

Tsfati, Yariv, Natalie Jomini Stroud, and Adi Chotiner. 2014. Exposure to Ideological News and Perceived Opinion Climate: Testing the Media Effects Component of Spiral-of-Silence in a Fragmented Media Landscape. *The International Journal of Press/Politics* 19 (1): 3–23.

Walther, Joseph B. 1996. Computer-Mediation Communication: Impersonal, Interpersonal, and Hyperpersonal Interaction. *Communication Research* 23 (1): 3–43.

Waters, Dustin, and Mark Berman. 2016. Dylann Roof Found Guilty on All Counts in Charleston Church Massacre Trial. *The Washington Post*, December 15. https://www.washingtonpost.com/news/post-nation/wp/2016/12/15/jurors-begin-deliberating-in-charleston-church-shooting-trial/?utm_term=.cb55248a9782. Accessed 2 Jan 2017.

Watson, David, Lee A. Clark, and Auke Tellegen. 1988. Development and Validation of the Brief Measures of Positive and Negative Affect: The PANAS Scales. *Journal of Personality and Social Psychology* 54 (6): 1063–1070.

Weber, Patrick. 2013. Discussions in the Comments Sections: Factors Influencing Participation and Interactivity in Online Newspapers' Reader Comments. *New Media & Society* 10 (6): 941–957.

Williams, Sherri. 2015. Digital Defense: Black Feminists Resist Violence and Hashtag Activism. *Feminist Media Studies* 15 (2): 341–344.

Williams, Kipling D., Joseph P. Forgas, and William von Hippel. 2005. *The Social Outcast*. New York: Psychology Press.

Wojcieszak, Magdalena E., and Vincent Price. 2012. Perceived Versus Actual Disagreement: Which Influences Deliberative Experiences? *Journal of Communication* 62: 418–436.

Wotanis, Lindsey, and Laurie McMillan. 2014. Performing Gender on YouTube: How Jenna Marbles Negotiates a Hostile Online Environment. *Feminist Media Studies* 14 (6): 912–928.

Yourish, Karen, Larry Buchanan, and Alicia Parlapiano. 2016. More Than 160 Republican Leaders Don't Support Donald Trump. Here's When They Reached Their Breaking Point. *The New York Times*, August 28. http://www.nytimes.com/interactive/2016/08/29/us/politics/at-least-110-republican-leaders-wont-vote-for-donald-trump-heres-when-they-reached-their-breaking-point.html. Accessed 12 Dec 2016.

Yun, Gi Woong, and Sun-Yeon Park. 2011. Selective Posting: Willingness to Post a Message Online. *Journal of Computer-Mediated Communication* 16 (2): 201–277.

Zadro, Lisa, Kipling D. Williams, and Rick Richardson. 2005. Riding the 'O' Train: Comparing the Effects of Ostracism and Verbal Dispute on Targets and Sources. *Group Processes and Intergroup Relations* 8 (2): 125–143.

Zajonc, Robert B. 1980. Feeling and Thinking: Preferences Need No Inferences. *American Psychologist* 35: 151–175.

Zajonc, Robert B. 1984. On the Primacy of Affect. *American Psychologist* 39 (2): 117–123.

Zamith, Rodrigo, and Seth C. Lewis. 2014. From Public Spaces to Public Sphere: Rethinking Systems for Reader Comments on Online News Sites. *Digital Journalism* 2 (4): 558–574.

Zukin, Cliff, Scott Keeter, Molly Andolina, Krista Jenkins, and Michael X. Delli Carpini. 2006. *A New Engagement? Political Participation, Civic Life and the Changing American Citizen*. New York, NY: Oxford University Press.

Index

A
Affective intelligence theory, 35, 118, 136
Amazon Mechanical Turk, 150
Anonymity, 61, 64, 90, 91, 107, 110, 118–120, 179
Arendt, Hannah, 32
Austin, 44, 96, 142, 162, 163

B
Basket of deplorables, 9
Belongingness hypothesis, 63
Bias-perception conflict spiral, 37
Bigotry, 57, 63
Black, Laura W., 31
#BlackLivesMatter, 34, 39, 86
Blogging, 38
Bullying, 4, 6, 8, 10, 13, 175
Burr, Aaron, 59

C
Capital letters, use of to signify yelling, 90, 107, 111, 112, 115, 116, 153, 160, 180
Central Intelligence Agency, 10
Chicago Sun-Times, 82, 180
Cincinnati Enquirer, 57
Civil marriage, 87
Civil Rights Movement, 58
Civil War, 58, 86
Clinton, Hillary, 3, 88, 133, 136
Cognitive dissonance, 30, 36, 160
Computer-mediated communication, 11, 40, 58, 59
Confederate battle flag, 86, 87, 89, 91, 105, 149, 150, 155
Congress, 32, 58, 87
Content analysis, 11, 12, 40, 82, 106, 179
Crosscutting viewpoints, 3, 36
Cross-pressures, cross-pressures hypothesis, 37, 134
Cues-filtered-out approach, 60
Cyberbullying, 14, 18, 183
Cyberghetto, 38
Cyber racism, 86
Cybertopia, 38

D
Daniels, Jessie, 86
Davis, Kim, 88
Defensive effect, 4, 12, 134–138
Deindividuation, 11, 60, 61, 64, 119
Deliberation, 4, 11, 12, 16, 21, 30–44, 48–50, 69, 70, 82–86, 88, 90–94, 105–108, 112, 113, 115–117, 119,

120, 122, 125, 126, 168, 176–178,
180, 182, 183, 185, 186
Deliberation-Participation Paradox,
37
Deliberative arena, 30, 175
Deliberative democracy, 30, 176
Deliberative moment, 11, 30, 34,
41, 82, 84, 116, 176, 177, 180
Deliberative moment zone, 84, 177
Digital deliberation, 38
De Tarde, Gabriel, 30, 62
Digital divide, 38
Digital inequality, 39
Disabling comments, 81
Disagreement, 4, 6, 11, 12, 30, 31, 34,
36, 37
Dispersed crowds, 30

E
Echo chamber, 3, 39
Eisenstadt, Marnie, 29, 30, 40, 41
Election, 3, 9, 10, 32, 41, 88, 133, 139
Emotions, 5, 7, 12, 35, 40, 59, 63, 64,
84, 86, 118, 135, 136, 138, 140,
154, 156, 157, 160, 161, 178, 181,
182
Evidence, 11, 12, 30, 31, 33, 34, 36,
39–41, 47, 83, 84, 90, 108,
116–118, 122, 133, 134, 139, 161,
176–179, 183
Evolutionary psychology, 7

F
Facebook, 5, 9, 14–16, 19–22, 33, 39,
40, 42, 45, 50, 58, 61, 65, 66, 69,
81, 89, 92–94, 98, 110, 118, 120,
122, 123, 127, 133, 137, 139, 141,
162, 165, 179, 185–187, 189
Face theory, 71, 72
Face-to-face communication, 38, 60

Fake news, 4, 9
Federal Bureau of Investigation, 10
Federalist Papers, 32
Fox News, 89, 98, 105, 109–112, 114,
118, 119, 121, 124, 178, 179

G
Gastil, John, 31
Gay rights, 8, 87
Geer, John G., 117
Gender, 39, 83, 107, 109, 110, 116,
151, 153, 177, 179
Global warming, 137
Goodes, Adam, 58, 66
#GorillaLivesMatter, 58
Grabbing genitals, 9, 133
Guardian, 40, 82, 92
Gutmann, Amy, 177

H
Habermas, Jürgen, 62, 117, 176
Haley, Nikki, 87, 96
Hamilton, Alexander, 59
Harambe the Gorilla, 58
Hate speech, 6, 83, 84, 177
Homophobic speech, homophobia, 6,
83, 84, 90, 108, 116, 177
Huffington Post, 89, 105, 109–111,
114, 115, 118, 121, 124, 178, 179
Hurt feelings, 63, 136
Hyperpersonal, 60

I
Immigration, 34, 61, 86, 119
Indiana, 88
Information richness theory, 60
Insults, insulting language, 6, 8, 12, 37,
83, 84, 90, 108, 109, 113, 116, 117,
134, 135, 137, 160, 177, 181

J
Jensen, Elizabeth, 81
Jones, Leslie, 8

K
Kentucky, 88
Kristof, Nicholas, 3

L
Lawrence v. Texas, 87
Legitimate question, 12, 84, 90, 108, 113, 116, 117, 178
Leonard, Tom, 59
Logevall, Fredrik, 58
Losing face, 71, 72, 144, 163

M
Madison, James, 32, 34
Marginalized groups, 32, 38, 39
Marriage equality, 33, 87, 88
McCain, John, 9
Memes, 33, 58, 133
Mississippi, 87, 88
Mommy blogging, 39
Montgomery, Scott, 81
MTurk, 150
Mutz, Diana C., 9, 59

N
Nasty woman, 9
National public radio (NPR), 81
National security agency, 10
NBC News digital, 89
Need to belong, 7, 136
New Yorker, The, 29, 38
New York Times, The, 3, 40, 68, 89, 105, 106, 110–112, 114, 115, 119, 121, 124, 133, 140, 178–180

New York Times v. Sullivan, 58
Nir, Lilach, 43, 44, 46, 47, 140, 188, 189
North Carolina, 88

O
Obama, Barack, 33, 108, 182
Ohio, 57
Ostracism model, 17
Outrage media, 4, 9, 58

P
Pitts, Leonard, 63
Politeness theory, 63
Political attack ads, 4
Presidential election, 9, 88, 137, 175
Public debate, 4, 5, 11, 12, 30, 38, 58, 82, 116, 117, 133, 150, 176, 180, 182, 183
Public deliberation, 5, 14, 16, 21, 31–34, 39, 41, 83, 84, 91, 116, 176
Public sphere, 30, 40, 41, 62, 117, 176
Public talk/talking, 31, 83
Putin, Vladimir, 10

R
Racist speech, racism, 57, 86, 87
Reality television, 5, 9
Reason, 5, 10, 11, 31, 32, 35, 36, 83, 84, 118, 134, 136, 138, 139, 160, 161, 182, 183
Reciprocal, 30
Refugees, 137
Religious freedom acts, 88
Reuters, 82, 180
Roof, Dylann, 86, 95
Rudeness, 4, 6, 10
Russia, 175

S

Same-sex marriage, 12, 85, 87, 89, 91, 105, 106, 109–112, 114, 115, 119, 121, 124, 125, 137, 149, 150, 155, 157, 159, 161, 162, 165, 178
Schudson, Michael, 32, 139
Self-esteem, 5, 7, 17, 63
Sexist speech, sexism, 6, 57, 83, 84, 90, 108, 109, 116, 117, 177
Silencing effect, 37, 157
Snapchat, 41, 175, 177
Social identity Model of Deindividuation Effects (SIDE), 60
Social relationships, 5
Sociometer Theory, 63
South Carolina, 86, 87, 89
Spiral of silence, 134
Steiner, Peter, 38
Stereotypical speech, 108, 109
Stonewall Inn, 87
Straight panic, 87
Streep, Meryl, 175
Super Tuesday, 85, 88, 105, 109, 111, 112, 114, 115, 119, 178
Supreme Court, 12, 58, 85, 87, 88, 105, 106, 108, 178
Sympathetic nervous system, 136
Syracuse, 29

T

Talk radio, 4, 9, 59
Texas, 33
Thompson, Dennis, 34, 177
Trolling (trolls), 83, 84, 177

Trump, Donald, 3, 6, 9, 10, 58, 59, 88, 133, 175
Tunnel vision, 3
Twitter, 5, 8, 33, 39, 58, 59, 81, 90, 175

U

USA today, 89, 105, 109–111, 114, 115, 118, 119, 178, 179

V

Virtual public sphere, 30
Voting, 37, 38

W

Walther, Joseph B., 60
Washington Post, 81, 180
Weak ties, 38, 60
Weight watchers, 60
Whole Earth 'Lectronic Link (WELL), 41

X

Xenophobic speech, xenophobic, 6, 83, 84, 90, 108, 109, 116, 117, 122, 178

Y

#YesAllWomen, 39
Yiannopoulos, Milo, 8

Made in the USA
Coppell, TX
05 December 2021